Dissent in Organizations

San Diego Christian College
Library
Santee, CA

Key Themes in Organizational Communication

Charles Conrad, *Organizational Rhetoric*
Jeffrey W. Kassing, *Dissent in Organizations*
Michael Kramer, *Organizational Socialization*
Vincent R. Waldron, *Communicating Emotion at Work*

658.45
K19d

Dissent in Organizations

Jeffrey W. Kassing

polity

Copyright © Jeffrey W. Kassing 2011

The right of Jeffrey W. Kassing to be identified as Author of this Work has been asserted in accordance with the UK Copyright, Designs and Patents Act 1988.

First published in 2011 by Polity Press

Polity Press
65 Bridge Street
Cambridge CB2 1UR, UK

Polity Press
350 Main Street
Malden, MA 02148, USA

All rights reserved. Except for the quotation of short passages for the purpose of criticism and review, no part of this publication may be reproduced, stored in a retrieval system, or transmitted, in any form or by any means, electronic, mechanical, photocopying, recording or otherwise, without the prior permission of the publisher.

ISBN-13: 978-0-7456-5139-2
ISBN-13: 978-0-7456-5140-8 (pb)

A catalogue record for this book is available from the British Library.

Typeset in 11 on 13 pt Sabon
by Servis Filmsetting Ltd, Stockport, Cheshire
Printed and bound by MPG Books Group, UK

The publisher has used its best endeavours to ensure that the URLs for external websites referred to in this book are correct and active at the time of going to press. However, the publisher has no responsibility for the websites and can make no guarantee that a site will remain live or that the content is or will remain appropriate.

Every effort has been made to trace all copyright holders, but if any have been inadvertently overlooked the publisher will be pleased to include any necessary credits in any subsequent reprint or edition.

For further information on Polity, visit our website: www.politybooks.com

Contents

Detailed Contents vi
List of Illustrations x
Preface xii

1 Why is Organizational Dissent Relevant? 1
2 What is Organizational Dissent? 27
3 How Do We Make Sense of Organizational Dissent? 56
4 What Triggers Organizational Dissent 87
5 How Do Employees Express Dissent? 116
6 Upward Dissent Anyone? 144
7 Can Organizational Dissent Be Managed Well? 174

References 200
Index 215

Detailed Contents

List of Illustrations x

Preface xii

1 Why is Organizational Dissent Relevant? 1
The Case of Sibel Edmonds: Dissent Gagged 8
The Case of Dr Jeffrey Wigand: Dissent and Credibility 11
The Traitorous Eight: Dissent Births an Industry 14
Society and Dissent 16
Repression and Dissent 20
Dissent in Organizations 23
Discussion Questions 26

2 What is Organizational Dissent? 27
Organizational Conflict 31
Upward Influence 35
Employee Resistance 40
Employee Voice 43
Whistleblowing 47
Differentiating Dissent 50
Discussion Questions 54

3 How Do We Make Sense of Organizational Dissent? 56
Classical Approaches 58
The Classical Management Perspective 58

The Human Relations Perspective 59
The Human Resources Perspective 61
Contemporary Approaches 62
The Systems Perspective 62
The Cultural-Interpretive Perspective 64
The Critical Perspective 65
The Discursive Perspective 66
The Identity Perspective 68
Theoretical Explanations for Organizational Dissent 71
The Decision-Making Elephant: Situational Factors that Influence Employees' Decisions to Express Dissent 75
The theory of independent mindedness 76
Unobtrusive control theory 76
Social responsibility and moral reasoning 79
The Feeling Elephant: Motivational Factors that Move Employees to Dissent 79
The exit-voice-loyalty-neglect model of employee dissatisfaction 80
Procedural justice 81
The Sensemaking Elephant: Explanatory Factors that Help Employees Make Sense of Organizational Dissent 82
Impression management 83
Organizational sensemaking 83
Discussion Questions 85

4 What Triggers Organizational Dissent 87
Economic, Political, and Socio-Cultural Factors Affecting Dissent 88
Barriers to Organizational Dissent 92
What are Dissent-Triggering Events? 95
Dissent-Triggering Events 97
Employee Treatment 100
Organizational Change 101
Decision-Making 102
Inefficiency 103

Role/Responsibility 103
Resources 104
Performance Evaluation 105
Preventing Harm 106
Supervisor Inaction 108
Supervisor Performance 109
Supervisor Indiscretion 110
Dissent and Ethics 110
Discussion Questions 114

5 How Do Employees Express Dissent? 116
Models of Organizational Dissent 117
Forms of Organizational Dissent 124
Dissent Goals 128
Individual, Relational, and Organizational Influences Affecting Dissent Expression 129
Organizational Dissent in Alternative Organizing Structures 134
Communication Technology and the Expression of Organizational Dissent 139
Discussion Questions 142

6 Upward Dissent Anyone? 144
Direct Factual Appeal 146
Solution Presentation 148
Circumvention 150
Threatening Resignation 156
Repetition 162
Recommendations for Employees Expressing Organizational Dissent 167
Discussion Questions 172

7 Can Organizational Dissent Be Managed Well? 174
How Much Dissent Can an Organization Tolerate? 177
Mechanisms Used to Solicit and Capture Organizational Dissent 181

Organizational Recommendations for Cultivating Dissent 193
Time Again 198
Discussion Questions 199

References 200

Index 215

List of Illustrations

Tables

3.1 Organizing perspectives and organizational dissent 71
4.1 Typology of dissent-triggering events 99
6.1 Typology of relational outcomes 154
6.2 Typology of organizational outcomes 155
6.3 Recommendations for employees expressing organizational dissent 169
7.1 Organizational recommendations for cultivating dissent 196

Figures

2.1 The relationship of organizational dissent to other concepts 51
3.1 Theoretical explanations of organizational dissent 75
4.1 Dissent-triggering events and individual tolerance for dissent 97
5.1 Decision premises and assessment of dissent-triggering events 120
5.2 Typology of organizational dissent 125
6.1 Constructive versus destructive circumvention 153
6.2 Factors affecting repetition 163
6.3 Empirical findings regarding repetition 164

7.1 Factors determining underrepresented, optimal, and overloaded dissent conditions 180
7.2 Variation in voice mechanisms 182
7.3 Variation in type of dissent accommodated by voice mechanisms 183
7.4 Determinants of the viability and efficacy of voice mechanisms 192

Box

2.1 Working conceptual definitions 32

Preface

Over twenty-five years ago, the man largely recognized as the father of organizational communication stridently called for a rethinking of our pedagogy. In an article entitled "Rocking boats, blowing whistles, and teaching speech communication," Charles Redding (1985) argued that organizational communication pedagogy needed to change. He was one of the first to recognize that dissent could be good for organizations. Furthermore, he admonished communication instructors for perpetuating the "management knows best" ideology and encouraged us to have students spend time thinking about things that would cause them to speak out at work – to dissent. This book is a response to that call. It is grounded in the popular but still rebuffed premise that organizations can benefit from dissent. And it embraces the often touted yet seldom realized assertion that employees should be freed up to express dissent. This book aims to provide students and other readers with an understanding of the principles and practices that shape organizational dissent in contemporary workplaces.

Chapter 1 examines how organizational dissent has been positioned historically and in popular culture. It presents several relevant case studies that illustrate the spectrum of reactions to dissenters and the possible outcomes of dissent expression and then moves to consider the role and place of dissent in society generally, as well as why it remains fundamentally unwelcome in organizations.

Chapter 2 presents a working definition and conceptualization of organizational dissent that provides a reference point for the remaining chapters. This chapter examines several concepts that are related to, but remain distinct from, organizational dissent: organizational conflict, upward influence, employee resistance, employee voice, and whistleblowing. It closes with a discussion of how each of these concepts relates to and overlaps with organizational dissent, which helps differentiate dissent as a unique construct.

Chapter 3 places organizational dissent in the broader context of leading organizational perspectives. This chapter illustrates how organizational dissent functions within classical and contemporary approaches to the study of organizations. It then considers how theories drawn from across disciplines explain and shape dissent expression. In particular, the chapter reviews theories that address situational, motivational, and explanatory factors associated with dissent expression.

Chapter 4 tackles the issue of what causes dissent. Before providing a review of actual dissent-triggering events, it establishes the context within which events become triggers. This is accomplished by examining the economic, political, and socio-cultural factors that affect organizational dissent, as well as a set of commonly experienced barriers that exist within organizations. Finally, the chapter reviews eleven familiar dissent triggers, using employee narratives to illustrate how each occurs in contemporary workplaces.

Chapters 5 and 6 look at how employees actually express dissent. Chapter 5 begins by reviewing prevalent models of organizational dissent – discussing the factors that determine and moderate dissent expression. It then presents an overview of the forms of organizational dissent expressed by employees. This chapter closes by examining dissent expression in alternative organizational structures and via communication technologies and social media. Chapter 6, in turn, focuses specifically on the risk-laden choice of expressing upward dissent to management. It includes an in-depth review of five different upward dissent strategies. The chapter concludes by offering a set of recommendations for employees who choose to express dissent.

Chapter 7, the final chapter, steps back from an individual perspective to address what organizations can do to accommodate dissent. It begins with a discussion of how much dissent organizations can tolerate and then reviews several mechanisms organizations use to solicit and capture dissent. The chapter ends by providing particular strategies organizations can adopt to cultivate dissent.

Across chapters organizational dissent is explored through case studies, popular examples, and employee narratives. These features of the book help situate dissent as an everyday occurrence rather than something unusual. They reveal how commonplace and routine dissent can be, but do so in a way that concurrently highlights how risky and complicated it remains. Accordingly, the case studies, examples, and narratives powerfully animate the conceptual foundations of the text.

The author thanks Tim Hegstrom for mentoring from afar and for carrying the organizational dissent torch. He is grateful to his colleagues in Communication Studies at Arizona State University who have tolerated or joined him in expressing organizational dissent, and to his students who have helped collect data over the years. He is privileged to have worked with the fine people at Polity – Andrea Drugan for her editorial expertise and Lauren Mulholland for managing logistics. Thanks are due also to the group of reviewers who gave generously of their time and helped strengthen the work.

1

Why is Organizational Dissent Relevant?

> He that wrestles with us strengthens our nerves, and sharpens our skill. Our antagonist is our helper.
>
> – Edmund Burke

Although they were written in 1790 as part of a political pamphlet contesting the French Revolution, Burke's words still resonate clearly today – some two hundred plus years later. They capture the very essence of why dissent or disagreement with the majority viewpoint is so critical to society generally and the healthy functioning of organizations in particular. As we close out the first decade of the twenty-first century we remain mired in a global economic crisis. Countries have amassed staggering deficits. Giant organizations deemed "too big to fail" have been resuscitated at great expense. Banks have collapsed. The housing bubble has burst. Container ships sit idle and empty as international trade has waned. And entire industries, such as the US-based automobile manufacturers, have been bailed out. In all of this, there is little mention of any dissent about the organizational decisions, strategies, and choices that have brought us here. There is a disturbing absence of whistleblowers sounding the alarm and trying to warn us. Yet if we turn back the hands of time just a few years we will arrive at a point when whistleblowers, those ordinary employees courageous enough to publicly question their organizations, were front and center in our public consciousness.

Three women stand, arms folded defiantly, on the cover of

the December 30, 2003, issue of *Time* magazine. They are not politicians, movie stars, or pop music idols. They are not Olympic athletes draped in gold medals. They are not supermodels or corporate czars. They are "Persons of the Year" – designated as such because they blew the whistle on their respective organizations. Coleen Rowley, Cynthia Cooper, and Sherron Watkins did not aspire or ask to be on the cover of the weekly news magazine. According to *Time* reporters Richard Lacayo and Amanda Ripley:

> They were people who did right just by doing their jobs rightly – which means ferociously, with eyes open and with the bravery the rest of us always hope we have and may never know if we do. Their lives may not have been at stake, but Watkins, Rowley, and Cooper put pretty much everything else on the line. Their jobs, their health, their privacy, their sanity – they risked all of them to bring us needed word of trouble inside crucial institutions. (2002, p. 32)

The actions of these women are characterized fairly as courageous in light of the public and institutional scrutiny they suffered. But at a very simple level they acted not so differently from most employees. They saw issues at work that they felt should be addressed and they simply chose to express organizational dissent.

Lacayo and Ripley (2002) are careful to point out that they were reluctant heroes, cast into the spotlight only when their memos were leaked. Yet they believed in the idea that their workplaces served the world in some significant way, and they were ready to hold those organizations accountable for transgressions. The fact that they were all women is interesting as well. It cannot be easily dismissed by the short-sided notion that they would have less to lose in the workplace than their male counterparts, as all three were the primary breadwinners in their respective households. A closer look at each of their cases is warranted.

Coleen Rowley was enamored with the FBI from a young age. But in the wake of the tragic events of 9/11 she found herself lamenting the bureau's failure to take seriously concerns raised by agents in her Minneapolis field office prior to the terrorist attacks. As part of a joint inquiry by the House and Senate Intelligence Committees, she and others were invited to Washington for a private interview. Rowley had so much to tell. She wanted to make sure she would not leave anything out. After two and half sleepless nights worrying about what she might forget, sometime around 3 a.m. Saturday morning she headed to her office to jot down some notes. She began writing and continued until her husband called at 7 p.m. the next evening. She had been at it for sixteen hours, and by the end of the weekend her notes extended to thirteen pages. She realized that she had produced something more than just a series of notes – it was a declaration about the current state of affairs at the FBI. She dropped the memo off the next day in Washington for FBI Director Robert Mueller and two members of the Senate Committee on Intelligence. The memo was leaked to the press and two weeks later she was back in Washington testifying in open hearings.

In the months that followed Rowley was applauded by lower-ranking employees in the bureau, appreciative that she had exposed some of the heavy-handed top-down management practices that had become so pervasive at the FBI. She was thanked and winked at by these colleagues. In contrast, she was attacked by former agents, who encouraged her to resign. In the first interview she granted, Rowley told *Time* magazine reporters: "Loyalty to whoever you work for is extremely important. The only problem is, it's not *the* most important thing. And when it comes to not admitting mistakes, or covering up or not rectifying things only to save face, that's a problem" (Ripley and Sieger, 2002, p. 37). Her memo flew in the face of the bureau's loyalty-above-all-else credo. Yet it exposed the FBI to much needed scrutiny, which resulted in an overhaul of the agency.

To Rowley's right in the cover image is Cynthia Cooper. Cooper returned to her hometown of Clinton, Mississippi, after a divorce and went to work for WorldCom there. In 1994 she started their internal-audit department, working strategically to convince her superiors that internal audits could save the company millions of dollars in wasteful spending. She was successful. The long-distance telephone service company continued to expand and prosper throughout the 1990s.

A few years later, with the long-distance market saturated with a host of carriers, earnings declined. Cooper learned of WorldCom's fraudulent accounting practices by accident. She received a complaint from the director of the wireless division, who claimed that corporate accounting had removed $400 million from the division's reserve account. Cooper's unit was responsible for operational audits but not for audits of the organization's financial reports. That task had been outsourced to Arthur Anderson. When she contacted a representative from Anderson about the matter she was told that it was not a problem. Unconvinced, she confronted Worldcom's CFO and was told "everything was fine and she should backoff" (Ripley, 2002, p. 47).

The CFO's hostility gave Cooper pause. She decided to investigate the issue further, mounting her own team to secretly pore over Andersen's work. Much to their dismay they discovered an accounting ploy used to make the company look much more profitable than it actually was. Annual operating costs were disguised as capital expenditures that were to be stretched over several years. The deliberate mislabeling of expenditures resulted in a $2.4 billion profit for the year rather than a $662 million loss. The CFO and controller were unable to explain the miscalculation to WorldCom's board of directors and were dismissed.

Over the summer Cooper's audit memos were released to the press and she became the face of WorldCom's fraud. When called by a WorldCom representative and told the press wanted to make her a hero, she responded, "I'm not a hero, I'm just doing my job" (Ripley, 2002, p. 49). While Cooper did end up in the limelight, she found little solace in her efforts. In July of 2002 WorldCom submitted the largest bankruptcy filing in US history (Romero and Atlas, 2002). Shareholders lost billions of dollars and thousands of employees lost their jobs. In the office Cooper was greeted at times with a cold shoulder. Water cooler conversations ceased. Many of the remaining employees questioned her tactics, believing instead that the company could have borrowed its way out of the crisis. Others were bemused by the fact that she had seen so little recognition from corporate officers. One colleague told *Time*, "What gets me angry is that after all she has done, you would think she would be rewarded" (Ripley, 2002, p. 50).

The third person in the cover photo is Sherron Watkins. She was the first whistleblower to sound the alarm in a year marked by corporate scandal, and the most celebrated (Morse and Bower, 2002). In addition to the recognition from *Time*, she was named by *Glamour* magazine as one of its 2002 "Women of the Year" and by Barbara Walters as one of her "10 Most Fascinating People" of 2002. On Valentine's Day 2002 Watkins testified before Congress about the company she had loved. Her testimony detailed the auditing fraud perpetrated by Enron – one of the largest corporations in the United States – where she was the vice president of corporate development. After uncovering irregularities with some of the firm's accounting practices the previous summer, she crafted a seven-page memo to warn then CEO Kenneth Lay. He decided to have Enron's law firm investigate. In September he told Enron employees that the company was in strong financial shape, but in early December Enron filed for Chapter 11. Enron imploded, leaving $30 billion in debt and 21,000 employees jobless.

Blowing the whistle is costly to both employees and organizations. It can, however, lead to important and necessary reform. Whistleblowing by Karen Silkwood led to reform in the nuclear power industry. Dissent from David Franklin led to reform in the pharmaceutical industry. And the efforts of Watkins and Cooper described above resulted in what Cooper called "a corporate-governance revolution" that led to reform in oversight of corporate financial reporting (Lacayo and Ripley, 2002, p. 33). The Sarbanes–Oxley Act now requires stricter standards regarding the accuracy and reporting of financial statements by all US public companies.

Whether real or fictionalized, whistleblowers continue to inhabit our popular imagination. We can find them in novels like John Grisham's *The Rainmaker* (1995), where lawyer and protagonist Rudy Baylor's case against an insurance company hinges on key testimony from a corporate insider, or on Capitol Hill in Michael Neff's recent book *Year of the Rhinoceros* (2009), where young idealist Manny Eden begins his career in public service by going to work for the Office of Whistleblower Counsel. We can find them in popular films such as *The China Syndrome* (1979), *Silkwood*

(1983), and *The Insider* (1999). The dates of these films indicate that whistleblowers do not make regular appearances on the big screen, but when they do their stories have the gravitational pull to attract some of Hollywood's biggest stars (Jack Lemmon, Meryl Streep, and Russell Crowe respectively). And in each case their performances have garnered Best Actor/Actress nominations. Indeed, the whistleblower's story is powerful stuff.

Take the film *The China Syndrome* (1979), which examines the failed attempts of fictionalized nuclear power plant shift manager Jack Godell. The shift manager becomes alarmed about safety concerns at a California nuclear power plant after an emergency shutdown and implores the foreman not to restart the reactor until a thorough investigation can be completed, but is unsuccessful. He decides to go to the media with his concerns and avoids an attempt on his life en route to giving testimony at a safety hearing. Godell hastily returns to the plant and finds it has been restored to full capacity. In desperation he commandeers the gun of one of the security guards, takes over the control room, threatens to destroy the plant, and demands to be interviewed by the press. As the interviewers set up, a staged emergency shutdown is triggered, allowing for a SWAT team to breach the control room. In the film's climactic scene Godell is shot and killed. The safety of the plant still hangs in the balance but the immediate crisis has ended.

Godell is not the only whistleblower to die on screen in service to a greater cause. *Silkwood* (1983) chronicles the true story of Karen Silkwood, an employee who sounded the alarm about safety concerns at the Kerr-McGee Corporation's nuclear fuel production facility in Crescent City, Oklahoma. Initially she took her concerns to the union. When the union failed to act she prepared additional documentation which she planned to bring to the media. She died in a suspicious car accident the night before she was to hand over the explosive documentation to a reporter from the *New York Times*. The damming information she had collected was reputed to have been with her at the time but, mysteriously, was not recovered at the accident scene.

While not all whistleblowers end up in stand-offs or in suspicious accidents, their stories continue to intrigue. Consider the strange but true story of Mark Whitacre, whose escapades were reported in the book *The Informant* (Eichenwald, 2000) and provided the material for the 2009 black-comedy motion picture of the same name. Whitacre worked for agri-business powerhouse Archer Daniels Midland (ADM) in the mid-1990s, rising to the position of president of the bio-products division. In November of 1992, at the behest of his wife, who threatened to go to the FBI herself, Whitacre revealed the details of an elaborate price-fixing scheme perpetrated by ADM and it competitors. He became an informant, taping secret meetings of the price-fixing activities over the next three years, and provided the FBI with hundreds of hours of evidence. However, the evidence was suspect, as Whitacre was indicted for defrauding ADM of $9 million while serving as an informant for the FBI. The pressure of informing apparently gave rise to bizarre behavior, a suicide attempt, and the disclosure that he was suffering from bipolar disorder. Whitacre did not believe he should see any prison time for his transgressions and that he should be treated favorably due to his cooperation with the FBI. Thus, he fired his original lawyer, who was waging a successful case with the intention, and likely outcome, of ending up with reduced prison time. Whitacre hired another lawyer and ironically ended up serving almost nine years in prison – three times longer than the three-year sentences dispensed to the corporate criminals against whom he helped build a case. Whitacre managed to curtail his mental illness, served his jail time, and now heads up a biotechnology firm in California.

The public is captivated by a good whistleblower tale. Such stories usually involve the protagonist in a lopsided battle against powerful institutions – institutions buttressed by resources that clearly outstrip those available to the whistleblower, a hero or heroine thrust reluctantly into action, yet undeterred. They are classic David versus Goliath accounts – juxtaposing rich and poor, big and small, good and evil, dishonesty and candor, and corruption and integrity. They portray the underdog snarling at the bully. But this is the archetype that overshadows the customary expressions of dissent that occur daily in every organization. Not all of us – in fact, very few of us – will become whistleblowers. Most of us will confront problematic issues in the workplace, however, and have to decide whether to express dissent or to remain silent about such issues. The purpose of this book is to look at the normative practices deployed to express dissent in contemporary workplaces. This first chapter serves to survey the popular and mediated representations of organizational dissent, to illustrate the prevalence of dissent within society generally, and to demonstrate the relevance of dissent in modern organizations. To begin, we can look to several case studies to determine some of the common themes evoked by portrayals of whistleblowers in popular culture.

The Case of Sibel Edmonds: Dissent Gagged

Sibel Edmonds began working as a translator for the FBI shortly after 9/11. Fluent in three languages, she was hired to help with a backlog of documents and to respond quickly to those that were mounting up as interrogations of detainees intensified in the days following the attacks. Although Edmonds did not see herself working necessarily as a professional translator, she took on the responsibility out of a sense of patriotic duty (Rose, 2005).

In an interview on *60 Minutes* that aired several years later (Kohn, 2004), Edmonds reported that translators were told by their supervisors to let work "pile up." In so doing they could demonstrate the need for more translators and help the department expand. Despite these directives Edmonds diligently pressed on with the arduous task of completing lengthy translations. Her immediate supervisor did not appreciate these efforts and apparently erased completed translations from her computer file after she had left the office. "The next day, I would come to work, turn on my computer, and the work would be gone. The translation would be gone," she told *60 Minutes.* Frustrated with having to start over on completed translations, she approached her supervisor and was told to consider it a lesson.

To this point Edmonds's case is a simple and clear example of organizational dissent – an instance in which an employee disagrees with a workplace policy or practice and shares that discontent with others in the office. But her case quickly became much more complicated. Two months into the job she was visited at home by a fellow translator from work. The coworker and her husband came to Edmonds's home on a Sunday morning and proceeded to invite her to get better acquainted with certain organizations – organizations that were the very subject matter of the wiretaps she was translating. Acting favorably toward these organizations would allow Sibel and her husband, they were told, to live well and retire early. In short, she was being propositioned to engage in espionage. When she later refused the invitation she recalls that her coworker got very angry and threatened her and her family.

The situation worsened when Edmonds realized that this particular coworker was in fact leaving crucial information out of translations that would implicate those being investigated by the FBI. Edmonds reported her concerns about the inaccuracies in these translations to her supervisor. In the documentary film *Kill the Messenger* (Hahon et al., 2006), which recounts her ordeal, she states that she was told to "hush it, and not talk about it." She then shared these transgressions with members of middle management. Retaliation started: assignments were taken away, her documents and work disappeared, and her computer was confiscated. Undeterred, Edmonds took her concerns to the highest level – Director of the FBI Robert Mueller. On Friday March 22 at 4 p.m., six short months after she had begun working for the FBI, Sibel Edmonds was fired and escorted out of the building. Although her official notice of termination gave no specific reason for her dismissal, one of the men who escorted her out that day revealed that she had taken the situation too far. She no longer worked for the FBI.

Edmonds filed a lawsuit against the FBI for wrongful termination, which prompted an investigation into the case by the Department of Justice. However, her case was short-lived, as her dismissal was quickly sanctioned by Attorney General John Ashcroft when he invoked the states secrets privilege, essentially barring the case from going forward on account of national security concerns. Not only was Edmonds's case stalled, but she was gagged from speaking about it or the alleged incidents. She was later called by Congress to provide closed-door testimony before the 9/11 Commission. Their report, released on July 24, 2004, stretched to 567 pages, but there was no mention whatsoever of Sibel Edmonds's claims.

Incensed by these omissions, and backed by a large cohort of 100 or so other disaffected intelligence agency employees, in 2004 Edmonds started the National Security Whistleblowers Coalition (www.nswbc.org). Although she had been gagged, her story did eventually garner the attention of media outlets. She made appearances on CNN, MSNBC, and National Public Radio, and the *New York Times*, *USA Today*, and the *Washington Post* covered her story as well. The result of this ongoing saga and her efforts to keep freedom of speech, particularly as it pertains to national security, pertinent to the American public have made her a bona fide celebrity whistleblower. As such, Sibel Edmonds now maintains a website (justacitizen.com) where she blogs regularly about free speech issues.

Edmonds's organizational dissent mushroomed from a simple complaint about the honest representation of her work to an unusual case of espionage and national security. Yet it reveals some common facets of organizational dissent. She did not set out to blow the whistle: she simply wanted to address some concerns that troubled her – a simple concern that involved misrepresenting the work she completed and a more complex issue that involved the potential for translators to compromise national security. Her situation follows a clear trajectory that is true of most whistleblowing cases (Stewart, 1980). They begin with some disclosure to management and move to more advanced levels of involvement only when the employee is ignored. When this occurs with significant and important issues that are not easily dismissed, we can expect that employees will, as Edmonds did, take their concerns up the chain of command. They will look for responsiveness from higher-positioned people in management. This often results in the type of retaliation that Edmonds experienced. Shunned by coworkers and ignored by management, but still convinced that issues deserve to be addressed, dissenters eventually look outside their organizations for validation and support. After all else fails, employees will solicit the attention of industry-governing bodies or the media. When they do, they become whistleblowers. This same pattern is apparent in other whistleblower cases like the one considered next.

The Case of Dr Jeffrey Wigand: Dissent and Credibility

Dr Jeffrey Wigand, having served as vice president for research and development for Brown & Williamson Tobacco Corporation for four years, was the first high-ranking former executive of a tobacco company to expose industry trade secrets. Working on the frontlines of R&D at one of America's largest tobacco companies provided him with a genuine insider's perspective. After his departure from the tobacco industry Wigand cooperated with governmental agencies investigating the tobacco industry by providing a key deposition. His assistance was instrumental in bringing about the landmark $368 billion settlement between the attorneys general of forty states and the tobacco industry.

In 1995 Wigand sat for an interview on *60 Minutes* to air his concerns about the practices in the tobacco industry. The interview, however, was shelved for six months after CBS executives determined that it would be too risky to run due to concerns about the network being sued for breach of Wigand's confidentiality agreement. They eventually aired the story in early February of 1996 (Bergman, 1996). Wigand's claims revealed what had long been suspected in the tobacco industry – that tobacco companies knew that cigarettes were harmful to people's health, that they knew nicotine was addictive, and that they had gone to great lengths to hide this knowledge in corporate correspondence and secret documents.

In the *60 Minutes* interview Wigand recounted being hired to help develop a safer cigarette – one that had less harmful side effects. Yet the minutes from a meeting of scientists from around the world who worked for British American Tobacco, the parent company of his employer, were stripped by a corporate lawyer of any discussion of this possibility. Any record of efforts to develop a "safer" cigarette inferred from a public liability standpoint that current cigarettes were unsafe. The lawyers' meddling continued, editing and reviewing – striking any reference to "less hazardous" or "safer" in the reports that Wigand produced. Tired of this interference, Wigand approached the president of the company to voice his concerns. He was told in very clear terms that the company was no longer pursuing a safer cigarette as it would expose their existing products. Wigand states, "I got angry" but "I bit my tongue." He was earning over $300,000 at the time, living comfortably and supporting his wife and two daughters well. He decided not to push the matter further.

Wigand went back to work and refocused his efforts on the additives that were being put into cigarettes. There was mounting evidence that one particular additive, used to sweeten the taste of the tobacco, was a known cancer-causing agent. In response to these developments, Wigand says that he sent a memo to the president claiming that he could no longer in good conscience continue with the practice of adding a known carcinogen to the product. He was told by the president of the company that he should continue looking for a substitute, but that the additive would stay in the product because removing it would affect sales. With this decision the president had made a clear breach of public health. The same corporate officer was later promoted to CEO, and he moved quickly to have Wigand fired in March of 2004. As part of a severance package Wigand was required to sign a strict confidentiality agreement.

But Wigand's story was too compelling to ignore. Congress and the Food and Drug Administration were investigating the tobacco industry in the spring of 2004. Wigand talked to the investigators and shortly thereafter received death threats against his family. He received two menacing phone calls. According to Wigand's diary, the first claimed, "Don't mess with tobacco anymore. How are your kids?", whereas the second said, "Leave tobacco alone or else you'll find your kids hurt. They're pretty girls now." Wigand began carrying a handgun for protection, yet the threats did not deter him from testifying on November 29, 1995, in a case brought by the State of Mississippi against the tobacco industry. The case sought reimbursement for public healthcare costs related to smoking-induced illnesses. Prior to the trial Mike Moore, the attorney general of Mississippi, told *60 Minutes* that "the information that Jeffrey has, I think, is the most important information that has ever come out against the tobacco industry."

In the subsequent months his former employer went on the offensive. According to the *Wall Street Journal*, the company hired a private investigation firm to comb through Wigand's past, a public relations firm to provide press releases on his misdeeds to the media, and a scientific consultant to review his research for signs of plagiarism. The culmination of these efforts, a 500-page dossier titled "The Misconduct of Jeffrey S. Wigand Available in the Public Record," was delivered directly to the newspaper. The report alleged that Wigand had filed false reimbursement claims, shoplifted, and falsified statements on his resume and during a videotaped job interview. However, after an internal review of the content the *Wall Street Journal* concluded: "A close look at the file, and independent research by this newspaper into its key claims, indicates that many of the serious allegations against Mr. Wigand are backed by scant or contradictory evidence. Some of the charges – including that he pleaded guilty to shoplifting – are demonstrably untrue" (Hwang and Geyelin, 1996). Yet Brown & Williamson's public relations representative claimed on *60 Minutes* that Wigand's life was "a pattern of lies." The smear campaign against Wigand was widespread, picked up nationally, and appeared even in the local market of Louisville, Kentucky, where he was teaching high-school science at the time. Wigand's defiance cost him dearly. His reputation was questioned, his credibility challenged, and his personal life fractured. He ended up divorced and living apart from his two daughters.

According to his website (http://www.jeffreywigand.com), Dr Wigand now provides educational seminars designed to inform the public about cigarette design, the use of tobacco additives, and nicotine addiction and manipulation. He started SMOKE-FREE KIDS – a nonprofit foundation designed to address and combat the tobacco industry's efforts to introduce children and youth to smoking and tobacco products. In addition, he has worked as a consultant for state and national governments seeking to create smoke-free zones in public spaces.

Like Edmonds, Wigand would have preferred to have his company address the issues rather than to have been thrust into the limelight. He, however, was up against an incredibly powerful industry that had no interest in making the changes he was suggesting. We can see from his case that whistleblowing is a high-stakes game. Both Edmonds and Wigand were restricted from speaking about their experiences and suffered retaliation. Wigand's case highlights another aspect of whistleblowing: discrediting the dissenter (Near and Jensen, 1983). His former employer went to great lengths to discredit him in the hopes that people would become suspicious of his allegations. Regardless of whether or not this strategy proves successful, it certainly takes a toll on organizational dissenters. These two cases demonstrate how dissent leads to whistleblowing and how it can put employees under considerable duress. But this is not always the case.

The Traitorous Eight: Dissent Births an Industry

Historian Adam Goodheart (2006), in a guest column for the *New York Times*, designated September 18, 1957, as one of ten days that changed history. What makes this particular date special? According to Goodheart – the revolt of the nerds. It was on this day that eight dissenting scientists walked out of Shockley Labs. They subsequently started Fairchild Semiconductor and invented the microprocessor. It was the birth of Silicon Valley, the electronics industry, and the digital age. The eight departing scientists became known as the "traitorous eight" in Silicon Valley folklore. Today, countless high-technology firms, including National Semiconductor, Teledyne, and Intel, can trace their lineage to Fairchild Semiconductor (Addison, 2009).

Hired only eighteen months earlier, the eight men were Robert Noyce, Jean Hoerni, Victor Grinich, Julius Blank, Eugene Kleiner,

Gordon Moore, Jay Last, and Sheldon Roberts. All under thirty, they comprised a collection of scientists and engineers with complementary skills in physics, metallurgy, chemistry, and electrical and chemical engineering. They had been hand-picked by William Shockley, a well-known scientist who co-invented the transistor, to join the company he had started, Shockley Transistor Laboratories. The men were attracted by Shockley's promise to build transistors using silicon and new untested technologies.

Under Shockley's management the eight men soon discovered that he "was a difficult boss" who was "subject to fits of temper" (Berlin, 2001, p. 70). He was a scientist by trade and had little experience managing people or running the daily operations of a business. Yet all was forgiven when Shockley was awarded the Nobel Prize for physics in 1956 for his work on the transistor. The eight scientists celebrated alongside Shockley and were reminded of how prestigious it was to work under his tutelage. But Shockley's unpredictable behavior and mismanagement continued. At one point he suspected that a lab accident was in fact an act of sabotage. To get to the bottom of the suspected plot against the lab he subjected employees to lie-detector tests.

Moreover, the promise of working at the cutting edge was short-lived. Shockley decided to focus the company's efforts on a product he had invented. Employees raised concerns, noting that his device was much more expensive to mass produce than the silicon transistors they had been hired to develop. Furthermore, they indicated that the customer base for his device was small in comparison to the possible applications of the silicon transistor. Shockley was obsessed, though, with his own invention and paid no heed to these suggestions.

In May of 1957 the eight scientists took their concerns about Shockley's management to Arnold Beckman, the investor who had fronted the money for Shockley Labs (PBS, 1999). Beckman agreed to seek a new manager and to move Shockley into a new director's position. Two months later Beckman retracted his offer – realizing that removing Shockley would be detrimental to the scientist's reputation. The situation for the eight was now untenable. They had unsuccessfully circumvented their supervisor, and they knew they would need to go. The men began to negotiate with other possible investors and found a partner in New York industrialist Sherman Fairchild, who agreed to make an initial investment of $1.3 million to start a new company, Fairchild Semiconductor. Robert Noyce led the group at Fairchild, becoming its first head of research and development. His hands-off leadership style, emphasis on innovation, and entrepreneurship defined the firm and set the parameters for a management style that would be emulated in many other Silicon Valley companies in the decades to follow.

For the traitorous eight, organizational dissent led to uncharted territory. It set them on a pioneering course that brought about the development of an entire industry. Certainly the computer and digital age would have arrived eventually had the men not left Shockley Labs. But their dissent put them right at the center of it all. They were key players because of their willingness to press on with their vision of innovation realized through silicon-based applications. They did not bow to the authoritative management practices and the dictates of innovation espoused at Shockley Labs. Their dissent, construed as treasonous, was necessary to distance them from a world-renowned Nobel Prize winner who did not share their foresight. Given their historical significance, it is worthwhile noting that their having been branded as traitorous says something about the place and role of dissent in our society. It is paradoxical. The dissenters profiled in these cases were vilified by some and lionized by others.

Society and Dissent

Dissent is all around us. It is in our government, in our schools, in our leisure activities, and in the organizations where we work. It is a fact of modern life – some would say a necessary evil. It is dissent that keeps us from falling prey to the perils of conformity (Sunstein, 2003). Some measure of conformity is necessary in collectives, but it can be dangerous when overplayed. Conformity narrows the availability of opinions and leads to easier and quicker, but often suspect decisions. Dissent, on the other hand, replenishes the wellspring of opinions. Decisions may come more slowly, but they will be vetted more rigorously. The antidote for conformity, dissent allows us to think and speak for ourselves rather than to ingest and reiterate the positions of others. It is a fundamental component of human interaction. Perhaps that is why it features so prominently in many of our public institutions.

The UK Parliament's House of Lords has been keeping track of dissent for quite some time. Members can register their dissent to decisions in one of three ways: first, by signing their name to the record of decision under the Latin heading "dissentientibus" (first recorded in 1549); second, by signing their name next to a reason or reasons that were added to the record (first appeared in 1641); and, third, by signing next to some but not all reasons provided on the record. Although expressing dissent has been standard operating procedure in the House of Lords for several centuries, there have been measures put in place to keep it in check. For example, in 1722 a standing order was introduced that required members to register their protests in the clerk's records by 2 p.m. the following day. Protests or signatures accompanied by reasons were never terribly prevalent, but have waned considerably since decision lists began to be published in 1857. The last large protest, which included fourteen signatures, occurred in 1911. The practice has declined further, with only five protests since, and the last three being signed by only one member (Jones, 2008).

Dissent is also a fundamental component of the way in which the US Supreme Court functions (Ray, 2002). Judges regularly enter their "dissent" on decisions that the court reaches, but that has not always been the practice. Before the 1930s the Supreme Court favored *per curiam* decisions that presented a single argument for their legal decisions. Accordingly, the court's opinion would be devoid not only of dissent, but also of authorship – presenting a single, clear and unified voice. This practice began to change, however, with the first dissent offered by Oliver Wendell Holmes, Jr, in 1909. It was almost two full decades before another dissent accompanied a *per curiam* opinion, in 1938. The reluctant one-paragraph dissent offered by Holmes returned as an eighteen-page opinion provided by newly appointed Justice Hugo Black. He had been only three months on the job before offering his dissent, and other justices questioned the authenticity and authorship of his unprecedented lengthy offering. They apparently misjudged their colleague. Black would go on to serve on the Supreme Court until 1971 – offering twenty-seven separate dissents over the years. A tradition of dissent on the court was born. Justice William Douglas, appointed only a year after Black, bolstered that tradition considerably, and in his thirty-six-year term on the court he penned an impressive seventy-one dissents. The act of offering a Supreme Court dissenting opinion has become so commonplace, in fact, that it now registers as part of most dictionary definitions of dissent.

The White House is not immune to dissent. It has been heard by several sitting US presidents regarding foreign policy decisions (White, 2007). Secretary of Defense Charles E. Wilson advised President Dwight Eisenhower not to escalate the US presence in Vietnam. Similarly, Under Secretary of State for Economic and Agricultural Affairs George Ball openly criticized President Lyndon Johnson's Vietnam policy. As ambassador to the United Nations, Adlai Stevenson implored President John F. Kennedy to take a less hawkish approach toward Cuba. Author Mark White, in his book *Against the President* (2007), considers the role of dissent in foreign policy decisions. He speculates that, if accepted, such dissent might have resulted in different foreign policy regarding the Vietnam War and the Bay of Pigs. In essence, it would have reshaped modern US history as we know it.

Dissent has been important in schools and universities as well. In September of 1958 nine African American women intentionally took their children out of Harlem neighborhood schools and started an alternative unaccredited school. They were fed up with their complaints about decrepit facilities and overcrowding being ignored by the school board. In October, after their children had been absent from public schools for thirty-five consecutive days and had been declared truant, parents involved in the boycott were subpoenaed by the New York City Board of Education. They were charged with violating the state's compulsory education law and with criminal neglect. Although the majority of the cases landed in the hands of a judge who viewed them as simply an issue of truancy and ordered the children back to school, two cases did not. In these cases, Judge Justine Polier found the parents innocent of the charges and affirmed their right to challenge the school board. Her ruling exposed the inequities in the system as a result of segregation. The success of the boycott "began to mobilize widespread dissent that would fuel the movement for a decentralized education system controlled by local school boards" (de Forest, 2008).

In higher education we can look to the events of May 4, 1970. On that day the Ohio National Guard opened fired on a group of protestors at Kent State University, killing four. Students had gathered to protest US involvement in the Vietnam War. Reflecting upon the tragic events, former university president Michael Schwartz (1982–1990) concluded that "A central lesson in all of this was the importance of the defense of the rights of individual dissent as a basic, unifying and organizing principle of the university itself" (Schwartz, 1996, p. 177).

In popular culture today dissent can take many forms. The Crosby, Stills, Nash and Young lyric "Four dead in Ohio" keeps the aforementioned events at Kent State University in our public consciousness, as does the photograph of an unnamed dissident standing in front of a line of tanks in Tiananmen Square in 1989. Dissent even factors significantly in our leisure activities. All major sports, for example, require referees. And all referees must brace themselves for the onslaught of dissent directed at them by fans, coaches, and athletes. Wolfson and Neave (2007) found that dissent was endemic to refereeing, and refs reported that they expected dissent from players, coaches, and fans. To deflect such criticism they relied on external attributions of others, taking into account others' lack of knowledge about rules of the sport and their propensity to show bias for their team.

Although prevalent in popular culture, dissent should not be taken lightly. It is a fundamental driver in dissident groups that set themselves apart from mainstream politics and ideologies. Yet dissent functions even within these groups as a catalyst for factions to splinter. In fact, dissent often causes dissident groups to fracture into military and political factions. This occurred when a more militarized agenda led Hamas to sever from the Palestinian Liberation Organization (PLO) and The Irish Republican Army (IRA) to split from political party Sinn Fein (Siqueira, 2005). Similarly, the Gush Emunim grew out of the National Religious Party in Israel when members felt that the party was not zealous enough about resettlement of lands in the West Bank. Gush Emunim fervently believed that resettlement of occupied territories was the highest duty of Israelis and ended up in several confrontations with police over their pursuit of that goal (Schnall, 1977).

But not all dissent within dissident groups leads to militarization. Consider the case of Sayyid Imam al-Sharif (Brachman, 2009). Sharif co-founded al Qaeda alongside his former protégé Ayman al-Zawahiri. He split with Zawahiri years later after falling out over the direction of al Qaeda, but not before penning two highly influential texts that articulated the ideological foundation of Islamic terrorism that took root in the early 1990s. His works made clear that jihad entailed martyrdom and attacks on non-Islamic states. Jailed since 2001, Sharif began writing again, but his subsequent writings challenged al Qaeda's version of jihad, claiming that it violates Islamic law. Terrorism expert Jarret Brachman states, "In a remarkable series of prison writings renouncing violence and attacking al Qaeda on Islamic theological grounds, Sharif has done more to expose the terrorist group's obscurantism and hypocrisy than almost anyone else" (ibid., p. 40). The propensity for dissent to result in political and military activism often leads to its repression.

Repression and Dissent

Political scientists and sociologists have recently advanced models that seek to explain how and when states respond to public dissent (Carey, 2010; Maher and Peterson, 2008; Pierskalla, 2010). In classic models of repression, opposition groups grapple with the risks of protest versus the costs of inaction, while governments struggle to determine whether or not accommodation or repression will curb the escalation of conflict. Of course, escalation is influenced by a regime's capacity to squash protest and its willingness to engage in open conflict with the public (Pierskalla, 2010). Governments or regimes tend to be threatened by and to repress dissent that is organized and violent (Carey, 2010). States that have a history of using violent repression are more likely to continue to do so. The result is that they tend to face more violent forms of dissent in response (Maher and Peterson, 2008). Violent repression occurs more often in countries that offer fewer civil liberties, while states with democratic apparatus tolerate and absorb citizen dissent more readily (Pierskalla, 2010; Maher and Peterson, 2008).

Conflict and human rights scholar Sabine Carey (2010) outlines several types of public or domestic dissent, which vary in terms of violence, level of organization, and number of people involved. Demonstrations, for example, are peaceful nonviolent gatherings of a limited number of people, whereas strikes are nonviolent gatherings that are more highly organized and by definition involve larger groups. Riots, in turn, are spontaneous, violent activities which generally lack organization. Guerilla attacks are violent and, although they appear highly sporadic, are in fact highly organized by a sponsoring agent. They are therefore more thoroughly planned and organized than riots. Revolutions are large-scale, violent, and organized. They are larger in scope and more far-reaching than guerilla attacks. In a comparative study of how different types of public dissent result in more or less repression, Carey found that only guerilla attacks increased the probability of repression. Nonviolent forms of dissent (demonstrations and strikes) as well as spontaneous ones (riots) did not produce enough threat to warrant repressive responses. Moreover, counteracting revolution with repression figured as too high-cost, whereas alternatives like negotiation or seeking exile seemed more appropriate.

But public dissent is no longer domestic. There is evidence to suggest that the global economy and national inequalities affect the state's repression of dissent (Kowalewski and Hoover, 1994). In a watershed moment, a loose amalgam of environmentalists, church groups, trade unionists, anti-poverty groups, nongovermental organization (NGO) members, and concerned citizens protested at the 1999 Seattle meeting of the World Trade Organization (WTO). An estimated 40,000 to 50,000 people were involved in the protests at the WTO's third ministerial conference, and the massive protests resulted in widely publicized riots. The protesters from such divergent backgrounds gathered out of a shared and growing sentiment that corporate interests had hijacked the move to bring international trade and investment into more equitable arrangements (Gandz, 2001).

Dissent, then, is embedded in our institutions, features in our leisure activities, and occurs on domestic and global stages. It is ubiquitous within society. Why, then, do we think of it as such radical behavior? Why is it forbidden fruit? Perhaps because it can expose wrongdoing, highlight errors, reveal shortcomings, and illuminate faults. In short, it can be scary and threatening, not to mention incredibly risky (Waldron and Kassing, 2011). Nevertheless dissent can build camaraderie through contentious but respectful deliberation. It can ensure sound decisions through thoughtful reflection. And it can lead to innovation through honest and introspective consideration of alternative perspectives.

One reason why the value of dissent is often overlooked is because it remains comparatively restricted in modern organizations – the places where we tend to spend a considerable amount of our time. While dissent is institutionalized in many of our governance structures and performed routinely in our leisure activities, it is not nearly as welcome in organizational settings. We are more comfortable shouting our disapproval from the bleachers at a sporting event than we are expressing dissent from the swivel chair in the office conference room. We are more likely to share our discontent with the school board, the homeowner's association, or the local politician than we are to express dissent to management, supervisors, or CEOs. It is strange really. Those of us who live in democratic societies that not only advocate but also demand freedom of speech seem to check our dissent at the door when we step into work. Within organizational settings we tend to remain silent (Milliken et al., 2003). Yet dissent is equally important within and outside organizations. Thus, the final section of this chapter considers some of the reasons why organizational dissent is relevant in the modern workplace.

Dissent in Organizations

Organizations exercise considerable control over our lives (Deetz, 1982; Mumby, 1988). This can be overt, when a supervisor dresses down a subordinate for being late or for failing to meet expectations, or it can occur much more subtly, through unobtrusive means like conformity and social pressure (Tompkins and Cheney, 1985). In these instances the mechanisms of control reside in collaborative work, and employees consent to evaluate and depend on one another for mutual and corporate success (Barker, 1993). This happens when employees unequivocally buy into the mission of the firm with little critical reflection. Some even contend that the power of organizations extends to defining our very selves (Mumby, 1988). As language communities, organizations function to position and constitute our existence as social actors in these places. Thus, organizations are a principal influence on our lives both inside and outside of formal workplaces. We are vested in organizations – those for which we work, but also those that we patronize (e.g., restaurants, health clubs) and those that intersect with our lives in other meaningful ways (e.g., school systems, government agencies).

Historically, organizations have deprived employees of rights readily afforded outside of the workplace – rights like free speech, protest, and privacy (Ewing, 1977; Sanders, 1983). "Management knows best" has long been the fundamental operating premise governing organizations (Ewing, 1977). Employees have come to understand that they should not rock the boat (Redding, 1985). In an early examination of freedom of speech issues in the workplace, Sanders looked at some 200 federal appellate cases. He concluded that court decisions revealed a general assumption "that conflict and dissent are always bad and no good can come from them"

(1983, p. 260). Because organizations are collectives and act as such, there continues to be an inherent tension that pits the opinion of the individual against the force of the collective (Finet, 1994). Not surprisingly, the interests of the organization tend to prevail.

Michels (1962) speaks of the "iron law of oligarchy" that inherently emerges in organizations. This occurs as organizations grow and become more administratively complex. The added complexity results in increased specialization and more expert leadership. As a consequence there is less input into decisions for most organizational members. Organizations, in essence, become more bureaucratic with less provision for employee opinion. This apparently happens even in organizations that have intentionally constructed highly democratic operating structures (Cheney, 1995). Thus, there is a natural tendency in organizations toward supervision and control – a point well made by organizational communication patriarch Charles Redding (1985), who reminded us that, in most organizations, most employees are subordinate to someone. A humorous anecdote shared by the president of a small manufacturing company helps to illustrate this point. The president recounted taking suggestions from the senior management team during a meeting early in his tenure and remembers telling the group that "he would have to check on that." He then had an epiphany of sorts, as he realized in that moment that he was ultimately in charge. There was no one else with whom to check. His story highlights a basic fact of organizational life – very few of us sit, free of supervision, at the top of the reporting chain. We may manage and supervise some employees, but we also tend to be subordinate to someone higher in the chain of command.

So we devote time, energy, and resources to the organizations with which we interact and end up with little opportunity to affect how they operate. But we ought to have some say. From a moral standpoint, expressing dissent is an important component of our basic human right to practice freedom of expression (Redding, 1985). This is one reason why many contemporary organizations have moved toward more democratic forms of organizing (Cotton,

1993). In these arrangements employees are empowered to contribute to organizational decision-making and to do so through open disagreement and clear debate (Pacanowsky, 1988). They are encouraged to dissent, and dissent becomes a critical factor contributing to how organizations function. Yet empowerment is as much perception as process (Chiles and Zorn, 1995). Employees can quickly feel disenfranchised when the promise of empowerment is not realized (Harlos, 2001), when they recognize that the structures set up to provide greater participation are in essence just that, merely structures. We can expect dissent to occur in these instances too – that is, when employees confront the disconnect between unfulfilled expectations about meaningful involvement and the lip service that characterizes an organization's espoused efforts to function more democratically (Kassing, 1997).

Organizational dissent, then, will emerge from any number of motives. It can occur as an act of contestation against organizational constraints or transpire as an expectation of the give and take that characterizes highly participative organizations. It can erupt, as well, when promises of employee empowerment fall short. All of this is to say that few organizations will be immune to dissent. Whether organizations are more or less restrictive, more or less participative, or simply pretending to be participative while still functioning restrictively, there will be dissent (Kassing, 1997). For organizations that tolerate and are receptive to dissent it can be a valuable tool for providing corrective feedback about practices and policies that are not working well (Hegstrom, 1995). It can alert management to shortcomings in leadership, as Coleen Rowley sought to do with the FBI. It can signal challenges associated with organizational change, as the "traitorous eight" attempted to address with Shockley Labs. Or it can shine a light on unethical practices, as Dr Jeffrey Wigand hoped to do with Brown & Williamson. These employees ended up as whistleblowers or exiting their firms, or both, as their dissent went unheeded. Opportunities to correct organizational faults were forfeited at great cost to both the organizations and the dissenters. But when communicated effectively and handled appropriately, dissent should be rewarding, not costly.

Discussion Questions

1 What can be learned about organizational dissent from examining the cases of whistleblowers? What are the risks associated with and benefits derived from blowing the whistle on one's organization?
2 How have whistleblowers been represented in the media and popular culture? What is it about the whistleblower story that captures our imagination? Do these treatments of whistleblowers resonate with your personal experience of acting as or knowing others who have acted as whistleblowers?
3 The "traitorous eight" case shows how dissent can lead to industry development and innovation. What other cases are there that reveal the positive benefits companies and industries have derived from organizational dissent?
4 Why are dissenters vilified by some and celebrated by others? Why do the expression of dissent and the expectations associated with it prove paradoxical at times? Why is dissent threatening to some audiences and welcomed by others?
5 What makes organizational dissent challenging? How is it different from dissent expressed in other spheres of our lives (e.g., schools, churches, neighborhoods, etc.)?

2

What is Organizational Dissent?

> The dissenter is every human being at those moments of his life when he resigns momentarily from the herd and thinks for himself.
>
> – Archibald Macleish

Early in the film *Jerry Maguire*, the protagonist finds himself summarily dismissed from the sports agency he criticized in his 25-page "mission statement." Maguire made 110 copies, one for everyone in the company, of the document he decided to call "The Things We Think and Do Not Say: The Future of Our Business." In it, he questioned the operating premises of the sports agent industry. Although there is no scene depicting him being fired, we know this is the case as he appears in front of his colleagues with the clichéd box of belongings in hand. Before leaving, though, he stops and professes in front of what appears to be the entire company:

> Don't worry, don't worry. I'm not going to do what you all think I'm going to do, which is just flip out [flailing wildly for effect]. Let me just, let me just say, as I ease out of the office I helped *build*. I'm sorry, but it's a fact that there's such a thing as manners. A way of treating people. [Pointing to the fish tank:] These fish have manners. These fish have manners. In fact, they're coming with me [walking toward fish tank]. I'm starting a new company and the fish will come with me. You can call me sentimental. The fish, they're coming with me. [Awkwardly scoops a fish out of the tank.] OK, if anybody else wants to come with me, this moment will be the moment of something real,

> and fun, and inspiring in this god-forsaken business – and we will do it together. (Crowe, 1996)

Maguire then repeatedly utters the infamous line: "Who's coming with me?"

Jerry Maguire's dissent captures our imagination. We can see ourselves in his shoes, contesting flawed practices, questioning to the end, not going down without a fight. But his situation and circumstances have been highly dramatized for effect. After all, would all of the employees of a company be in one place to allow for such a performance? Dramatic effect aside, Maguire's actions reflect some of the commonly held myths about organizational dissent. He is adversarial, openly protests, and feels strongly that the ethics of his business need a good hard look. But other aspects of this episode belie some of the commonly held myths about organizational dissent. Maguire expressed dissent, via his personal manifesto, to everyone in the company – not just to management. And he hoped it would help the firm alter its course. His dissatisfaction gave way to dissent, but a desire to make things better clearly was apparent.

The purpose of this chapter is to clarify what organizational dissent is. To do so will involve outlining the conceptual parameters. But, before that, it may help to debunk some of the common myths associated with organizational dissent:

1. *Dissent involves conflict.* It certainly can, but does not always (Kassing, 1997; Redding, 1985).
2. *Dissent targets the ear of management.* To the contrary, it can be expressed just as readily to coworkers of the same rank or to friends and family outside of work (Kassing, 1997).
3. *Dissent occurs primarily in response to ethical issues.* Employees dissent about numerous workplace issues of which ethics is just one (Kassing and Armstrong, 2002).
4. *Dissent results from dissatisfaction.* Sometimes, but it can be offered in a spirit of helpfulness as well (Redding, 1985).
5. *Dissent entails open protest.* It may. Yet it can be comparatively quiet, murmured around the office and among colleagues (Kassing, 1998).

6 *Dissent is adversarial.* On occasion, but it is equally possible that it can be constructive in nature. Dissent may be delivered, for example, with suggestions for improving the situation (Kassing, 2002).

Myths take hold because they leverage some degree of truth, and myths about dissent are no exception. There is some truth to each. Dissent can lead to conflict, be directed to management, center on ethical issues, involve protest, evolve from dissatisfaction, and be adversarial. But is it always a disgruntled employee facing an ethical issue that confronts management? Do all dissenters choose open protest? Does all dissent lead to explicit conflict? Contemporary research on organizational dissent suggests otherwise (Kassing, 2007).

So what is organizational dissent? The quote from the Pulitzer Prize winning poet Archibald Macleish that begins this chapter is fitting. It reflects the notion that organizational dissent mandates a separation or distancing from the majority. It demands taking a stance that is in opposition to the prevailing position. It requires disagreement and contradiction. Dissent derives from the Latin *dissentire*, *dis* meaning apart and *sentire* meaning to feel (Morris, 1969). Dissent, then, denotes "feeling apart" – in the work context, feeling apart from one's organization. With this distancing, dissenters situate themselves in opposition to their respective organizations. But, as a communicative act, dissent does not stop with merely feeling apart. It requires expressing why one has chosen an oppositional stance (Kassing, 1997).

Conceptual definitions can be slippery, holding for some people but not for others. We do not always agree on definitions. They are anchored in how people interpret their settings and can be quite fluid. But we need working definitions to allow for discussion of related concepts. Therefore it may be helpful to think of definitions as a matter of scope. If we broaden or narrow the scope of what constitutes a given behavior we are suggesting that it comprises more or fewer actions. This is true with organizational dissent and the related concepts considered in this chapter. Focusing to a particular degree, as we would do with a telephoto lens on a camera, provides some scope for each concept. We can focus a telephoto lens to see more or less, just as we could broaden or narrow a definition to include more or less. Thus, for each of the concepts discussed in this chapter it is important to note that multiple definitions exist, that common characteristics apply across definitions, and that conceptualizations can be adjusted in scope or focus.

Organizational dissent, according to one commonly held definition, refers to "Expressing disagreement or contradictory opinions about organizational practices, policies and operations" (Kassing, 1998, p. 183). This is a simple definition that stipulates three key conditions: first, for organizational dissent to take place it must be expressed to someone; second, that expression must involve the disclosure of disagreement or contradictory opinions; and, third, the disagreement or contradictory opinions must be leveled against organizational practices, policies, and operations. What remains absent from this definition is also key. It does not specify to whom one communicates dissent, thereby allowing for the possibility that it may be directed at multiple audiences, not just management. Nor does it specify ethical issues particularly, as these form just one of many that will elicit dissent. Rather, it casts a broad net – indicating that dissent can be expressed in response to practices, policies, and operations. Practices tend to be thought of as informal ways of operating. They emerge as employees determine how best to accomplish tasks. Operations and policies, on the other hand, often refer to the formal ways in which organizations function. Punching in on a time clock, for example, would be a formal operation, whereas taking a shorter lunch break and clocking out early would be an informal practice. A company policy might require employees to clock in for forty hours per week. The configuration of how many hours per day is not, however, stipulated, allowing employees to exercise some flexibility in the practice of scheduling their hours. Some may start early, others may stay later. Some may work fewer but longer days. Others may work a consistent number of hours each day. A mandate that changes the policy, operation, or practices of accounting for one's hours could result in dissent.

Organizational conflict, upward influence, employee resistance, employee voice, whistleblowing – these are the usual suspects when it comes to conflating organizational dissent with similar, yet distinct concepts. From behind the glass of a police lineup these five concepts would look similar to dissent – perhaps difficult to discern, but distinct nonetheless. With a working definition of organizational dissent set, the purpose of this chapter is to distinguish dissent as a unique construct. There are a host of concepts that have been used synonymously and at times interchangeably with organizational dissent. Exploring the nature of each will help to draw out the delineations between organizational dissent and related constructs and will bring clarity to the notion of organizational dissent examined in the remainder of this book. The sections that follow, then, treat each of these concepts, paying particular attention to the overlap with and distinction from organizational dissent. Box 2.1 provides a helpful set of working definitions for each.

Organizational Conflict

Conflict is a well-researched topic across disciplines (Putnam and Poole, 1987). We know that it originates from a variety of sources, follows predictable patterns, and manifests in both positive and negative ways. Definitions of conflict abound, most of which share several common components (Lewicki et al., 1992). Conflict occurs when people hold mutually exclusive goals and when incompatible values are at play. These discrepancies between parties can be real or simply perceived – that is, perceived incompatibility can trigger conflict as readily as a real impasse (Putnam and Poole, 1987). But conflict cannot occur unless the parties are interdependent – that is, dependent on one another for particular resources and outcomes. Real or perceived interference with the goals of each party requires interdependence.

Visualize two basketball games being played at the same time. They are unfolding side by side on two courts in a single gymnasium. A player interferes with an opponent who is attempting to

Box 2.1 Working conceptual definitions

Organizational dissent
"Expressing disagreement or contradictory opinions about organizational practices, policies and operations" (Kassing, 1998, p. 183).

Organizational conflict
"The interaction of interdependent people who perceive opposition of goals, aims, and values, and who see the other party as potentially interfering with the realization of these goals" (Putnam & Poole, 1987, p. 552).

Upward influence
"A deliberate attempt by a subordinate to select tactics that will bring about change in a more powerful target and facilitate achievement of a personal or organizational objective" (Waldron, 1999, p. 253).

Employee resistance
". . . can encompass anything and everything that workers do which managers do not want them to do, and that workers do not do that managers wish them to do. It can take in both collective and individual; it can embrace actions that are specifically designed to thwart management (such as strikes and work-to-rules), and those which may not be (such as absenteeism)" (O'Connell Davidson, 1994, p. 94).

Employee voice
"Actively and constructively trying to improve conditions through discussing problems with a supervisor or coworkers, taking action to solve problems, suggesting solutions, seeking help from an outside agency like a union or whistle-blowing" (Rusbult et al., 1988, p. 601).

> Whistleblowing
> "The disclosure by organization members (former and current) of illegal, immoral, or illegitimate practices under the control of their employers, to persons or organizations that may be able to effect action" (Near and Miceli, 1985, p. 4).

shoot on the first court. The player is called for a foul because interference here literally affects the opponent directly – keeping the opponent from scoring. The interference is meaningful because it impedes the goal of both parties to win the game. But the interference on this court does not affect the outcome of the other game in any way. The games are independent of one another, not interdependent. A foul in one game is not interference in the other. In the workplace, conflict would not emerge when a coworker from another division that is completely separate from our division continues to leave early. Although this coworker's early departures likely detract from the overall effectiveness of the organization, they do not affect every workgroup directly. If that same worker continuously leaves early and he or she is in our direct workgroup, we may have a problem. We are dependent on said coworker for getting certain tasks done, and his or her desire to leave early competes with the group's need to get a certain amount of necessary work completed. It is incompatible with the goals of the group. It will lead to conflict between group members and the individual who insists on leaving early.

Interdependence, then, is a critical element of any conflict. So too is interaction. Conflict warrants that some type of interaction occurs between organizational parties. These parties can be entire groups, like management and labor or management and unions, or they can be single individuals (Sheppard, 1992). Considering conflict from the perspective of the individual has led to extensive research on the strategies people use in conflict interactions (Rahim, 1986). There is some discrepancy in conflict studies about what drives people's preferences for using particular conflict strategies (King and Miles, 1990; Womack, 1988). Some consider conflict styles to be trait-like, enduring, and used across situations and contexts. A contrasting perspective holds that conflict strategies are bound by the situation and context. People vary how they approach a given conflict based upon situational and contextual factors – giving particular consideration to the target of conflict. A trait perspective suggests that an employee would not deviate from a preferred style regardless of whether she was questioning why her supervisor cut her hours or dealing with a coworker who regularly finishes off the coffee without making another pot. A situational/contextual perspective indicates that this employee would vary how she handles conflict based on situational factors as well as the source of conflict. Indeed, much more is at stake in a conflict with a supervisor over having ample hours than is at stake in a conflict with a coworker over coffee. Nonetheless, interaction between parties or individuals – regardless of the strategies used – must transpire for conflict to occur.

Although interdependence and interaction have to be in place, it is really incompatibility of goals and values that sets conflict in motion. Groups and employees that are interdependent and interact regularly can work harmoniously without conflict and often do so with regularity. Once incompatibility enters into the equation, though, we can expect conflict to disrupt the status quo. Incompatibility can take many forms. A manufacturing worker may find that a management directive that requires him to be cross-trained is incompatible with his goal of being proficient at a single task. A middle manager told by senior management that she can no longer provide bonuses to her sales team will find this dictate incompatible with her goal of maintaining a high level of productivity in the sales division. In both cases, but for different reasons, these employees find their goals to be incompatible with management's goals. How they feel about such incompatibility shades their orientation to conflict.

Some organizational parties, traditionally stakeholders and senior managers, view conflict as a disruption, a system breakdown that needs to be fixed (Sheppard, 1992). From this perspective conflict is something to be resolved, not managed. However, most workplace conflicts go unresolved, and conflict tends to build emotionally when it extends over time (Gayle and Preiss, 1998). An alternative perspective emphasizes conflict management. This position holds that conflict is dynamic and ongoing. This is an important distinction, as "Conflict resolution implies reduction or elimination of conflict, whereas the management of conflict does not necessarily imply reduction or elimination or conflict" (Rahim et al., 1992, p. 424). Thus, perspectives differ on whether conflict is something to be extinguished completely, like a house fire, or to be managed more like a chronic illness. Some combination of the two perspectives is appropriate in contemporary organizations. Certainly most organizations will function better if they are not hampered by certain conflicts, yet realistically they cannot be free of all conflicts and need to consider how enduring conflicts can be managed best.

Enduring conflicts can be particularly challenging, since emotion figures significantly in how people recall organizational conflict and likely affects how they handle themselves in subsequent workplace conflicts (Gayle and Preiss, 1998). Some argue in fact that we do not realize we are in conflict until we become emotional about something and that emotion drives how important a given conflict will be for us (Bodtker and Jameson, 2001). The emotions we display and experience during conflict can reshape or redefine the relationships between disputants. This reformulating of boundaries informs how we will engage in conflict in the future. Organizational conflict, then, occurs when incompatibility arises between interdependent groups who interact regularly. It can be strategic, yet emotional. And it may occur regularly and be enduring.

Upward Influence

Upward influence concerns informal influence attempts, rather than formal grievance procedures. Though it is informal, upward influence can be quite strategic and intentional (Krone, 1992; Waldron, 1999). It is a deliberate attempt by an individual subordinate to bring about change in a more powerful person or target.

Thus, it is oriented up the chain of command and driven by both long- and short-term goals. As such, it can have serious implications for superior–subordinate relationships, affecting the bond between leaders and followers. While influence can certainly be part of the give and take that transpires during union and management negotiations, upward influence is much more individualized in focus. Influence attempts between groups within organizations or targeted at organizational groups fall outside the scope of traditional definitions of upward influence.

Several factors affect upward influence. Among these are power differentials, goals, relationship history and quality, and organizational culture (Waldron 1999). Are we attempting to influence a team leader, a direct supervisor, or a member of upper management? The power differential elongates in each case. With regard to our goals, do we want to request to leave early to pick up our kids, to have a day off to attend a funeral, or to ask for an extra week of vacation time? The objective here – time off – remains consistent while the size of the request varies with our goals. Are we attempting to solve the immediate problem of not having a sitter for our kids, trying to find time to grieve and share our condolences, or seeking to extend our family holiday plans? The underlying goals vary considerably – problem-solving, providing comfort, and relaxing. And what about our relationship history with a given supervisor? This will be an important consideration as well. How long have we worked with this supervisor? And what history is there regarding the issue at hand? Has she repeatedly refused our requests for time off or has she been helpful in meeting those requests? Do we respect our supervisor or merely tolerate working for her? Of course, organizational culture cannot be overlooked. Does our organization support family–work life balance or frown on it? Are supervisors commended or admonished for showing scheduling flexibility? Organizational culture will shape how supervisors respond to upward influence.

Several studies have revealed that there are many ways in which employees go about practicing upward influence (Kipnis and Schmidt, 1985; Kipnis et al., 1980; Porter et al., 1981; Schriesheim and Hinkin, 1990). Ingratiation tactics combine conformity, being agreeable, flattery, praise, friendliness, and liking. Together these efforts signal deference to and affinity for a supervisor. Whereas ingratiation targets the ego, the rationality tactic focuses on reason and logic. This involves providing reasons, presenting information, and offering explanations in order to create the impression of competence. Another approach, exchange or bargaining tactics, entails offering rewards, exchanging resources, and promising to make sacrifices. This approach leverages debt or reward to create influence. Coalition tactics, in turn, leverage the support of others. That is, finding and demonstrating support among peers serves to bolster one's claim or request. This tactic relies on the simple premise that there is strength in numbers. A supervisor may have difficulty rebuffing an influence attempt that has the support of several employees instead of just one. The tactics discussed to this point rely on something other than being direct. But being direct is just as viable a tactic. Called assertiveness, this involves offering challenges or directives and making threats. It can be coercive when one uses power derived from social capital or technical expertise. Finally, employees can choose to go over the head of their immediate supervisor to some higher authority. This has been labeled an upward appeal.

Tactics are specific behaviors. They can be grouped and used together. When grouped together they comprise strategies (Kipnis and Schmidt, 1985; Waldron, 1999). Early strategies were differentiated as hard, soft, or rational. A hard strategy communicates intent directly and wields power overtly. It relies predominantly on assertiveness, but can include upward appeal and bargaining tactics. In contrast, a soft strategy is more covert and indirect in nature. It involves attempts to manipulate one's role relationship with the target. People who use soft tactics try to make themselves appear more attractive to the person they wish to influence through ingratiation. They also may use exchange tactics – promising future favors in order to activate a norm of reciprocity. Both hard and soft strategies combine the exchange tactic with other tactics, but the nature of exchange and how it is used varies. In hard strategies, exchange is competitive. In soft tactics, it is manipulative and serves to create some indebtedness with one's supervisor. Rational strategies are designed to offer the supervisor some course of action that would benefit the supervisor as well as the subordinate. It entails using logical appeals and reason.

Although people vary in the tactics they choose and how often they use them within given strategies, stylistic preferences do emerge. Employees, who use all tactics somewhat equivalently and exercise little judgment in selecting them, adopt a shotgun style (Kipnis and Schmidt, 1988). In contrast, a bystander style involves comparatively little use of all strategies and tactics. In between are tactician and ingratiatory styles, the former characterized by a preference for rational tactics, the latter by a heavier use of friendly tactics.

Employees are evaluated. They are at risk, then, when attempting to influence someone like their supervisor who directly evaluates them (Waldron and Kassing, 2011). For this reason they may edit and obscure their influence attempts. Thus, upward influence can become quite political and strategic in nature. Employees may be open about or work to obscure the means of influence or the desired outcome of the influence attempt, or both (Krone, 1992). They practice open upward influence when they are clear and apparent with both their means of influence and the desired outcomes. As an example, consider an employee who wants a raise. With an open influence tactic he sets up a meeting with his supervisor and directly asks her to consider giving him a raise. The means (a direct request) and the desired outcome (a raise) are obvious to the supervisor.

Strategic upward influence, in contrast, involves some degree of concealment. This can happen when an employee is open about the means of influence, but not about the desired outcome. In this case, an employee requests a meeting and directly speaks with his supervisor. The means of influence are evident, a direct meeting and a discussion. Yet the desired outcome remains obscured. During the meeting the employee requests additional recognition for what he deems to be extra work he has undertaken. He does not directly ask for a raise but certainly hopes and likely believes that the supervisor, upon realizing what he has contributed, might respond by offering one.

Strategic influence also happens when employees conceal influence attempts, but not what they hope to gain. When asked if she would be interested in a newly created position, for example, an employee reveals that she would be, but does not make a direct request for consideration. In the interim, she asks supportive colleagues to "put a good word in for her" with the supervisor. Their reports prove quite influential and result in her being awarded the position. Her upward influence is strategic because she obscured the means of influence (building support for her qualifications through the testimony of colleagues) while being clear about her desire to receive the promotion.

Now consider a situation in which an employee suggests during a staff meeting that peer reports should weigh more heavily in performance evaluations. She then proceeds to convince, and if necessary coerce, coworkers into providing her supervisor with favorable reviews of her work. In so doing she has managed to conceal her means of influence (manipulation of information provided by colleagues) as well as her desired outcomes (increasing the likelihood of receiving a merit raise due to a favorable performance evaluation) from her supervisor. Not surprisingly, this is referred to as political upward influence (Krone, 1992). It involves obscuring both the means of influence and the desired outcome. As the example indicates, this type of influence involves long-term deception and ongoing manipulation – a concerted and deliberate effort to perpetuate a false image with one's supervisor.

Although the tactics, strategies, and styles of upward influence tend to be individually based, this may not be the case with outcomes. Outcomes can be highly individualized, but also relational and collective. Upward influence can result in increased trust and security within relationships as well as in policy and procedural changes that benefit entire work groups or improve organizational decision-making (Waldron, 1999). In sum, upward influence is strategic, intentional, and occurs between individuals – a lower-ranking employee and a higher-ranking supervisor or manager.

Employee Resistance

Employees resist in order to deflect abuse, to regulate the amount and intensity of work, to defend autonomy, and to expand bases of control (Hodson, 1995).Very simply, such resistance is about how employees deal with the many constraints apparent in contemporary workplaces. Schedules, tasks, policies, and the like can be constraining, and all can engender employee resistance. Murphy (1998), for example, examined how flight attendants at a major airline resisted constraints regarding corporate and industry policy. Apparently, a Federal Aviation Administration (FAA) policy mandates that flight attendants serve drinks to pilots to keep them from getting dehydrated during flights. Female flight attendants, however, resisted this policy by engaging gendered stereotypes. They playfully teased male pilots about being unable to get their own drinks. To avoid such ridicule pilots adopted the practice of serving themselves. The flight attendants' resistance was simple and comparatively harmless, but at the same time important and powerful. Contesting a policy with clear gendered overtones relieved them from a secondary task and allowed them to concentrate on the primary responsibility of focusing on passengers. It also served to provide a means for the female flight attendants – operating in a highly feminized line of work where on average only six males are hired for every 100 females – to shift the power dynamic with predominantly male pilots. Even subtle shifts such as these can be significant with regard to our identities.

We all hold valued identities of ourselves. We may see ourselves as independent, hard-working, and competent – not as someone who should be given directives and timelines and have our efforts evaluated. But this is exactly what happens in modern organizations. Such constraints, Ashforth and Mael (1998) suggest, threaten our valued identities and therefore require some measure of resistance. They note that employees may face threats related to respect, self-esteem, individuality, autonomy, or competence. Resistance, in turn, serves as a buffer against the encroachment of the organization on one's sense of self. Some would say it is necessary to keep our sanity at work.

Collinson's (1994) case study of a heavy vehicle manufacturing operation in the United Kingdom helps to make this point. Historically in this organization shopfloor workers had been treated as expendable, easily replaced if need be – thought of as unthinking machines and as such excluded from any significant role in decision-making. They had become used to being treated as second-class citizens, so they quickly dismissed the culture campaign waged by the new American-based management group that emphasized teamwork and communication as mere propaganda. Management's personal approach was seen as a Yankee plot to increase productivity. Ironically, shopfloor workers refused invitations to have some say in the production process and work arrangements. In their eyes, it threatened the valued identity of being a working-class shopfloor employee, distinct and notably different from the management class. They refused to call managers by their first names and rebuffed offers to join managers for smoke breaks – all of this because they held that the shopfloor was the site of real, authentic work based in experiential hands-on knowledge and that a promotion to the managerial ranks would entail compromising their independence. Having intimate knowledge of just how long actual tasks would take allowed them to manipulate the work rate and the bonus scheme by doing just what was necessary, but not more, to achieve a given benchmark. In short, they had developed a valued identity as shopfloor workers, one they protected fiercely through resistance by clearly distancing themselves from management.

Resistance can take many forms. It may be overt or covert, collective or individual, planned or spontaneous (Prasad and Prasad, 1998). An employee may keep his coffee cup that clearly says "I'd Rather Be Fishing" in prominent view of his supervisor during staff meetings, or an outspoken group of coworkers may routinely bad-mouth their supervisor around the office. The coffee cup declaration is overt, likely planned, and individual. Gossiping about the boss is covert, collective, and spontaneous. How obvious and premeditated resistance is, as well as how many people are involved, are only a couple of ways to make sense of employee resistance. In addition, resistance can be targeted or diffuse (Ashforth and Mael, 1998). It is targeted when directed at the source of threat, diffuse when displaced to other audiences. Evidently, targeted resistance tends to result in substantive change, whereas diffuse resistance buffers the identity of the resister but rarely results in any significant change. Resistance can be considered facilitative or oppositional. Facilitative resistance involves acts that benefit the organization or the public interest. Whistleblowing is a prime example of facilitative resistance – it is an ethical concern shared with the organization or some governing body so that necessary corrections can be made. In contrast, oppositional resistance serves narrow self-interests. Absenteeism, for instance, would be oppositional. While it helps a single employee feel less constrained by his or her workplace, it serves the interests only of that specific person. Finally, resistance can be thought of as authorized or unauthorized. The former occurs within the established organizational norms (e.g., complaining to one's boss, filing grievances), whereas the latter involves behavior that falls outside of the bounds of what is organizationally acceptable (e.g., violence, theft). Although somewhat commonplace, stealing office supplies certainly is not sanctioned by most organizations.

Albeit helpful, these distinctions conceal the complexity of employee resistance, failing to allow for the possibilities that resistance can seep from individual to collective, can move from covert to overt, can begin spontaneously but shift to something planned (Putnam et al., 2005). Furthermore, resistance need not be targeted at a single entity, but can be directed to multiple targets. And it need not be directed at the focus of resistance, but can be staged in a theatrical sense for a much broader audience. Moreover, the examples and discussion to this point suggest that resistance classically involves lower-ranking employees contesting constraints imposed or enforced by those with higher status. However, Ashcraft's (2005) examination of airline captains demonstrates how resistance can occur even among dominant and empowered classes of employees, particularly when they feel their privileged status is threatened.

Airline pilots, who are predominantly white males, historically exercised complete control on board their respective aircrafts.

However, with the introduction of cockpit or crew resource management (CRM) came an industry-wide overhaul of the philosophy, training, and practice of running an airline crew. CRM grew out of increasing safety concerns as mounting evidence indicated that tragic outcomes could have been adverted if reticent crew members had challenged rather than deferred to the authoritative role of captains. As a result the captain's authority was softened so that crewmembers could begin legitimately questioning it. Ironically, captains reported embracing the very policy and philosophy that undermined their status. They did so by situating CRM as a "captain's generous gift to his subordinates" (Ashcraft, 2005, p. 80) and by talking about CRM as a personal choice, rather than as a mandate imposed upon them. It was deemed a necessary choice given the out-dated authoritarian approach that had blanketed the industry previously. Captains' zealous adoption of CRM, positioning themselves as benevolent purveyors of its practices and philosophy, demonstrates how resistance can be achieved through consent. Perverse as it may sound, their control of how CRM played out served as a form of resistance toward the policy.

Thus, resistance is many things, but not always an isolated act from a subordinate designed to produce a specific outcome. Rather it is a "routine, yet complex embedded social process" that contributes to the very fabric of organizing (Mumby, 2005, p. 32). Processes of control are resisted, demanding counter-control. So, it is not always the act of resistance that is important, but rather the process. "As such, the process of resistance – the *fact* that one resists – often matters more than any substantive change or outcomes" (Ashforth and Mael, 1998, p. 102). After all, resistance is as much about dealing with constraints for the sake of one's identity as it is about effecting organizational change.

Employee Voice

Originally conceptualized as one way in which dissatisfied consumers respond to falling product or quality service (Hirschman,

1970), voice has shifted to embrace employees' reactions to dissatisfying workplace conditions (Gorden, 1988). It is considered one of several responses to dissatisfaction, the others being exit (leaving one's place of work), loyalty (remaining supportive despite dissatisfying conditions), and neglect (engaging in behaviors that further contribute to organizational decline). Neglect might include excessive absenteeism, chronic lateness, social loafing, reduced effort, or increased error (Gorden, 1988; Farrell, 1983).

Voice can refer to formal procedures or arrangements that allow for employees to be involved in policy- or decision-making, or it can refer to informal efforts by employees to have some say in their workplaces (Dundon et al., 2005). The former perspective treats voice as an organizational process, the latter as an employee behavior (Van Dyne et al., 2003). Formal mechanisms might be unions, joint consultative committees made up of management and non-management employees, problem-solving groups, collective bargaining, grievance systems, or an ombudsman. Informal processes, alternatively, entail speaking up and may take the form of championing ideas, providing constructive feedback, engagement with management in meaningful ways, taking charge, issue selling, and making constructive suggestions – all of which result in having an authentic say about organizational practices (Dundon et al., 2005; Van Dyne et al., 2003).

While formal voice procedures can be helpful in giving employees a proverbial seat at the table, often they are viewed with distrust. In an examination of one such procedure, researchers found that employees in an Australian credit union felt that the CEO's open-door policy and the company's staff consultative committee were more symbolic than substantive in nature. Designed to make employees feel comfortable about bringing complaints or suggestions to management, these mechanisms were critiqued for making "it appear anyone can talk up" and questioned as to "whether you would feel confident confiding in any of them" (Winter and Jackson, 2006, p. 429). Formal voice mechanisms, then, do not guarantee opportunities for employee voice – which likely contributes to why they appear to be faltering.

Workplaces have changed considerably in the last two decades (Van Buren and Greenwood, 2008). Industry has shifted away from manufacturing and production, a historic stronghold for unions, toward service and information. For this reason and others, unions have been on the decline. Additionally, companies have begun to use global rather than local workforces. This affects employee voice in at least two ways: first, employees are geographically distributed, making it difficult to organize and achieve collective voice; second, the threat of moving jobs out of country looms large if employees demand too much. Furthermore, the employment contract has changed. Employees take personal responsibility for their career development, commit to a particular kind of work rather than a specific employer, and expect job insecurity. This is in contrast to generations past, who could expect lifetime employment and job security with the same company (Cavanaugh and Noe, 1999). With the evolution of the social contract and slippage among unions, companies have followed suit by demonstrating preferences for staffing and employment flexibility – evidenced by downsizing and outsourcing (Van Buren and Greenwood, 2008). These factors, coupled with the aforementioned suspicions about formal voice mechanisms, have undermined their effectiveness and availability.

Given the changes in workplaces and the advent of social media and computer-mediated-communication (CMC) technologies, it is not surprising that employee voice has migrated elsewhere (Bishop and Levine, 1999). Company-wide bulletin boards, for example, allow for discussion and complaints to be broadcast beyond one's immediate workgroup to a much larger audience. Furthermore, these technologies facilitate employees locating others with common concerns, regardless of how geographically dispersed they may be. A customer-service phone representative in India, for instance, can connect with reps in the Philippines and the United States to discuss issues with the script provided for handling incoming calls. Their thoughts on the shortcomings of the script could eventually be shared with management. Voice prevails, despite time zones, segmented operations, and cultural idiosyncrasies.

Waning interest in formal voice mechanisms has given way to greater appreciation and examination of aspects of informal voice. In an early effort, Gorden (1988) argued that voice should be differentiated along two dimensions: it can be active or passive and at the same time constructive or destructive. Making suggestions, expressing dissent, and providing critical feedback exemplify active constructive voice. These are active behaviors offered in the spirit of being constructive. In contrast, listening, compliance, and cooperation are forms of passive constructive voice. These behaviors are constructive as well, but passive by comparison. On the destructive side, active destructive voice includes complaining to coworkers, duplicity, and bad-mouthing, whereas passive destructive voice involves apathy, calculated silence, and withdrawal. The active behaviors here are clearly destructive, the passive behaviors less destructive by comparison but certainly unhelpful to the workgroup and organization.

A more recent typology expands upon these differentiations by emphasizing the motives – changing a situation, fear, or resignation – that drive employee voice (Van Dyne et al., 2003). Akin to active constructive voice, prosocial voice stems from a motive to improve a given situation, not merely to criticize it. Defensive voice derives from fear – with the goal of protecting oneself. It involves skirting responsibility, making excuses, giving justifications, and offering explanations, as well as shifting blame and attention to others. It resembles active destructive voice. Finally, acquiescent voice arises from feelings of resignation, believing and accepting that voice will make little difference. Defeatist in nature, it results in support and agreement offered without question or challenge even as doubts persist. It aligns with passive destructive voice.

In conclusion, employee voice may exist within formal mechanisms or informally through communication practices. Informally, one may provide constructive feedback, offer suggestions, or champion ideas. Regardless of form, the intention remains the same – to have some genuine say about how work gets done in organizational settings.

Whistleblowing

Of all the concepts considered in this chapter, whistleblowing is closest to dissent. It is in fact a form of dissent (Redding, 1985; Kassing, 1997). Definitions of whistleblowing share one predominant theme – primarily, reporting wrongdoing or misconduct within organizations. To whom employees report wrongdoing is a matter of debate: it can be reported externally to outside agencies such as media sources or regulatory bodies, but also internally to coworkers, to supervisors, or through formal reporting procedures established within organizations (Park et al., 2008). Traditionally, though, whistleblowing involves the disclosure of organizational wrongdoing to audiences outside the organization (Stewart, 1980).

In addition to being considered as internally or externally expressed, whistleblowing can be differentiated as formal or informal (Park et al., 2008). Formal whistleblowing transpires via established channels that exist within organizations, whereas informal whistleblowing occurs when employees tell trusted colleagues about organizational wrongdoing. Colleagues, in turn, may decide to use formal reporting channels, advise the coworker to do so, or suggest that the coworker leave the situation alone. It is important to note, however, that whistleblowing does not usually start with complete public exposure of organizational wrongdoing. Rather it culminates as such after several steps have been taken. Employees initially become aware of some wrongdoing and report it to a supervisor. When the immediate supervisor fails to respond or address the situation, employees move their concerns up the chain of command and speak to someone else higher in the organization. When upper or senior management is unresponsive the employee goes outside the organization, sharing the concern with media, a regulating body, or both (Stewart, 1980). This multi-step process demonstrates how internal whistleblowing eventually moves to external whistleblowing.

Two other considerations are relevant – first, an individual's association with their organization. Is the whistleblower a current or former employee? Jeffrey Wigand, of Brown & Williamson, was no longer an employee of his company when he blew the whistle. Neither was FBI linguist Sibel Edmonds. Both were fired for reporting organizational wrongdoing. But Coleen Rowley of the FBI, Cynthia Cooper of WorldCom, and Sherron Watkins of Enron were members of their respective organizations when they became whistleblowers. Thus, current or former employees can blow the whistle. Most, though, report the wrongdoing while still employed, before being fired or exiting the organization. The second consideration is to what degree an individual's name or identity is revealed when reporting wrongdoing (Park et al., 2008). When employees disclose their name or other identifying information they have engaged in identified whistleblowing, and when they conceal such information whistleblowing remains anonymous. Employees may choose to remain anonymous because whistleblowing involves accusations of misconduct, incompetence, or fraud. It is an indictment not to be taken lightly (Jubb, 1999).

So what drives employees to blow the whistle? Many reasons. It happens when employees believe that the public interest overrides organizational interests (Stewart, 1980), when they feel organizational wrongdoing can not be ignored. Whistleblowers explain such decisions by saying things like: "I did it because I had to," "because I had no other choice," "because I couldn't live with myself if I hadn't done anything," and "what else could I do? I have to look at myself in the mirror every morning" (Alford, 2007, p. 226). Emotions, primarily anger derived from witnessing wrongdoing, play a role too (Henik, 2008).

Apparently, some organizational members are more likely to blow the whistle than others. Those who hold higher status positions, who have worked for an organization longer, and who have higher performance ratings are more likely to do so than their counterparts who do not share these attributes (Mesmer-Magnus and Viswesvaran, 2008). Higher status, longer tenure, and a strong track record make employees more credible and powerful – two other attributes that contribute to successful whistleblowing (Near and Miceli, 1995). Also of note, those who have greater job satisfaction act more often (Mesmer-Magnus and Viswesvaran, 2008). Somewhat paradoxical, this finding highlights the fact that whistleblowers do not act out of a general sense of dissatisfaction, but rather in response to direct disappointment derived from witnessing wrongdoing – that is, from a sense of loyalty.

Yet whistleblowing places people in a moral dilemma (Jubb, 1999). Integrity – or loyalty to oneself – winds up pitted against loyalty to coworkers, one's profession, the firm, and the general public. Moreover, someone who takes action when others fail to do so runs the risk of being accused by colleagues of being disloyal. Whistleblowers end up being labeled "sneaks, spies, squealers, and other despised forms of informer" (ibid., p. 77). They face the tricky proposition of balancing dual goals: a desire to see the organization change and the hope that one will avoid retaliation (Near and Jensen, 1983). From an emotional standpoint, they have to balance anger about observed wrongdoing and fear of retaliation (Henik, 2008).

Employees who blow the whistle end up facing harsh treatment. Their employers and coworkers punish them with multiple forms of retaliation – being isolated, harassed, demoted, and fired, to name a few (Stewart, 1980). Some estimates indicate that nearly 70 percent of whistleblowers are fired or forced out of their organizations (Rothschild and Miethe, 1999). Apparently, external whistleblowers – those who expose the organization publicly – are at particular risk. They experience more extensive retaliation over longer periods of time than internal whistleblowers (Dworkin and Baucus, 1998). But employees can offset actual or expected retaliation if they produce convincing evidence and draw the support of their supervisor (Mesmer-Magnus and Viswesvaran, 2008). Having the merit of one's complaint endorsed by a public agency and being successful in bringing about change also helps reduce retaliation (ibid.; Near and Jensen, 1983).

Despite the risk of retaliation, whistleblowers can be effective: credibility, legitimacy, and power lend support to their claims (Near and Miceli, 1995; Miceli and Near, 2002). So too does identifying oneself versus remaining anonymous. Providing convincing evidence, and having the support of others, is critical. The nature of wrongdoing factors into the likelihood of its being corrected as well (Miceli and Near, 2002). Corrections are more likely when wrongdoing is infrequent, short-lived, and of little impact, indicating that organizations are most likely to respond to whistle-blowing when corrections are feasible rather than widespread and systemic.

Because whistleblowing requires reporting organizational wrongdoing, it draws on our notions of what is ethical. We identify wrongdoing by sensing that something is unethical. This could take the form of stealing, passing qualified employees over for promotions, or distributing unsafe products. At its very core, whistleblowing involves making judgments about what is ethical, but not merely making judgments – acting on those judgments. Reporting is fundamental to whistleblowing. It does not happen, in fact, if there is no reporting. We can observe and personally question something in our respective organizations without reporting it. Once we do, though, we have engaged in whistleblowing.

Differentiating Dissent

Organizational dissent relates to all five previously discussed concepts, but differently with each. Figure 2.1 presents a visual representation of these relationships. In the case of conflict and upward influence, organizational dissent overlaps, but remains distinct in particular ways. Conversely, organizational dissent is subsumed by employee resistance and employee voice and is a subset of these concepts. Lastly, organizational dissent encircles whistleblowing – denoting that whistleblowing is a clear form of organizational dissent.

Organizational dissent can lead to or be part of conflict, but it is not synonymous with it. The coworker who dissents – disagreeing openly about his manager's leadership style – likely will experience conflict with that supervisor. An employee who disagrees with the way in which a supervisor attempted to resolve a conflict over the redistribution of assignments demonstrates how dissent can be expressed within an existing conflict. The employee who did not get a preferred assignment could call into question the fairness of the process or challenge the outcome – disagreeing with and dissenting about either or both. So dissent and conflict can

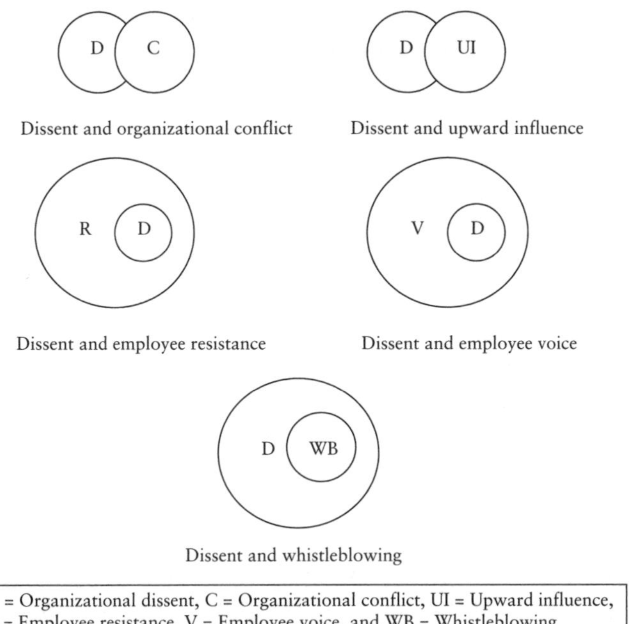

Figure 2.1 The relationship of organizational dissent to other concepts

coincide, but are not one and the same. In fact, organizational dissent can occur when parties have little interdependence and no interaction. A janitor, for example, who uncovers a paper trail of organizational wrongdoing while completing the night shift has little interdependence and no interaction with the offenders. Interdependence and interaction, though, are not conditions necessary for the janitor to express dissent about the wrongdoing. Moreover not all conflict involves dissent. Conflicting employees may disagree with one another and make accusations, false claims, and the like, but simply disagreeing with another employee does not constitute organizational dissent. The inner workings of conflict, the disagreement that accompanies most interpersonal conflicts, is not organizational dissent. So, although dissent and conflict accompany one another, they remain distinct.

Similarly, organizational dissent may be expressed as part of upward influence. In fact, upward influence and organizational dissent often coexist. The employee who wants to make a suggestion for improving the efficiency of staff meetings, for example, may first disagree with the current routine. Her dissent in this case is part of a larger effort to exercise upward influence regarding how staff meetings work. Similarly, promising future rewards to a supervisor for addressing a flawed hiring plan marries exchange tactics with dissent about troubling policies. Congruence can be seen as well in cases where employees express dissent by threatening to quit if their concerns about health and safety are not addressed adequately (Kassing, 2002). So dissent and upward influence can be present together and parallel one another. But much upward influence does not involve disagreement or sharing contradictory opinions. Trying to exercise influence to receive a promotion, additional pay, time off, and the like does not necessarily require one to express disagreement openly. This of course is largely a matter of how an influence attempt is framed. The employee who seeks a raise because he wants more money is enacting upward influence. The organizational member who sees her pay as out of line with that of her male counterparts will be expressing dissent about inequitable pay as she practices upward influence to seek a raise. So there is shared conceptual ground but not complete overlap between organizational dissent and upward influence.

Organizational dissent is a form of employee resistance. Expressing disagreement or contradictory opinions in effect derives, like employee resistance, from some perceived organizational constraint – a constraint that may be veiled in policies, practices, or operations. So it may be accurate to say that all dissent is resistance, but not to assume that all resistance is dissent. For example, working in a fashion that provides control of the workflow, as the manufacturing shopfloor workers profiled earlier in the chapter did, does not entail the expression of disagreement. To the contrary, it is a way of dealing with a constraint without being confrontational. It serves to provide some control in a constraining system. The shopfloor workers likely disagree with the constraints imposed upon them, but rather than contest these openly they chose to clandestinely manipulate the work setting.

In these instances resistance takes the form of manipulation rather than contradiction. This type of manipulation serves to bolster the identity of workers, but does not indicate disagreement or contradiction directly. Thus, organizational dissent is best positioned as a subset of employee resistance, since there are forms of resistance that would not be considered organizational dissent.

Similarly, organizational dissent is a subset of employee voice. Like employee voice, it derives from a basic desire to have some say about how and where we work. Both concepts stem from the same fundamental wellspring – the deep-seated ideal that employees should be meaningfully involved with their organizations. Dissent takes the form of disagreeing or contradicting to achieve this end, but not all employee voice does the same. Speaking up does not require disagreement. Employees can offer suggestions and champion ideas without expressing dissent. Dissent is a form of employee voice, not a necessary condition of it. Thus, not all employee voice should be conflated with organizational dissent.

Finally, whistleblowing is unique in its relationship to organizational dissent. Unlike the other concepts considered, it is in fact a subset of organizational dissent. Whistleblowing involves reporting organizational wrongdoing. Doing so requires one to contradict the standard operating procedures, to disagree with the status quo, to express dissent. Not all organizational dissent, however, leads to whistleblowing, which is merely one form of organizational dissent. It often serves as a signal that internal mechanisms designed to absorb and respond to organizational dissent have failed. After all, whistleblowing would not be necessary if concerns about wrongdoing were addressed promptly and effectively – if dissent were better accommodated in organizations.

Prior to reacting to his dismissal from his well-paid position as a sports agent in the scene that begins this chapter, Jerry Maguire dissented openly and publicly in a document he shared with all of his colleagues. The manuscript he eventually shared was written in the middle of the night after a breakthrough. In it he had a simple epiphany: to do right by clients, the company needed to get back to basics. He wrote: "Fewer clients, less money." Then he rushed off to make copies for everyone. The next morning while dressing he second-guesses his expression of organizational dissent and panics. He calls to stop delivery of the document, only to find that it has already been distributed. In the next scene Maguire hesitantly exits the hotel elevator with his head down and enters into a crowded lobby where all of his colleagues are gathered for the annual company conference. He is unexpectedly greeted with a slow and building round of applause and cheers, as coworkers chirp, "Finally, somebody said it," and "Good work, Maguire." He stands and soaks in the admiration, but the façade of congratulations is short-lived. A cutaway scene depicts two colleagues. The first asks, "How long do you give him?" and the second responds, "About a week."

This sequence of scenes captures some of the sensemaking that accompanies organizational dissent. Is dissent something that will be welcome and celebrated or will it lead to retaliation and marginalization? This depends on how employees and their respective organizations make sense of it – whether people see dissent as helpful and beneficial or as harmful and detrimental to the organization, whether they believe an organization accepts and tolerates dissent or resists and suppresses it. This chapter served to solidify an understanding of organizational dissent by situating it relative to related organizational constructs. The next chapter addresses the concerns raised above by exploring how we make sense of organizational dissent.

Discussion Questions

1 What factors are traditionally associated with organizational dissent? What are the fundamental features of organizational dissent? How do traditional conceptions align with actual workplace communication that constitutes organizational dissent?
2 What are the fundamental conceptual similarities that often lead to organizational dissent being linked to organizational conflict, upward influence, employee resistance, employee voice, and whistleblowing? What are the fundamental

conceptual differences that help distinguish these aspects of workplace communication from one another?

3 Think about your experiences at work, giving particular consideration to the events, issues, or policies that you found troubling and problematic. Now think about how you communicated about those issues. Using the descriptions provided in this chapter, would your communication be best characterized as organizational conflict, upward influence, employee resistance, employee voice, whistleblowing, or organizational dissent?

3

How Do We Make Sense of Organizational Dissent?

> In a democracy dissent is an act of faith. Like medicine, the test of its value is not in its taste, but its effects.
>
> – J. William Fulbright, US politician (1905–1995)

> Opposition is true friendship.
>
> – William Blake, *The Marriage of Heaven and Hell* (1793)

Though still relevant and popular, the parable of the Blind Men and the Elephant originally appeared in a collection of Buddhist scriptures dating back to 250 BC (Feistner and Holl, 2006). It has traveled from Buddhism through Islam and Hinduism, eventually reaching modern poetry. In the parable each man touches or feels a different part of the elephant and draws a distinctive conclusion of what it is. For some the elephant is a tree or a rope, for others a fan or a snake. There are as many versions as there are men in the tale. Although the parable itself is designed to show how differing perspectives account for varying realities, the many versions do so with equal power. In the Buddhist version the head is a large round jar, the ear a winnowing basket, the tusk a ploughshare, the trunk a plough, the body a granary, and the tail a pestle. Whereas there is a clear association with agrarian tools in this account, weaponry seeps into an Islamic version, where the ear is a shield and the trunk a club. And still more variation is revealed in Hindu versions. Here the ear is a fan, the trunk a snake, and the tail a flute or a rope. In the first known version in modern poetry the body becomes a wall, the tusk a spear, and the leg a tree.

Needless to say, there is great variation in how this parable is told. There is variation as well in the meaning it holds. In some accounts the emphasis falls on the quarreling that transpires as the blind men dispute their perceived conclusions about the elephant. In other versions it concerns seeing part for the whole, identifying the limitation that viewing only one aspect of an object places on one's understanding. Or it can be taken as a lesson in people's capacity to mistake limited interpretations for accurate ones. Thus, it can be about conflict, perspective, or observation.

Organizational dissent is much like this parable – its value disputed, its nature questioned, its relevancy fluid – depending on one's perspective. Is dissent a distasteful but necessary act of faith, as statesman William Fulbright suggests? Or is it a sign of friendship, as poet and painter William Blake proposes? What do we make of dissent? Is it good or bad, helpful or hurtful, necessary or inappropriate? Dissent can be many things depending on how we think and feel about it. It can be championed as something healthy and beneficial for an organization, like good nutrition would be for the human body. Or it can be viewed as a distraction, something that eats away at a company's core functions – a parasite with debilitating effects on organizations. Is it a punishable offense, then, or helpful criticism?

The purpose of this chapter is to make sense of how dissent fits within contemporary organizations. This of course will be a matter of perspective. Therefore there are two objectives for this chapter: first, to see how dissent sits within traditional perspectives that guide the study of organizational communication; second, to review selected theories that inform our understanding of organizational dissent. Understanding both should provide a greater sense of how the meaning and role of dissent fluctuate depending on the perspectives and theories that underpin organizing.

Classical Approaches

The Classical Management Perspective

Medieval craft guilds were the precursors of modern organizations (Hardy and Clegg, 1999). They dictated a very different form of organizing than what took hold during the industrial age. In these arrangements, a worker would start as an apprentice, learning the trade. A devoted and skilled apprentice could matriculate to become a journeyman and eventually a master craftsman – differentiated in rank and status merely by "greater ability, knowledge and experience in production" (ibid., p. 368). The work was task-continuous with each employee seeing a product through from start to finish – working on each and every task to complete the whole. But with the advent of industrialization and mass production employees were expected to do just the opposite – to perform a single or narrow set of tasks exclusively and repetitively. Known as specialization, this practice became one of the defining characteristics of early management approaches.

Specialization intensified the division of labor. No longer were people learning multiple tasks, sharing knowledge and instruction with others, and contributing to overall production processes, as with the guild structure. Rather they were reduced to a narrow range of tasks. Tasks in turn became segmented and standardized, easily performed by any number of employees or would-be employees, who needed to have only a narrow skill set, to master a standardized work process, and to do so with consistency. Deviation from this simple equation would result in replacement, because people could be replaced just as easily as parts of a machine.

Communication within this perspective was primarily top-down, task-centered, and formal (Miller, 2008). As such, purveyors of classic management would very likely find organizational dissent to be quite problematic. It would be highly disruptive to the aura and practice of authority mooring the classical management perspective. Moreover, disagreement would threaten predictability. It would be problematic for employees as well. As upward and apparently off-task communication, organizational dissent would be unlikely to result in any significant adjustments or changes. Additionally, working in conditions that already provided for the easy dismissal and replacement of employees, dissenters would almost certainly find themselves out of a job. From a classical management standpoint, then, organizational dissent would be disruptive and unwelcome for management and ineffectual and perilous for employees.

The Human Relations Perspective

The human relations perspective corrected for the mechanistic cog-like representation of employees in early approaches (Krefting and Powers, 1998; Miller, 2008). The emphasis shifted away from designing and controlling workflow to motivating and managing employees. The effect on productivity of meeting employees' needs and appealing to their motives moved front and center. Theorists held that workers were complex individuals with human needs – emphasizing the importance of self-direction, self-control, commitment, shared responsibility, creativity and problem-solving. In an important break from the classical management perspective, theorists argued that employees worked to meet higher-order needs, not merely for financial gain.

A family metaphor substitutes for the machine metaphor – placing relationships central to this perspective (Miller, 2008). Families provide opportunities for members to realize their goals and desires, but at the same time maintain hierarchies and patterns of social influence that govern behavior. Similarly, management bears the responsibility for defining the purpose of an organization while eliciting the cooperation of workers (Krefting and Powers, 1998).

Communication within this perspective differs considerably from the classical management perspective. Here, communication is not just task exclusive but also meets social needs. It is not merely downward but multi-directional. And it is informal more than formal. Would dissent, then, be welcomed? Not necessarily. The promise of being more humanistic actually obscures powerful yet subtle managerial compliance tactics (Krefting and Powers,

1998). Management still wields considerable, if not complete, authority. Unquestioned acceptance of authority is still paramount. Consent is important and necessary, but it is not achieved through heavy-handed managerial practices. Consent needs to be engineered through persuasion and incentives. It develops when management successfully aligns employee values and motives with those of the firm. Thus, managers may "endorse the role of voice while discouraging its exercise," because employees who dissent "demonstrate publicly that management has failed to elicit willing compliance" (ibid., p. 264). With a greater emphasis placed on meeting human needs and addressing employees' motives, we would expect dissent to flow freely. But this is unlikely, as dissent threatens "the order required for cooperation and performance" (ibid., p. 266). Dissent, then, is problematic because it publicly withdraws consent.

Within the human relations perspective dissent may appear welcome, but it essentially remains threatening. For this reason it may be co-opted. Stohl and Coombs (1988) found this to be the case with quality circles. In the mid-1970s quality circles emerged as a new form of assuring quality by inviting and relying on employee expertise. Traditionally, they involved bringing a group of employees together to address a specific quality issue. Employees would be drawn from across a company to mobilize multiple perspectives. They afforded and demanded a high degree of employee involvement in problem-solving and reportedly allowed for workers to develop the best solution possible, free of managerial constraint. Yet some questioned their capacity to allow for greater employee control and autonomy with regard to decision-making (ibid.). To find out if this was the case, researchers examined the content of training manuals, paying particular attention to the rationale companies provided for having quality circles. Findings revealed that training functioned as a mechanism to generate employee consent. Training manuals, while supposedly directing employees to choose whatever outcomes made the most sense for the organization, in fact tended to prioritize solutions favorable to management. In this instance, opportunities to offer contrasting perspectives end up subverted by the way in which management dictates participation. Dissent, then, may be invited and even welcomed, but not addressed or absorbed – that is, voiced but not heard.

The Human Resources Perspective

The human resources perspective builds upon its predecessors by taking into account the need for labor, but also the importance of appealing to workers' motives, desires, and goals (Miller, 2008). Whereas human relations centers on employees' feelings, human resources capitalizes on their intellect. Keeping employees satisfied and motivated is only part of the equation. Inviting them to think and act for themselves is also critical. Employees are neither cogs nor emotional vessels waiting to be fulfilled, but rather assets that make suggestions and provide feedback for improving the organization. By comparison, the human relations and human resources perspectives share much in common. Human relations, however, requires only superficial changes in management–labor relationships, whereas human resources demands fundamental changes in organizational structure, interaction, and functioning.

The human resources perspective calls for authenticity of participation and involvement. Therefore the many paradoxes that hinder participative organizational practices should be heeded (Stohl and Cheney, 2001). For example, the design paradox references the practice of top management creating participation programs meant to serve lower-level employees, who ironically have no say in the design of said programs. Similarly, the punctuation paradox concerns management's desire to do things more quickly than a slower participative process might allow. Management is not the only source of paradox. Employees working in participative workplaces also create and experience paradoxes. The autonomy paradox, for example, arises when a participative system demands subversion of one's individual autonomy in order to be productive as a group participant. And the commitment paradox occurs when dissent and disagreement wane as the pressure to conform and agree takes precedence. What should be recognized as a critical part of participation becomes a distraction.

In organizations operating from a human resources perspective there will be both task and social communication. Additionally, there will be innovative communication – serving to move the organization forward. Such communication may be about new products, new ways to organize, or new ways to complete or define jobs (Miller, 2008). Furthermore, communication will flow in all directions, between members in participative arrangements. It should follow, then, that dissent would be expressed comparatively freely. If organizations authentically seek the opinion and input of employees, then such feedback should on occasion take the form of organizational dissent, so dissent should be part and parcel of how organizations exercise human resources – how they realize participative work arrangements. Yet, dissent may be absent when participation reaches untenable levels, when it detracts from strong preferences for consensus as the commitment paradox surfaces. Organizational dissent also may occur when human resource-rich systems fall short of what they promise, when employees realize the shortcomings of their supposed participative workplaces (Kassing, 1997).

Contemporary Approaches

The Systems Perspective

Organizations can be thought of as intricate patterns of interaction (Farace et al., 1977; Katz and Kahn, 1978), patterns that occur with regularity, that are observable and routine. People, departments, divisions, and the like are connected to and through one another. Some organizations have streamlined and simple systems; others have complex systems. With the advent of communication technologies, systems are no longer limited by the physical confines of office space and now include whom we interact with across spatial and temporal boundaries – the people with whom we email, text, and video conference that work across the globe.

The systems perspective applies a biological metaphor – that of an organism – to how organizations function. Accordingly, the whole is greater than the sum of the parts. The organization is responsive to both internal and external forces and must strive to balance these. Like an illness affects an organism, so too does a product shortage, a labor strike, or a corporate scandal affect an organization. Furthermore, what happens in one part of the organization will affect other parts. Thus, feedback is a necessary and important function of organizing. And, like organisms, organizations grow, mature, decline, and eventually dissolve (Monge and Contractor, 2003).

There are several features of interest within organizational networks. Networks can be formal or informal. They can vary in terms of the number of members, how many connections exist between members, and how concentrated or dense those connections are. Some members can be highly connected, whereas others may be outliers with few connections. Acknowledging network features gives rise to a host of questions regarding dissent expression. Does dissent travel more readily in formal or informal networks? How does a dissenter's centrality in a network affect the way in which an organization absorbs dissent? Are these dissenters more vulnerable to retaliation or more insulated as result of their connections? And how does dissent in one part of an organization trickle across to other parts of the company? These are all questions relevant to how dissent functions within communication networks.

Researchers interested in dissent networks examined a collection of emails exchanged between Enron employees before the company collapsed (Garner et al., 2008). They found that just under 40 percent of the emails sent were copied to someone else – meaning that over one-third of dissent expressed was shared with multiple parties in the network. Yet the network itself remained relatively sparse, with people sharing dissent with only one or two others. Furthermore, a sizeable portion of the connections were one-way, with dissent expressed to another party but not reciprocated or confirmed. Additionally, there were many employees who remained unconnected to the central network. Thus, there were clear outliers who either chose not to express dissent or felt unable to do so, or both. This study begins to reveal how such networks function, but the questions raised above regarding how dissent traverses existing networks remain to be answered.

The Cultural-Interpretive Perspective

Understanding organizations as cultures has been another predominant metaphor (Putnam and Pacanowsky, 1983). Like cultures, organizations have rules, belief systems, and values that are captured through the enactment of rites, rituals, ceremonies, and the telling of stories. Employees at Disney, for example, are not mere employees serving customers who come to the park. They are cast members who have an important role in a show designed to create magic moments for guests (Van Maanen and Kunda, 1989). Although it is tempting to chalk up these differences to mere semantics, they have an important cultural function – they show how "organizational life is accomplished communicatively" (Pacanowsky and O'Donnell-Trujillo, 1982, p. 121).

Through communication, employees not only learn but also perform the culture of their respective organizations (Pacanowsky and O'Donnell-Trujillo, 1983). The idea of a performance is at once theatrical in the role-playing sense, but at the same time references the accomplishment or constitution of something. In this regard, crafting a story or developing an account helps members make sense of organizational occurrences. Performances capture routine organizational life and give shape to organizational cultures. Like a spider web, culture is spun – shaped, enhanced, dismantled, and reconstructed communicatively (Pacanowsky and O'Donnell-Trujillo, 1982). Organizational culture, then, is both structure and process. It is "not something an organization has; a culture is something an organization is" (Pacanowsky and O'Donnell-Trujillo, 1983, p. 146).

From this perspective, organizational dissent would be performed and accounted for by members – becoming a part of the organizational culture. How employees make sense of such dissent would be dependent on whether or not dissent was condoned within a given organizational culture. In cultures where it is restricted, organizational dissent would take on the flavor of employee resistance (see chapter 2), serving to protect valued identities, being widely circulated, and shared with only particular audiences. In contrast, in cultures that expect dissent and have in fact embraced it, stories about successful organizational dissent would abound (Pacanowsky, 1988). So the nature and relevance of dissent performances would depend on an organization's cultural orientation toward organizational dissent.

The Critical Perspective

The critical tradition builds upon the notion that communication shapes organizations, but does so with an eye toward how it functions to build and protect dominant power interests within organizations (Mumby, 1988). "Dominant power interests are served when a structured, coherent, acceptable vision of organizational reality is articulated, and oppositional views are systematically excluded" (ibid., p. 99). Communication that remains unchecked and uncontested gives preference to certain views of reality over others. Dominant meanings become fixed and oppositional views rarely stick. Power is not something a person or entity holds, but rather a structural quality of organizations that is reproduced in daily interactions. For it is within daily interactions that competing interests vie for privilege. Power, then, is the struggle over meaning (Deetz and Mumby, 1990).

Power therefore can be found in normal and routine organizational practices (Mumby and Stohl, 1991). A dominant social group is the one which can control the meaning systems that serve its own interests, the group that can fix meanings in ways that are beneficial to its members. Doing so requires appropriating both what should be included in dominant versions of organizational rationality and what should be absented. Mumby and Stohl's account about a male secretary shows how gender inequity gets perpetuated and substantiated through workplace interactions. The very presence of a male secretary produces tension. In a historically male-dominated workplace, men are managers and executives, not secretaries. Women are secretaries. All parties – managers, the male secretary, and the other female secretaries – confront an anomaly that reveals what has been absent: the clear gendered distinctions between the rank, status, and position of men and women.

Organizational dissent, from a critical standpoint, would be a form of employee resistance (see chapter 2) – a way in which employees would contest the embedded power within organizations. As such it would be as important for the identity of employees as it would be for realizing some actual change in power dynamics. This is not to say that it would be ineffectual. To the contrary, it could be extremely beneficial for employees, helping them to define themselves as individuals who may be constrained, but not necessarily controlled. Markham's (1996) examination of a small architectural design firm run by an owner/manager who was prone to emotional outbursts helps to make this point. Although offended and incensed by such outbursts, the designers did not construe them as indicative of an obvious personality flaw. Rather they accepted the behavior as a natural part of the artistic process – an unavoidable and inevitable outcome of failing to deliver what the owner/manager believed the client wanted. As members of a company that took pride in its participative management style, designers were expected to be self-starters, to begin and work on projects independently with little description, definition, and oversight. The company's philosophy of creativity and autonomy masked the owner/manager's inability to provide clear direction. Interestingly, a particularly volatile outburst led to one designer cussing the owner out and another threatening to quit. In this instance dissent could have served to challenge the unreasonable behavior, but it failed to fix a different meaning for the outburst. Instead the exchange became a commonly shared narrative that perpetuated the nature of emotional outbursts between the owner/manager and designers. The explosive working climate continued to be naturalized, with employees reasoning that it was all part of the way things were done. Dissent and employee resistance ended up being absorbed into the creative process. In the end dissent did not result in any significant change in managerial style, but it did serve to bolster the identity of designers fed up with being bullied.

The Discursive Perspective

The discursive perspective evolves from the central premise that "discourse is the very foundation upon which organizational life is built" (Fairhurst and Putnam, 2004, p. 5). The study of discourse involves the examination of talk in social action – the study of language in use. Whereas communication takes in broader activity, discourse analysis focuses very specifically on talk and discourse. Discourse exists at two levels: there is everyday talk and discursive action as well as discourses that background all interaction. These are connected intimately, as everyday talk contributes to the overall discourse or constellations of talk, ideas, and assumptions that powerfully define the world in particular ways. Therefore texts do not exist independent of one another. Rather they achieve meaning through interplay and interconnectivity – what has been called intertextuality (Monge and Poole, 2008).

Discourse can function in several ways. It can simply reflect organizational features and outcomes. It can constitute aspects of a particular organizational reality. And it can contribute to the social processes that anchor organizations (Fairhurst and Putnam, 2004). As a part of ongoing organizational discourse, dissent could function in any or all of these ways. This can be seen in a case study that examines a university's faculty senate (Castor and Cooren, 2006). In the mid-1990s a major university faced a significant budget shortfall. To address the concern, an acting dean decided to make cuts to several academic departments. The following year a group of faculty introduced a resolution calling for the faculty senate to issue a statement of disapproval regarding the dean's program review and subsequent elimination process. After much debate, the faculty senate rejected the motion and opted not to issue such a statement. But how they came to that decision is quite interesting and shows how organizational dissent features in discursive practices.

First, dissent reflected organizational features and outcomes. Certain faculty believed that the senate was an appropriate venue for faculty dissent to be leveraged against administration. Their attempt to use the senate as a vehicle for dissent reflected how the organization functioned, the opposing forces of administration and faculty playing out as they do on many campuses during senate meetings. Thus, dissent reflected the contentious nature and inherent opposition that characterized this particular organization.

Second, dissent constituted certain aspects of the organizational reality. The dissenting group of faculty who offered the resolution stipulated that the required protocol for alerting departments of a formal review, which was articulated in the faculty code, had been breached when the dean and his respective staff failed to send the appropriate letters to each department. Those leading the charge were trying to assign blame, to affix a particular meaning to the situation. In so doing, they were hoping their dissent would add another page to the budget-cut story and would constitute an alternative version of how the budget cut was handled, giving notice to the administration that future budget cuts better take into account faculty voice. Here, dissent served as a means for employees to shape organizational reality, to formalize aspects of the budget cut that they felt should be in an enduring document attesting to how it was wrongfully administered.

Third, dissent contributed to the social processes that anchor organizations. Interestingly, blame did not fall exclusively on the dean and his staff. Rather members of the senate found fault in the faculty code and the faculty response. The code was deemed too ambiguous, failing to stipulate the correct action required for the dean to inform departments. The faculty response was found lacking and was thought to be overdue, since the senate had failed to act the previous year when the budget cut had actually occurred. Moreover, there was talk about whether the senate served a judicial or legislative function. Members came to the realization during the debate that it was not the responsibility of the senate to pass judgment. Thus, organizational dissent functioned to mobilize faculty senate members to discuss and debate its charge. The social processes of debate and deliberation helped them clarify the role and purpose of the senate, thereby anchoring their organizational experience.

The Identity Perspective

Communication is fundamental to shaping our identities, as "one's organizational membership creates a very important social identity for many individuals" (Scott, 2007, p. 125). Organizational identification, though, is not unitary. It may be fragmented. We may find ourselves identifying to varying levels with workgroups, organizations, and professions (Scott, 1997; Cheney and Ashcraft, 2007). And the importance of a given identity appears to shift based on other participants in the interaction and the activities being performed (Scott et al., 1998).

Take professional identities, for example. What does it mean to be a professional? Historically, professionalism emerged as a counterpoint to aristocracy – as a way to achieve mobility through education, expertise, and association – that is, through merit rather than birthright (Cheney and Ashcraft, 2007). Credentialing and the classification of work fueled professionalism. So too did claims of "authoritative expertise" (ibid., p. 150). At the same time professionalism stipulated that one should act responsibly toward the public, and collective ethical standards for practitioners took shape. The Hippocratic Oath for doctors is a prime example. In today's organizations the terms "professional" and "professionalism" can be quite ambiguous. We can be told we are not professional enough, that our work appeared unprofessional, or that we failed to achieve the level of professionalism needed. In contrast, we may be complimented for looking professional, for acting professionally, and for having a professional presentation. Meanings of professionalism will be context and situation driven, like identity in general. Thus, professional identity may be layered over or mixed in with all other identities tied to our work.

Finally, how we define ourselves is linked closely to how we define the work that we do (Kuhn et al., 2008). Yet in contemporary work arrangements the meaning that work holds has been disrupted by a sense of impermanence. This is a feeling of instability brought on by changes in the workplace, including temporary work, contract work, virtual work, and outsourcing. These trends undermine traditional conceptions of where and when work gets done, and consequently erode identity. Definitions of work are evolving too (Broadfoot et al., 2008). Work is no longer something that happens exclusively in offices, factories, plants, or service centers. To the contrary, work takes place in homes, schools, houses, and social groups. It can be paid or unpaid. Workers, then, may have identities tied to numerous forms of work that cross over and intersect within the various spheres of their lives.

The discussion of employee resistance in the previous chapter made it clear that identity factors into organizational dissent. Indeed, research indicates that identity is a predominant goal when employees express dissent (Garner, 2009a). While identity threats can lead directly to dissent, they are unlikely to do so in a predictable fashion. Organizational dissent will be voiced, withheld, or transposed in response to the multiple identifications we hold at any given time in certain social contexts. If we are highly identified with a workgroup we may share dissent directly with coworkers as we problem-solve. If we are highly identified with our organization and take pride in its customer service reputation, we may dissent to a supervisor about a shortcoming in our training program. If we are merely serving time in an organization until we find a better alternative, a troubling organizational decision may garner little energy or desire to express dissent. In each case dissent fluctuates with the target and level of identification. Still, the ethical obligation to protect the public may lead to dissent in situations where employees find their professional and organizational identities at odds. When a company brings a product to market prematurely before all safety concerns have been resolved, the product engineers may express dissent. Westin (1986) found this to be the case with chemical and mechanical engineers, where one in ten reported dissenting in response to a perceived professional obligation.

Organizational dissent, like the elephant in the parable, will take on many different meanings as it unfolds in organizations that vary in how they orient to communication and organizing. These variations are captured in table 3.1. Accordingly, we can see that dissent may be ineffectual and risky, fundamental to participation, key to shaping organizational culture, reflective of organizational discourse, or instrumental to identity enactment. The next section considers a host of theories that help explain various aspects of organizational dissent.

Table 3.1 Organizing perspectives and organizational dissent

Perspective/approach	*Role/function of dissent*	*Dissent occurs*
Classical management	Disruptive and threatening, ineffectual and risky	Rarely
Human relations	Invited and welcomed, but not addressed; voiced but not heard	Occasionally, when consent-generating practices and mechanisms fail, but is neutralized and co-opted
Human resources	Strengthens organizational processes, contributes to participative organizing, signals shortcomings in participation	Commonly and extensively as part of the give and take of participation or in response to participation paradoxes
Systems	Integrates employees within dissent networks; effects existing networks	Within a dissent network or as a part of an existing network
Cultural-interpretive	Shapes organizational culture	As part of cultural performances, preserved through stories, rituals, etc.
Critical	As a form of employee resistance, contesting accepted meanings and/or protecting valued identities	When meanings compete for legitimacy; when employees confront constraints but retain some degree of control
Discursive	Reflects, shapes, or anchors the organization	As part of the everyday talk and discursive practices
Identity	Protects threatened identities	When identification is central to social interaction; out of professional obligation

Theoretical Explanations for Organizational Dissent

Hunting an animal by running it to death sounds absurd, but according to one theory that is exactly what Homo sapiens did for centuries (McDougall, 2009). The Running Man theory was crafted by a group of biologists, paleontologists, and anthropologists over the course of two decades. What was once scoffed at as pure folly now stands as a legitimate chapter in human evolution. The theory flies in the face of more commonly held theories which suggest that the human body, although capable of running, evolved primarily to walk. The human body is in many respects poorly designed for running. We are the only upright species that runs on two legs instead of four and the only species that does so without the helpful ballast of a tail. But stable internal organs, large buttocks, Achilles tendons, nuchal ligaments, and sweat glands set humans apart as unique and efficient running machines.

So, at first glance, our anatomy is inferior in key ways. But the aforementioned aspects of human anatomy hide our capacity for running. Stable organs allow us to regulate our breathing compared to other species. When large cats run, for example, all of their organs slosh back and forth like water in a bathtub, pushing air in and out of the lungs with each stride. Apparently all running mammals share this breathing restriction, save one – humans. Humans can regulate their breathing regardless of stride. Animals also must regulate their temperature primarily through breathing. They do not have the advantage of skin and sweat glands, the most efficient air-cooled system in the biological world, to help them cool down. That is why dogs have to stop running, lie down, and pant when they experience overheating. The muscular buttocks of humans recoup the ballast missing with the absence of tails. The nuchal ligament holds the head steady when people or animals move quickly. Similarly, the Achilles tendon adds spring to the legs – spring necessary for running. While some species have a few of these physical attributes, humans are the only one that possesses the entire collection.

Based upon the evolutionary evidence of these biological properties, the Running Man theory was able to challenge the conventional wisdom that humans had advanced as a walking species. The walking perspective recognized our capacity to run, but dismissed it as a significant feature of our evolution because we were slow and easily winded in comparison to likely prey – most of which could easily outrun us. But this reasoning focused on speed, not endurance. Additional evidence was necessary to overturn this bias, and evolutionary anthropology provided another important piece of the puzzle. Scientists have been able to decipher that our ancestors' diet changed dramatically to include meat 2 million years ago. But how did they get meat? Hunting tools date back only 200,000 years – meaning that our ancestors attained meat for roughly 800,000 years before they had the use of bows, arrows, and spears. According to the Running Man theory, hunting was accomplished through endurance running, not by catching but rather by outlasting prey. Outrunning in terms of distance instead of speed was a key to our success – what has been called persistence hunting.

Scientists pursuing the theory began to uncover folktales of indigenous people from the Americas, Africa, and Australia running animals to death. Then they started crunching numbers. What quickly became evident is that many species can outsprint humans, but humans can run faster and longer at slower speeds. Thus, humans merely need to keep prey in sight and continue pursuing it until eventually the animal expires from hyperthermia. Keeping it on the run overloads an animal's cooling system. If it is forced to continue running, it is unable to find ample time to pant and regulate its body temperature. According to scientific calculations this could happen on a warm day in as little as 6 miles. Thus, running was the weapon of choice for our ancestors long before other weapons were available. Running gave them an upper hand in the animal kingdom.

Many elements needed to come together for the Running Man theory to be substantiated. It is an interesting case to consider for several reasons. First, it illustrates how theories serve to explain phenomena – in this case how and why the human body evolved to be efficient at long-distance running. Second, it shows how theories draw from a variety of places to develop a consistent explanation for the phenomenon in question. And, third, it shows how dissent or disagreement with prevailing theories or perspectives is an important component of scientific inquiry – how dissent is at times necessary and beneficial for moving forward our understanding of the world.

Dissent can be perceived differently depending on one's

perspective. The act of dissent varies with regard to how people perceive it, what purposes it serves, and what changes or results it brings. Moreover, organizational dissent overlaps and parallels other important organizational phenomena, yet remains distinct (see chapter 2). So how do we explain this unique but variable form of communication? The second half of this chapter aims to address that question. It provides some theoretical explanations for why employees dissent, what motivates them to express dissent, and how they make sense of dissent. The selection of theories presented is representative, not inclusive. Unfortunately space prevents a more exhaustive examination of all theories that might be relevant to organizational dissent. Those chosen, however, clearly are.

The Blind Men and the Elephant parable emphasizes the perspectives of the blind men with little regard for the perspective of the elephant. To this point we have positioned the elephant as dissent and the blind men as the many ways in which it could be construed depending on one's orientation. But what makes the elephant express dissent in the first place? Elephants are reputed to be one of the most social and best sensemaking mammals on the planet (O'Connell, 2007). They have complex patterns of interaction to communicate different states of being, possibly even dissent. So we can extend the parable in the latter part of the chapter by giving some consideration to why the elephant would express dissent. Doing so requires placing the theories discussed into three broad domains: the decision-making elephant, the feeling elephant, and the sensemaking elephant.

The theories reviewed here, the broad domains which they occupy, and the major issues they introduce appear in figure 3.1. Next to the elephant's head we find the situational factors that affect employees' decisions regarding the expression of organizational dissent. Near the heart we see the emotional triggers that motivate employees to feel like dissent is necessary and warranted. At the bottom we find the footing for making sense of organizational dissent. These explanatory factors emphasize the processes employees use to make sense of expressing dissent.

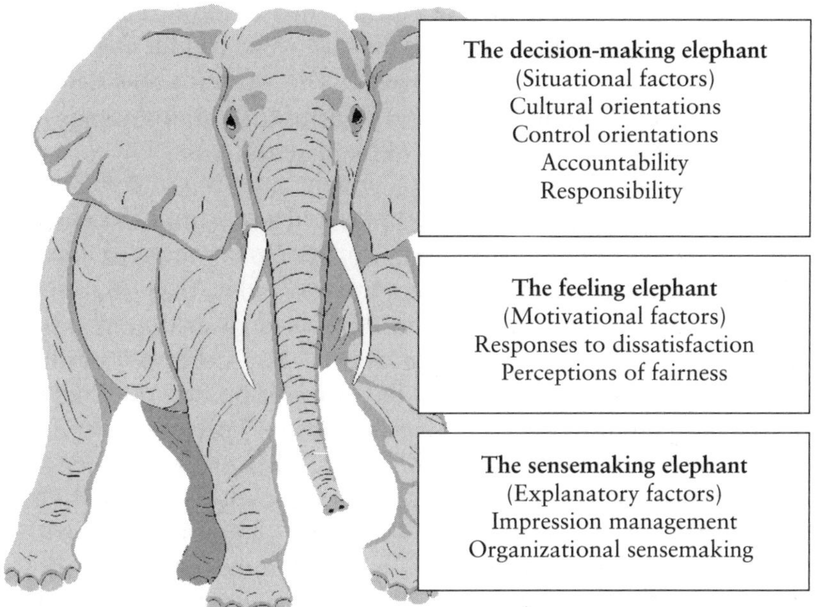

Figure 3.1 Theoretical explanations of organizational dissent

The Decision-Making Elephant: Situational Factors that Influence Employees' Decisions to Express Dissent

When employees give consideration to expressing dissent, what factors are at play? What do they think about and consider in these instances? The elephant confronted with the conundrum of how to access out-of-reach fruit decides to put its weight behind the problem by literally pushing into the base of tree in order to exert enough force to dislodge the fruit (O'Connell, 2007). What does the decision-making employee consider when deciding whether or not to express dissent? Culture, power, responsibility, and accountability would be some factors. Cultures differ with regard to the premium they place on free speech and responses to authority (Hofstede, 2001), as do forms of control within organizations (Tompkins and Cheney, 1985) and employees' estimations of responsibility and accountability (Graham, 1986). What place does free speech hold in our culture and workplaces? How is power exercised? Who is responsible and accountable for reporting flaws, missteps, and infractions? The theories covered here speak to these questions and reveal some of the underpinnings that anchor employee decisions to express dissent.

The theory of independent mindedness The theory of independent mindedness (Gorden and Infante, 1987, 1991) helps explain why employees, particularly employees from the US, would expect and seek opportunities to express organizational dissent (Kassing, 1997). The US in particular, but other Westernized countries as well, is steeped in a tradition of free speech. Therefore, employees from these cultures prefer supervision that affords freedom of expression. When this condition is met employees appear to be more satisfied, committed, and productive. They also see their workplaces as more participative in terms of decision-making, more committed to worklife and product quality, and more dedicated to employee rights. Organizations in the US and Europe have developed models to institutionalize free speech (Cotton, 1993). These include self-directed teams, quality of worklife programs, quality circles, and representative participation in the form of works councils or employee representatives on corporate boards. Essentially, whether they achieve this formally through work arrangements or informally through communication and supervisory styles, employees desire to have some say in the workplace. For employees socialized in free speech cultures, the desire to have some say in matters that affect them serves as the ember that at times ignites dissent.

Unobtrusive control theory How employees orient to control mechanisms stands as an important situational factor that affects the expression of dissent. Unobtrusive control theory explains how organizational control extends to less obvious and more subtle forms – that is, how control manifests when employees act in concert (Tompkins and Cheney, 1985). Control mechanisms in organizations have evolved from simple control exercised openly, personally, and arbitrarily through technical control to bureaucratic control. Technical control exists when control is embedded in the physical technology used by a company – the way in which machines, functions, and operations control people. Time clocks and assembly lines would be clear examples. Bureaucratic control resides in the social organization of a company – in entities like reporting chains of command, hierarchies, and formal policies.

In contrast, unobtrusive control suggests that identification is the key force that moves employees to act favorably toward their organizations. Organizations benefit when identification is high because employees choose courses of action and alternatives that favor the organization. For example, staying late several consecutive nights to meet a deadline on a key project instrumental to corporate success is an easy call for highly identified employees. Thus, management suspends more overt forms of control in lieu of practices that foster identity and belonging. In contemporary organizations that have instituted more participative systems like self-directed teams, control no longer resides in the formal mechanisms. Instead it emerges in the concertive power derived from organizational members policing one another.

When given the opportunity to "structure the system of their own control" (Barker, 1993, p. 412) employees rely heavily on achieving value consensus. In the long run, they often end up in systems that are more constraining and powerful than those for which management would have opted. Barker detailed how this happens in a compelling case study of a small circuit board manufacturing company that adopted self-managing teams. Accordingly, concertive control began with the consolidation of values – a shared sense of how the team should perform and behave. Values, in turn, became morally binding as they reflected the will of the team. The emergence of normative rules that provided guidelines for current and new team members followed. Control shifted from shared values to objective rules, which allowed team members to delineate behavior that was appropriate or inappropriate. Finally, these norms stabilized when teams formalized rules, codes of conduct, and sanctions for misbehavior.

For example, one team created a public absentee chart that kept track of member absences. Eventually, values shifted to norms and norms to rules. Control was clear even though it "resided in the peer pressure of the teams" (ibid., p. 435).

Thus, unobtrusive control functions when there are high levels of identification with organizations, workgroups, or teams. Control depends on consensus. Therefore, Kassing (1997) reasoned that organizational dissent happens in part when employees choose their own decision premises over those of the organization – when they decide that they need to do what is best for themselves or others versus what is best for the organization. There are times, then, when employees will dissent because they experience incongruence between organizational directives and their own instincts. Many whistleblowing cases begin here (Seeger, 1997). Employees determine that they cannot in good conscience continue to do something unethical because that is what their company expects of them.

Yet, this assumes incongruence rather than congruence. It is possible in more participative work arrangements, particularly when those arrangements are authentic, that providing feedback and input – even contradictory feedback like dissent – will be part of the value premises of a given organization. In such cases highly identified employees would choose to express dissent because it is seen as something beneficial to the company. In this instance, individual and organizational decision premises align and people willingly express organizational dissent. In an empirical test of these assumptions, data revealed that employees who perceived their workplaces afforded greater opportunities to provide input also reported high levels of identification and a tendency to express dissent to management (Kassing, 2000a). This may not always be the case, though, as participative systems often end up stunted by some of the aforementioned paradoxes: participation proceeds without dissent as consensus is easier and quicker to achieve. Furthermore, there could be a curvilinear relationship at work here. As organizing systems move toward more participative arrangements they become more apt to invite and tolerate dissent, but, as the case study described above points out, highly participative systems like self-managing teams end up stifling dissension.

Social responsibility and moral reasoning Social responsibility refers to our learned and innate tendencies to act responsibly and accountably (Harris, 1957). Accountability tends to refer to events that have happened in the past, responsibility to future events. One approach suggests that such behaviors are neither required nor prescribed. Rather they are extra-role, prosocial behavior exhibited on behalf of one's organization (Witt and Wilson, 1991). Others argue that accountability can be demanded but responsibility must be assumed (Graham, 1986). Additionally, to whom people should be socially responsible is a matter of dispute. Should people be accountable to an immediate authority or to those that they deem important? Responsibility and accountability will be important to how people practice and make sense of organizational dissent. Whether and how we choose to express dissent will be a function of who we orient toward with regard to accountability and responsibility. For instance, our felt obligations to coworkers seem to drive decisions to express dissent on many occasions (Kassing and Armstrong, 2002), as do our professional obligations (Westin, 1986).

Moral reasoning concerns how people justify their behavior (Kohlberg, 1984), particularly with regard to social perspective-taking and empathy (Gibbs, 2003). It can range from simple reasoning that remains superficial and egocentric to more complex reasoning that takes into account interpersonal relationships and membership in social systems. More complex moral reasoning incorporates norms, expectations, rights, and values. Not surprisingly, moral reasoning has featured prominently in whistleblowing research, often being cited as a reason why people decide to blow the whistle on their respective organizations (Gundlach et al., 2003).

The Feeling Elephant: Motivational Factors that Move Employees to Dissent

The feeling elephant enthusiastically greets other elephants it has not seen in some time with a ritualistic set of gestures akin to the way we offer a hardy handshake and a hug (O'Connell, 2007).

The theories profiled next illustrate the motivational factors that move employees to express dissent. They underscore the emotional triggers that cause organizational dissent by focusing on two key factors – dissatisfaction and fairness. Modern workplaces invoke dissatisfaction and fairness across issues. Concerns about satisfaction and fairness flow through organizations and can bubble up in regard to any number of specific problems like dress codes, organizational change, and outsourcing. The two theories featured here concern these overarching factors that often motivate organizational dissent.

The exit-voice-loyalty-neglect (EVLN) model of employee dissatisfaction How do employees behave when they face unsatisfactory conditions at work? In one of several different ways, according to this theory (Hirschman, 1970). They can choose to exit the organization by quitting, resigning, or finding a new job, or they can decide to stay and voice their concerns about the unsatisfactory conditions. Exit involves escaping unsatisfactory conditions, whereas voice requires one to stay and attempt to change those conditions from within the organization. Loyalty serves as a moderating variable, moving people to choose one option or the other. Employees feeling greater degrees of loyalty are expected to stay and voice their concerns, those feeling less loyalty to exit.

The model indicates simple and limited choices, thus other scholars have argued for refining it (Graham and Keeley, 1992; Gorden, 1988; Farrell, 1983). Some have argued that it is more accurate to think of exit and voice as two separate but related choices (Graham and Keeley, 1992), as it is quite possible someone could exit an organization and then voice discontent. Recall Jerry Maguire's exit from the sports agency profiled in the previous chapter. At the same time it is possible that an employee may choose to stay with an organization, but remain silent or choose a form of voice that does not directly influence or address the dissatisfying condition. Moreover, what happens when dissatisfied employees remain not out of a sense of loyalty, but rather because they have few other options? We often stay in jobs we find dissatisfying. We can build our credentials and experience as we bide our time until something better comes along. So how do employees who feel trapped or unable to leave their workplaces react to dissatisfying conditions? Sometimes with neglect – engaging in additional forms of decline such as tardiness, absenteeism, and increased errors (Farrell, 1983).

Furthermore, voice is not limited to communication designed to correct or address the target of dissatisfaction. Rather it will vary (Gorden, 1988), achieved in active or passive behaviors and via constructive or destructive means (see chapter 2). Despite these qualifications, voice does appear to stem directly from dissatisfaction with one's supervisor and job (Farrell and Rusbult, 1992; Leck and Saunders, 1992; Rusbult and Lowery, 1985) and occurs among loyal employees (Leck and Saunders, 1992). The EVLN model helps situate organizational dissent as behavior that emerges from unsatisfactory conditions – as a form of employee voice. It is only one of many possible responses, though. And dissent, like voice, can exist in several different forms. Employees can voice dissent in ways that resemble exit and neglect as well (Kassing, 1997).

Procedural justice Procedural justice concerns the ways in which people respond to decision-making. It very simply posits that people are more likely to be satisfied with and abide by decisions that they feel have been reached as the result of fair processes. This is true even when outcomes are unfavorable. Essentially, people find satisfaction more in fair treatment during the decision-making process than in the outcome of a given decision. This holds because fair decision-making procedures take into account one's organizational status, which is a key part of our organizational identity. In addition, fair decision-making processes demonstrate neutrality and trustworthiness. Relational criterion rather than a focus on outcomes, then, defines procedural fairness: "In other words, people determine procedural fairness by evaluating the quality of their treatment by authorities and not the outcomes of their experiences" (Tyler, 1998, p. 253).

Scholars have differentiated between different types of justice related to decision-making. Distributive justice refers to perceptions of fairness regarding outcomes, whereas procedural justice concerns the fairness of formal processes leading to decisions. Interactional justice, in turn, entails how supervisors communicate to subordinates about organizational decisions (Hubbell and Chory-Assad, 2005; Moorman, 1991). Evidence suggests that how people perceive decisions are made is as or more relevant to perceptions of justice than outcomes received (Krehbiel and Cropanzano, 2000). Furthermore, procedural justice leads people to act more cooperatively in team settings (Sinclair, 2003), to be more cooperative in conflict settings (Rahim et al., 2000), and to act more favorably toward their colleagues (Moorman, 1991).

Essentially, procedural justice is a powerful attribute of organizational decision-making, and one that relates clearly with organizational dissent (Goodboy et al., 2009; Kassing and McDowell, 2008). Organizational decisions are a well-documented trigger of organizational dissent (Kassing and Armstrong, 2002). How fair employees perceive decision-making processes to be will impact the amount of dissent they express as well as how they choose to share their concerns.

The Sensemaking Elephant: Explanatory Factors that Help Employees Make Sense of Organizational Dissent

The sensemaking elephant uses its feet apparently to hear sonar vibrations. It practices seismic listening (O'Connell, 2007). Accordingly, elephants have perfected a stance and orientation that allows them to place their foot just right on the ground so that they can hear sound waves traveling below the surface (e.g., the sounds of other elephants or vehicles approaching). Similarly, employees must gauge the vibrations traveling through organizations to make sense of dissent. Before, during, and after dissenting, employees try to make sense of their actions and those of others in the organization. In doing so, they give consideration to the impressions they form and the accounts they craft when expressing organizational dissent. The theories profiled below articulate how people work through these processes.

Impression management Impression management concerns "the process by which individuals attempt to control the impressions others form of them" (Leary and Kowalski, 1990, p. 34). Although we do not exercise impression management consistently across all situations, we do practice more of it in situations where acute self-awareness is necessary. For example, we will engage in more impression management during formal job interviews than we will over a meal with family or close friends. Stakes are high during job interviews, but comparatively relaxed over dinner. The stakes are high too when employees consider expressing dissent. People consider the potential benefits alongside the possible liabilities associated with presenting a given image (Schlenker, 1980). Therefore dissenters must balance the possibility of being perceived as adversarial with their desire to offer constructive feedback (Kassing, 1997). For this reason impression management should feature prominently in the decisions employees make about whistleblowing and expressing organizational dissent (Gundlach et al., 2003).

Impression management has served as the theoretical platform for several organizational dissent studies. Kassing (2002) reasoned that it would lead employees to use different strategies for expressing dissent to management. A follow-up study revealed that these strategies varied with regard to how competent employees perceived them to be (Kassing, 2005). And when employees express dissent about the same topic repeatedly over time, supervisors' responses affect the progression of how employees continue to express dissent (Kassing, 2009a). Employees gauge how often and in what ways they should continue to express dissent based in part on the impressions they seem to form with their supervisors. Other work revealed that dissenting by going around one's boss regularly resulted in negative impressions of subordinates (Kassing, 2007).

Organizational sensemaking It is through interaction with others that employees come to know and understand their organizations and their place within those environments (Weick, 1979, 1995). Sensemaking is about how something becomes a meaningful event for organizational members (Weick et al., 2005), about how we deal with "disruptive ambiguity" (p. 413) – with something that merits explanation and definition. Sensemaking most likely occurs when "the current state of affairs of the world is perceived to be different from the expected state of the world" (p. 414), specifically when people face situations that feel different from what they know. Breakdowns, discrepancies, surprises, interruptions, and the like breach the expectation of continuity in such a way that ongoing organized collective action becomes problematic.

Sensemaking begins when we notice a behavior and then attempt to bracket that behavior so that it stands apart from other understood activity. Once bracketed, events can be labeled and categorized. Possible meanings of and interpretations for bracketed behavior get culled in the selection process. Here stories or accounts remain tentative and provisional while they are vetted. Solidarity builds around vetted accounts in the retention process. Accounts, in turn, become more substantial because they relate to past experience, connect to significant identities, and serve as sources of guidance for future action and interpretation. Interestingly, sensemaking is not about getting a story or account "right" but rather about redrafting a story so that it has plausibility. This happens when explanations are comprehensive, incorporate data, and hold up to criticism (Weick et al., 2005).

Sensemaking is relevant to organizational dissent in at least two ways. First, it concerns how we make sense of organizational events that diverge from the expected. Events and issues that move employees to consider dissenting would qualify at times as unexpected. In fact, employees identified the goals of gaining information and seeking advice, behaviors resulting at times from unexpected events, as most relevant to organizational dissent (Garner, 2009a). Second, sensemaking is critical to how we form our identities at work, since it "occurs in the service of maintaining a consistent, positive self-conception" (Weick, 1995, p. 73). Employee resistance, of which dissent is a form, emerges from identity threats (Ashforth and Mael, 1998), and identity goals are important to dissenters (Garner, 2009a). Therefore sensemaking should figure into how employees account for dissent. This appears to be the case when employees choose to go around their supervisors. A recent study showed that employees bracketed supervisors' inaction, performance, and indiscretion in ways that rationalized and justified circumventing their bosses (Kassing, 2009b). For example, they developed accounts that achieved plausibility by emphasizing the identity attacks perpetrated by supervisors via bullying and harassment. Thus, sensemaking about unexpected events can lead to dissent, whereas accounting for dissent requires sensemaking that protects our organizational identities. These accounts, then, feed back into the organizational systems and influence sensemaking about future dissent episodes.

We may never touch an elephant. And we likely will never need to acquire food through persistence hunting. But we will come across dissent in the organizations where we work. The perspectives outlined here reveal the numerous ways in which dissent can be construed – as a disruption, an empowerment ruse, a legitimate form of participation, a feature of networked communication, a cultural artifact, a form of resistance, a constituting force, or a safeguard for threatened identities. The theories discussed move us closer to an understanding of the social and cultural factors that drive dissent, the motives that lead employees to express dissent, and the processes that help them make sense of dissent. The specific reasons why employees choose to dissent is the focus of the next chapter.

Discussion Questions

1 The author uses the metaphor of the Blind Men and the Elephant to show how perceptions can vary with regard to dissent. In your own work experience, how have managers and coworkers viewed organizational dissent? Did they view it as something healthy for the organization? As something detrimental? As a distraction? In your estimation, what attitudes

and perceptions seemed to be associated with the varying perspectives on organizational dissent?

2 With the perspectives on organizing and communicating in organizations changing over time, has the environment for expressing organizational dissent improved or declined? What makes expressing dissent now more or less risky compared with the circumstances of generations past? What aspects of contemporary workplaces promote or discourage organizational dissent?
3 Several theories are discussed regarding organizational dissent. Beyond these, what other organizational communication, management, organizational behavior, and/or human resources theories explain some facet of dissent? What additionally do these theories tell us about organizational dissent? About how and why it is expressed? And how people make sense of it?
4 The theories relevant to organizational dissent fall into three domains (decision-making, feeling, and sensemaking). Are there other relevant domains that have not been included in this chapter? How do those theories and perspectives complement what is presented here? How do they round out your understanding of organizational dissent?

4

What Triggers Organizational Dissent?

> Non-cooperation with evil is as much a duty as is cooperation with good.
>
> – Mahatma Gandhi

Ghandi's comment underscores one clear trigger of dissent – unethical behavior. But this is just one of many. Employees dissent for myriad reasons. Consider the account below provided by a pharmacist.

> The issue that caused concern was the overbearing micro-management of employees within a pharmacy. The corporate policy insisted that each customer interaction, whether face-to-face or over the phone, be conducted within a certain amount of time. If too much time was taken the computer system would make note of it. That went into a personnel profile and was used for evaluations conducted quarterly. Poor performance resulted in lost advancement opportunities as well as year-end bonuses. It was my belief that a customer-first policy means just that, customer first! Some interactions, especially related to health care and insurance adjudication just take time. Doctor's don't rush, nurses don't rush, insurance employees don't rush. Why must pharmacy employees?

There are several factors at issue here. Essentially a flawed policy drives organizational dissent. But the policy also has implications for the fair treatment of employees, quality customer service, potential harm to patrons, and the ethics of expediting healthcare delivery. Although the policy is the root of the concern, the fact that a computer system automatically logs infractions is troubling as well. Performance evaluations get tarnished while customer service suffers. All of which hides the practice of arbitrarily punctuating healthcare delivery. In short, the policy hurts the company, its customers, and its employees.

The excerpt powerfully illustrates how multiple factors come together to arouse organizational dissent. Whereas previous chapters have attended to theories and concepts, this chapter features actual stories collected by the author from employees in various industries and occupations. It relies heavily on employee accounts of organizational dissent to illustrate leading dissent triggers. In their own words, employees provide an informative tour of the many issues that can trigger dissent. Before looking at particular triggers, though, it will be useful to discuss general constraints that facilitate or restrict organizational dissent, as well as subtle and unobtrusive barriers that exist within organizations.

Economic, Political, and Socio-Cultural Factors Affecting Dissent

Although we often celebrate dissent from a participative standpoint, it resides in a larger organizational reality marked by the "material, political, and social constraints of global consumer-corporate capitalism" (Cheney and Cloud, 2006, p. 503) – alas, "communication is not everything to the organization and voice is not everything to the worker" (ibid., p. 504). Frankly, workers often have little say about the terms and conditions of their work, and in a capitalistic system they depend on their employers for survival. While many contemporary organizations have moved to empower employees, to harness their input, and to attend to their feedback, these same institutions hesitate to facilitate authentic discussions about wages, benefits, working conditions, and standards of living. So, organizational dissent can be restrained simply by the economic realities of modern society – as well as by the nature and power of markets and firms.

The web of market capitalism and globalization has allowed for what organizational communication scholars have referred to as "unbridled corporate expansion" (Cheney and Cloud, 2006, p. 527). Organizations are, after all, powerful institutional and cultural forces (Deetz, 1992). Their actions can have important consequences. Consider the series of corporate scandals – Dynegy, WorldCom, Tyco, Enron, and Adelphia – that plagued the business landscape at the turn of the twenty-first century. Journalists, politicians, and others provided several reasons for why these corporate scandals occurred and suggested particular solutions to address each (Kuhn and Ashcraft, 2003). First, firm-specific structures and cultures were blamed, and better enforcement of compliance mechanisms offered as the solution. Second, the character of particular employees who misled others was cited as offensive, with prosecution of guilty parties serving as the primary solution. Third, the pressures of market capitalism were referenced as the reason collusion between corporate officers and external auditors led to favorable and exaggerated financial reports – signaling the danger of institutionalizing firms and the need "to radically overhaul the role of firms in the economic system" (ibid., p. 24).

Interestingly, these varying accounts position firms and their accountability quite differently. Firms appear as "villains, unwitting accomplices, handy vehicles, and neutral containers" (Kuhn and Ashcraft, 2003, p. 25) – all of which give way to questions like "Why do firms exist?" and "What purposes are they meant to serve?" From an economic standpoint, firms exist to connect suppliers to consumers and employees serve as the agents of ownership, there to carry out production of goods and delivery of services. Firms are prone to scandal, in turn, because power is concentrated and executive decisions are obscured from most parties. A contrasting perspective, however, suggests that firms are moral communities, entities designed to serve the greater good, to provide opportunities for people to realize altruistic goals and for organizations to practice corporate social responsibility. From this perspective, organizational members are duty bound to each other "because they desire common ends and value common activities" (ibid., p. 35). Decisions are made with the input of all stakeholders. Clearly, dissent would serve a very different function within firms operating according to either of these premises.

Political constraints exist alongside economic ones. For example, in the US the free speech doctrine assures dissent (Sunstein, 2003), but this is not the case in other governments and countries. This doctrine prohibits the government from censoring speech. Speech can be banned only when a case can be made that it will lead to "imminent lawless action" (ibid., p. 98). Speech that persuades others to reject common beliefs or to adopt radical ones as well as speech that the government disapproves of cannot be barred. From a political standpoint, free speech "furnishes the foundation for democratic self-government" (ibid.). It protects not only the rights of the individual dissenter but also the public interest when it draws attention to fraud or deceit. In many parts of the world censorship principles stretch beyond protecting free speech and include the right to assemble in public places like parks and town squares. While this doctrine allows for speech to occur freely in public, its stipulations do not extend to private property – places where we work, for instance. In fact, police can intervene when we occupy public buildings, office complexes, or private land.

The absence of dissent can be downright dangerous in political and social terms. Without dissent, groups can go to extremes that would not be realized by individuals (Sunstein, 2003). History is replete with atrocities perpetrated by just such groups – the Nazis in Germany, the Khmer Rouge in Cambodia, the Serbian military in Bosnia. Groups move toward extremism when they distort information, attending more readily to arguments that support their positions while pushing dissenting opinions to the side. They build confidence in their views which in turn justifies more extreme attitudes and behavior (ibid.). For society, then, dissent is necessary to protect against both institutional and social forces.

But are we morally obligated to dissent or to blow the whistle? Is dissent mandatory? Scientist Mathieu Bouville (2008, p. 579) questions why whistleblowing often ends up positioned as "the choice between betraying one's company and one's humanity." There is much to lose by blowing the whistle – jobs, income, career prospects (Rothschild and Miethe, 1999). Suffering and retaliation are commonplace for organizational dissenters. So how can dissent be obligatory or mandated? Whether whistleblowing is deemed to be the right decision depends largely on whether or not dissent effectively brings about change (Bouville, 2008). Furthermore, we tend to judge whistleblowers' motives as more or less pure. When motives are pure, whistleblowing is a form of self-sacrifice – requiring saintly and heroic behavior. But being a saint or hero requires an individual to do more than their duty, not merely what is expected, mandated, or obligatory. So, while we may feel a moral obligation to report wrongdoing, expressing dissent is still a choice, not a mandate.

And what about the impact of culture on dissent? Well, not all cultures share the same orientation toward dissent (Moody et al., 2009). In cross-cultural comparisons, US managers appeared to be more likely to blow the whistle and reported less fear related to doing so than Croatian managers (Tavakoli et al., 2003). Dissent clearly involves exposing oneself to risk. People's tolerance for risk varies culturally too. Managers from India, for example, tend to be more risk averse and therefore reported being less likely to blow the whistle than their American counterparts (Keenan, 2002). Although added time spent in a given organization can lead employees to express dissent more readily (Kassing and Armstrong, 2001), organizational tenure may not have the same effect in all cultures. For instance, increased tenure resulted in greater dissent expression for workers in the US, but not for employees in India (Croucher et al., 2009).

Whether we orient to the individual or to the group is another significant factor that differs culturally. In Western cultures that tend to be individualistic, dissent is recognized as an important individual right. In contrast, dissent undermines cultural values like harmony and loyalty found in collectivistic cultures (Keenan, 2007). Yet there may be a demographic shift happening in traditionally collectivistic cultures. One study found that younger Chinese employees in the banking sector were more likely to express dissent than their older counterparts. While this can be attributed in some part to younger Chinese people being more individualistic, there is a collectivistic explanation as well. Apparently, younger generations are being taught to speak out in order to protect the welfare of the community rather than to remain quiet to preserve harmony (Zhang et al., 2009). Cultural differences, then, underpin orientations toward and practices of expressing dissent.

Barriers to Organizational Dissent

In conjunction with economic, political, and socio-cultural influences, there are additional forces that unobtrusively work to stifle and discourage dissent even when mechanisms are in place to recoup it. Although many factors could be added to such a list, some of the major reasons are profiled here: the trappings of leadership, binary thinking, diffusion of responsibility, futility, and misguided loyalty.

Leadership presents a particular challenge for organizational dissent. While certain forms of leadership facilitate and tolerate dissent, some of the more popular forms, such as transformational leadership, should be questioned (Tourish and Pinnington, 2002). Transformational leaders possess and communicate a clear vision – a vision that integrates employees into a collective governed by shared aspirations that guide everyday behavior. Goals are understood to be representative of what is best for the collective good, what is best for both leaders and followers. As a result, independent goals morph into collective ones. But this requires a clear leap of faith – a belief that everyone's goals are represented rather than simply usurped and replaced by those of a designated leader. Transformational leaders position themselves as messianic interpreters there to illuminate a corporation's shared faith. But what are the implications for dissent? Well, "the notion of universally held values suggests minimal to non-existent dissent, or dissent which is confined to the periphery of a firm's operations" (ibid., p. 148). Consent gets prioritized, while dissent becomes nonessential.

The tenets of transformational leadership "are remarkably

similar to the defining traits of cults" (Tourish and Pinnington, 2002, p. 156) – members' goals get sublimated by transformational leaders in much the same way as cult leaders uplift their devoted followers. Organizations that run the risk of becoming cultish will see communication flowing primarily from the leader to the followers and dissent falling by the wayside. Visionary companies that operate with cult-like cultures include Nordstrom and Disney (Collins and Porras, 1994). Historically these companies have thrived on account of organizational members' steadfast adherence to the company's cultural norms and practices. Members buy in completely or leave, because these companies "have such clarity about who they are, what they're all about, and what they're trying to achieve, they tend to not have much room for people unwilling or unsuited to their demanding standards" (ibid., p. 121).

A second barrier to organizational dissent is binary thinking. Historically established binaries such as consent/dissent, leader/follower, and control/resistance constitute the backdrop against which we make assumptions about organizational dissent (Collinson, 2005). We assume that dissent and consent preclude one another, but this is not necessarily the case. Employees can openly protest and withhold consent, but they also may disguise dissent, appearing to consent while disagreeing subtly through absenteeism, loafing, disengagement, and humor. Thus, the two coexist, "inextricably linked within the same ambiguous practices" (ibid., p. 1431). Similarly, we take for granted that followers resist leaders, but there is evidence to suggest that supervisors at times contribute to and support employee resistance (Kassing, 2007; Larson and Tompkins, 2005). Binary thinking, then, limits our understanding of who disagrees and how. Dialectic thinking, which emphasizes the tension and interplay between opposing ideas, is better suited to understanding organizational dissent (Collinson, 2005). It could prove beneficial by showing how dissent can be expressed concurrently by managers and employees, leaders and followers, executives and staff. Dialectical thinking also may reveal how dissent can contribute simultaneously to control and resistance.

With hierarchical structures in place, modern organizations

promote the diffusion of responsibility (Gandossy and Sonnenfeld, 2005). This occurs when employees discard their individual responsibility for calling suspect behavior into question. When they observe higher-ranking members within their firms failing to address problematic issues, lower-ranking employees take little or no responsibility for observed misconduct. Employees wash their respective hands of wrongdoing, thereby reducing any misgivings they may have had about neglecting to act on the issue. Complicity gets routinized and institutionalized throughout. Responsibility dilutes more and complicity compounds further when performance review and compensation bond exclusively with objective performance measures. Such arrangements promote a culture of cheating, pressuring employees to perform and achieve according to particular standards or else suffer professionally and economically. Strong incentives move people to look the other way when misconduct arises, particularly when it will disrupt the incentive system to which members have become accustomed. Diffusion of responsibility, then, elevates conformity while devaluing dissent.

Employees may be hesitant to express dissent when they believe their efforts will prove futile. Dissent can be rendered futile within organizations in a few short steps. Because dissent can be face-threatening, managers often dismiss opportunities to hear new ideas and encourage challenges (Kassing, 2005; Tourish and Robson, 2006). Dissenters recognize and respond to supervisory reactions accordingly, curtailing dissent when necessary (Kassing, 2009a). In the absence of critical upward feedback, management falsely assumes adherence and authenticates its stance as correct. When these convictions cement, dissent "will be viewed as resistance to be overcome rather than useful feedback" (Tourish and Robson, 2006, p. 716). What follows? Top leadership believes that there is one truth to explain most organizational shortcomings and only a few top managers have a full understanding of this truth. Dissenters are seen as misinformed or misguided and therefore need to be silenced. The rigidity of a communication system that marginalizes dissent gets fortified profoundly by "narratives that demonize" any critical opinions that surface (ibid.). All of this happens habitually within organizations through routine interactions – powerfully establishing an organizational culture that eschews dissent.

Lastly, there is the barrier of loyalty. Organizational dissent, particularly in the form of whistleblowing, smacks of disloyalty in certain circles (see chapter 2). Employees are tasked with choosing between their integrity and their company (Bouville, 2008; Jubb, 1999). But Vandekerckhove and Commers (2004) argue that this is an inappropriate choice to advance. Rather, employees should balance loyalty to the mission statement and the implied promises it makes about operating in the public's best interests against the company's conduct. Loyalty affixed to the physicality of the company and the people who inhibit it is misguided; the object of loyalty should be adjusted to emphasize adherence to a firm's mission statement. Misconduct that disrupts the code of conduct implied by a mission statement demands a reassessment of one's object of loyalty – directing it away from the firm and toward the general public. Accordingly, dissenting employees do not betray their companies. Instead, they highlight the betrayal of the public's interests perpetrated by the organization. Most companies, though, demand loyalty to the organization as an entity more than what it represents. But loyalty and dissent can in fact complement one another in organizational settings. Decision-making groups, for example, reported making better decisions when loyalty and dissent were pronounced (Dooley and Fryxell, 1999). Loyalty need not be, but often is, a barrier to expressing dissent.

What are Dissent-Triggering Events?

So what becomes a dissent-triggering event? Frankly, many things – so many, in fact, that it might be easier to answer the question: What is not a dissent-triggering event? Perhaps the lack of chocolate milk in the office vending machine. But even this seemingly trivial feature of organizational life can lead to dissent. If chocolate milk remains absent after repeated requests, then an employee may feel justified in expressing dissent. Why? Because it's no longer about chocolate milk; now it's about inattentiveness and inaction on the part of management. The chocolate milk may be the proverbial straw that breaks the camel's back, the signal once and for all that someone needs to say something about a company's failure to address basic employee requests. The point being, dissent triggers have a way of shape shifting as employees emphasize their seriousness and principled nature (Kassing, 2009b).

While we may not be able to chronicle all things that act as dissent triggers, we certainly can identify a group of regular culprits. Before departing on a review of what those are, though, some consideration should be given to what exactly a dissent-triggering event is and how it functions. A dissent trigger is an event that initiates the process of organizational dissent – an event that propels employees to feel that they must speak out and express dissent (Graham, 1986; Kassing, 1997; Redding, 1985). An occurrence becomes such an event when it exceeds our individual tolerance for dissent – that is, when we deem the occurrence serious enough to expose ourselves to the risk that dissenting about it might provoke (Redding, 1985). The likelihood that the issue will be addressed is also relevant (Graham, 1986).

Thus, at least three factors come together to determine dissent triggers: risk of retaliation, issue seriousness, and the likelihood that the issue will be addressed. Retaliation is an enduring consideration for dissenters (Near and Jensen, 1983), one that exerts considerable influence on employees' decisions to express dissent (Graham, 1986; Kassing, 1997). Risk of retaliation, therefore, determines in large part the level of our tolerance for dissent. If the risk is high, our tolerance for dissent rises and we become more selective and restrictive about the topics that will move us to dissent. If the risk is low, our tolerance dips and we feel more secure and comfortable expressing dissent about a larger cross-section of issues (see figure 4.1). The seriousness of the issue and the likelihood that it will be addressed position an event in relation to our tolerance for dissent, such that more serious issues that are likely to be addressed will end up surpassing all but the uppermost tolerances for dissent that exist in high-risk conditions. Conversely, when the risk of retaliation and tolerances for dissent are comparatively low, events that are less serious and easily

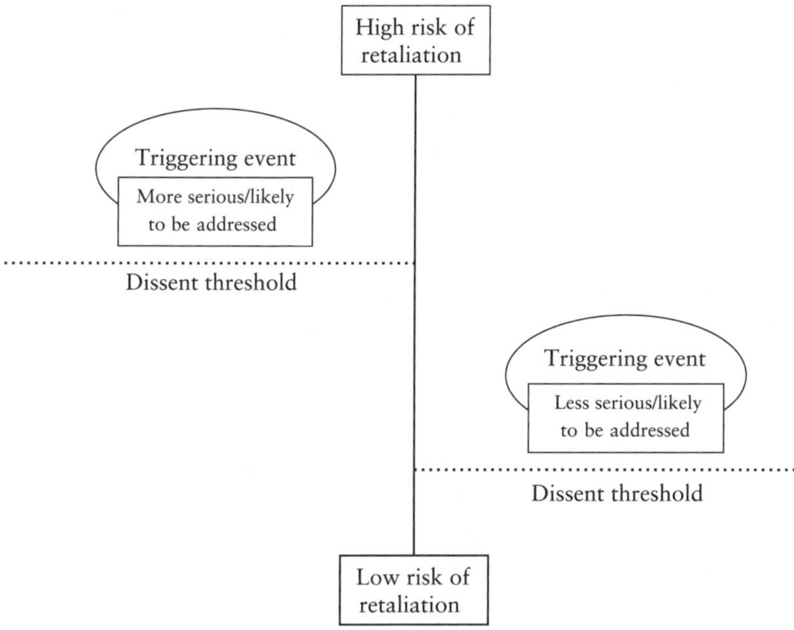

Figure 4.1 Dissent-triggering events and individual tolerance for dissent

dismissed can trigger dissent – the aforementioned chocolate milk, for example.

Dissent-Triggering Events

There are multiple and various dissent-triggering events (Hegstrom, 1999; Redding, 1985; Sprague and Ruud, 1988). These seem to fall into three domains: those that include organizational processes like decision-making, coordinating organizational change, and distributing resources; those that concern personnel matters like employee treatment, role responsibilities, and performance evaluations; and those that entail wrongdoing, malfeasance, and unethical behavior. There is considerable overlap, however, between and among these domains, as the chapter's opening vignette illustrated. An organizational process implicated both personnel matters related to performance evaluations and ethical concerns regarding the treatment of customers.

Another distinction made in the literature has to do with the nature of dissent. Principled dissent is expressed in response to issues that violate a standard of justice and honesty – as a matter of principle (Graham, 1986). But personal motives can drive organizational dissent as well (Hegstrom, 1999; Sprague and Ruud, 1988). Personal-advantage dissent references the practice of expressing dissent in order to achieve some personal gain (e.g., a raise, a better schedule, time off). Additionally, whether an organization tolerates or restricts disagreement will have some bearing on which events trigger dissent. In a study designed to determine these effects, Hegstrom (1999) discovered that employees expressed personal-advantage dissent only about pay and benefits and principled dissent only about ethical issues in organizations that restricted dissent. Interestingly, in organizations that permitted dissent, personal-advantage dissent extended to include concerns about the nature, amount, and expectations of work and principled dissent stretched to include concerns about organizational viability. Thus, what we choose to disagree about, regardless of whether the issue is principled or personal, shifts with how receptive our respective organizations are to dissent. While differentiating dissent as principled or personal advantage helps to frame organizational dissent and the motives that compel it, these differences suggest a distinction that does not always hold up. Sometimes principled and personal-advantage dissent comingle and intertwine, becoming difficult to parcel out from one another (Hegstrom, 1999).

After a review of previous dissent research, Kassing and Armstrong (2002) developed a typology of nine dissent-triggering events: employee treatment, organizational change, decision-making, inefficiency, role/responsibility, resources, ethics, performance evaluation, and preventing harm (see table 4.1). This sizeable group was found to collapse into three broader classifications: other-focused triggers entailed dissenting across topics but in response to concerns about coworkers; functional dissent triggers referenced organizational functions like decision-making, managing organizational change, correcting inefficiency, and examining and reevaluating job

Table 4.1 Typology of dissent-triggering events

Employee treatment	Dissenting about how employees are treated within one's organization – particularly with regard to fairness and employee rights
Organizational change	Dissenting about organizational changes and the implementation of those changes
Decision-making	Dissenting about organizational decisions and how decisions are made within one's organization
Inefficiency	Dissenting about inefficient work practices and ineffective processes
Role/ responsibility	Dissenting about one's work role and responsibilities or the roles/responsibilities of others
Resources	Dissenting about the use and availability of organizational resources
Ethics	Dissenting about unethical practices that exist within one's organization or about expectations to act unethically
Performance evaluation	Dissenting about how one's work or coworkers' efforts, or both, are evaluated; dissenting about the performance review process
Preventing harm	Dissenting about things an organization does that endanger employees, coworkers, or customers
Supervisor inaction	Dissenting about supervisors' failures to respond directly to initial and often repeated expressions of dissent in a timely manner or to respond to the degree employees expected
Supervisor performance	Dissenting about routine and prolonged displays of supervisors' poor management, communication, and/or organizational skills or supervisors inappropriate enactment of managerial roles
Supervisor indiscretion	Dissenting about ethically, legally, and morally questionable behavior on the part of one's immediate supervisor, including theft, harassment, and abuse of or neglect for organizational policy

Source: Adapted from Kassing and Armstrong (2002) and Kassing (2009b).

descriptions; and protective dissent triggers included ethical issues and issues that endangered employees, coworkers, and customers. Additional dissent-triggering events surfaced in another study that examined the reasons employees provide for circumventing their bosses (Kassing, 2009b). Since employees were sharing why they decided to go around their immediate bosses to express dissent, it is not surprising that the triggers revealed in this work centered on supervisors. Supervisors were found at fault for inactivity, poor performance, and indiscretion.

Dissent-triggering events, then, can take many forms, can reference personal or principled issues, and can coincide and intersect. With these qualifications in mind, several leading dissent-triggering events are discussed in the remaining section of this chapter.

Employee Treatment

Employee rights and fair treatment are important to most employees (see chapter 3). They preserve some sense of civility in organizational systems that naturally subordinate people (Redding, 1985). When violated, they produce dissent. It is not surprising, then, that employee rights and fair treatment have emerged as predominant dissent-triggering events in previous research (Kassing and Armstrong, 2002; Sprague and Ruud, 1988). Issues of employee rights and fairness surface in the following account.

> I was called into my supervisor's office, with the department head present as well, last year. And given a verbal warning regarding being seen outside the hospital talking on my cell phone, missing time clock punches (I had missed one in 6 months), and not taking lunch breaks. I explained to the 2 supervisors that my coworkers missed punches more than I did and that they talked on their cell phones not only outside the hospital but inside as well. I felt like I was being singled out. I asked them to investigate everyone and see if I was indeed the only one violating these rules. I explained to them that I felt that the warning was baseless and hollow and that I was being picked on and singled out.

Ironically, this hospital worker admits to policy infractions. Nonetheless she contests the way in which her supervisors admonish her. She sees this as an affront because in her estimation she is being singled out. With regard to fairness, she notes that her coworkers are much worse offenders. With a nod toward her rights as an employee, she suggests that management conduct a full investigation of everyone. Although confrontational, these do not seem like unreasonable requests as they bring issues of fair and equitable employee treatment into relief.

Sometimes employee treatment is an issue among and between coworkers. Dissent can be mobilized on these occasions as well. The story below chronicles one such instance.

> I was working for a lumber company. The rule was to rag on the new guy, but no one ragged on me for whatever reason. A friend of mine got a job there also. He was treated like crap. They stole his tools, his lunch and told him to do things that were not in his job description. I stood up for him. I went to the supervisor and told the supervisor that things needed to change.

In this situation an employee dissents to management out of concern about how a colleague is being treated unfairly by coworkers. Research indicates that employees are actually more likely to dissent to management about the treatment of coworkers than about ethical issues (Kassing and Armstrong, 2002). Employee treatment, then, both for oneself and for one's coworkers, is a significant trigger of organizational dissent.

Organizational Change

Organizations seem to be in a constant state of flux, consistently enduring some form of change. Restructuring, downsizing, and shifts in corporate culture are wrought with contradiction and can have lasting effects on employees (Fairhurst et al., 2002). In fact, one study revealed that resistance to change was the leading reason employees reported expressing dissent (Sprague and Ruud, 1988). Workers resisted changes related to personnel reassignment, manufacturing processes, and project warranties. In addition to resisting actual organizational changes, employees can dissent about the way in which changes are implemented. Evidence of both is apparent in the following excerpt:

> I recall this situation at a job I previously had as a loan processor representative. At the time our department had undergone many new changes. Including a new lead manager, quality control monitoring,

> and call time adjustments. The new manager was very strict and had high expectations. He expected the department to learn the new training program in a limited amount of time. It was a stressful time and needing to cram in the new training programs topped it off.

This young loan processor laments the amount of changes faced by employees, the supervisor's expectations regarding those changes, and the timing of them. Change in and of itself can be disruptive, and, indeed, compounded by how supervisors orchestrate change and the timelines set for accomplishing it. Any of these issues related to organizational change can spark dissent.

Decision-Making

While many organizations have moved to arrangements that involve employees in decision-making procedures (Cotton, 1993), decision-making still remains a significant prompt for organizational dissent (Kassing and Armstrong, 2002). Employees dissent about how decisions are made as well as about the quality of those decisions. Are decisions fair? Are they equitable? Are employees involved in the decision-making process? Poor decisions can range from being clearly illegal, immoral, or unethical to being merely insensitive, impractical, and irritating (Redding, 1985). Here is an example of a poor decision that led to dissent on the part of a restaurant chef.

> I am the head chef for a restaurant in town. The general manager decided to switch food providers, in order to cut costs. The meat and produce we began to receive was very unsatisfactory. Particularly compared to what we had received previously before switching providers. I confronted management and told them they needed to switch back or I would leave.

For management, the decision to switch food providers translates to cutting costs; for the chef, it means poorer ingredients with which to work. So, while management sees the benefits in the bottom line, the chef sees it in the actual dishes he is able to create. What seems to be a viable decision at one level of the organization does not make good sense at another – particularly at the level that affects the quality of food served. This decision is not unethical, but it is certainly problematic – insensitive to the needs of the chef and impractical with regard to producing quality dishes – and as a result is irritating enough to elicit dissent from the chef.

Inefficiency

Employees have first-hand knowledge and experience with organizational procedures and practices. They develop an intimate sense of what works well and what does not work so well. They become aware of inefficiencies in their respective organizations and at times feel the need to speak out about how their organizations function – "to start doing something" (Sprague and Ruud, 1988, p. 179). An account provided by a healthcare worker illustrates how and when this can happen.

> I worked in healthcare in lower management and the problem was that I did not have enough staff to deliver proper care to patients. I asked my regional managers several times to give me more help and my request was ignored. I told them, that in order to deliver proper care to patients and not endanger coworkers, I needed more help.

Rebuffed at first, this dissenter's observations regarding staffing shortages that were compromising patient care sparked her to persist with her claim. The example demonstrates how managers at one level of the organization can see inefficiencies directly. Meanwhile those same inefficiencies remain unobservable and unknown to absent or removed managers like the regional managers in question. When employees question organizational efficiency they often problem-solve at the same time – offering solutions to address the observed issues (Kassing, 2002). The request for more staff represents a possible solution in this case.

Role/Responsibility

Organizations routinely need to designate roles and assign responsibilities in order to function. But this is not an exact science and often proves stressful for employees (Miller et al., 1990). Stress can result simply when we have too much work to do. But it also occurs when role ambiguity and role conflict are present – that is, when we struggle to determine what we should be doing and how we should rectify competing expectations. In all cases, roles and responsibilities can lead to organizational dissent (Kassing and Armstrong, 2002). In previous research, employee concerns about roles and responsibilities manifested in dissent expressed about scheduling, goal-setting, and equitable distribution of work and pay (Hegstrom, 1999).

The excerpt below, drawn from the account of a young retail salesman, portrays these concerns well.

> We were short on staff members. My colleagues and I were asked to cover and clean up bigger portions of the store because of the shortage of people. I spoke to my immediate managers and then to the store manager. I explained the situation to them both. I told them that if I was to have more responsibilities, I wanted a pay raise. They told me they couldn't give me a raise. But told me they would hire more people so that I wouldn't have such a heavy load. They hired two people, but they were seasonal hires only. After they were let go, I had to get back to covering a larger portion of the store again. I felt this was not fair, I felt like I was being taken advantage of.

The salesman struggles with the fact that his responsibilities have grown while his role has not changed. His request for a raise highlights this discrepancy. Management's decision to hire new people represents an attempt to reset his responsibilities. Yet this is only a temporary fix, as additional responsibilities creep back into his workload once the seasonal employees depart. In the end, feeling taken advantage of seems entirely justifiable given the fact that he has taken on extra responsibilities twice. How roles and the associated responsibilities ebb and flow is relevant to our workload and the stress it may produce. When they are out of phase, dissent will follow.

Resources

While it is helpful to have clear roles and designated responsibilities, it also is important to have appropriate resources available.

Organizations rely on material resources to help employees complete tasks. Desk space, copy machines, and communication devices are a few. These resources derive from allocated budgets – how much a company sets aside to facilitate the production of goods and services along with what gets allocated for advertising, corporate sponsorship, employee training, benefits, etc. There are many directions in which resources can flow, and employees often notice and speak out when there are not enough resources directed at them or when the flow of resources is restricted (Hegstrom, 1999). A teacher's account shows how this can happen.

> I teach gifted students for a public school district. Gifted funding is tied in with special education. Therefore contracts for these classes come from a separate pool of money than regular education classes. I was given no money for supplies for my gifted classes and had to buy my own materials with my money. I found out that our principal was allocating all special education funds to students with special needs. I talked to him about this and he refused to alter our school's funding policy. I told him that if gifted funds were not freed up for next year's budget, I would transfer to another school and explain to personnel there my reasons for leaving my present position.

School supplies – an important resource necessary for teaching all students regardless of whether they are regular, gifted, or special needs students – are absent from the budget for gifted students. To fulfill her teaching responsibilities, this teacher is forced to buy her own materials. She contests the lack of resources and the policy that perpetrates this discrepancy. Her account reveals how resources function as a powerful cause for organizational dissent.

Performance Evaluation

While we need resources to perform our job, we also become resources for our organizations – more or less productive contributors to the ongoing enterprise. Therefore evaluation of our performance becomes necessary. This process, however, is far from perfect. Employees may find fault with their actual evaluation, finding it lacking or poorly conducted, or both. Or employees may find aspects of the performance evaluation process or how it is administered flawed. That seems to have been the case for the employee who shared the report below.

> I agreed to work for a low hourly wage for 1 month as an evaluation period after which my performance would be reviewed and I would receive a 30% raise. But the owner procrastinated. I had to insist they schedule the review. I informed the manager that I would quit if it was not scheduled in the next week. The review was scheduled with the manager and owner the following day.

Many companies adhere to similar policies – reserving higher pay and perhaps benefits for employees who remain and excel during a probationary period. This company, however, seems to disregard the stipulations of the probationary period. After clear efforts to delay the review, the employee demands that her manager schedule it. As a dissent trigger, performance evaluation can easily overlap with employee treatment as issues of fairness and employee rights come to the fore in performance evaluations and the processes that govern them.

Preventing Harm

Employees blow the whistle when they determine that an organization's actions will harm the public in some way (Stewart, 1980). In addition, employees dissent when they are put in harm's way, when coworkers are exposed to harm, and when customers are endangered in some way (Sprague and Ruud, 1988). For example, the following employee was concerned for his own safety.

> My job was in field service, both domestic and international. I was offered an advanced position with the company that involved relocation but promised diminished travel. After working for a year my travel never slowed down. At one point I felt that the owner did not have my safety in mind when making decisions regarding my foreign travel. I talked to the owner about my concerns regarding where they were sending me. I told him that if the choice were my job or my safety then I would quit.

Regularly dispatched to countries for which the US government had issued travel advisories, this engineering consultant questioned his organization's concern for his safety. For him, dissent was necessary to prevent possible harm he might experience traveling to dangerous destinations on behalf of his employer.

Clearly, we want to protect ourselves at work, but we also have a tendency to look out for the well-being of our coworkers (Kassing and Armstrong, 2002). Consider the case below.

> I worked at a nuclear power plant in the containment building. To leave the building or go into your section of the building you had to step into a screener to detect exposure to radiation. If you did not get a green light, you could not proceed. I could not pass the screening and my supervisor said "don't worry about it, it's been raining and sometimes the alarm goes off because you're wet." He told me to just go into the office. I told him I would rather quit than take the chance of contaminating others.

This employee draws the line with her supervisor when he suggests that she should disregard safety protocol and risk harming her colleagues. She dissented in this situation out of desire to protect others in her workplace. Uncertain of whether or not she was contaminated, she refused to expose her coworkers to any harm. Although they were selfless in this instance, desires to keep ourselves and our coworkers from harm go hand in hand at times. For example, we may join a protest or sign a petition that questions the safety of working conditions. This affects us individually and all of our coworkers.

Finally, we can choose to dissent out of a desire to protect customers and clients. This happens when an organization's practices or products endanger people. In late 2009 and early 2010, Toyota Motor Corporation, the car manufacturer who built its reputation on quality, came under fire when over 6 million vehicles needed to be recalled on account of safety issues with accelerator pedals in several models. Organizational dissent within Toyota, or any company facing product deficiencies, would be warranted in such instances. These dangers need not always be about health and safety, though. Sometimes they revolve around honesty and integrity with customers, as the excerpt below reveals.

> I was giving information about my company's prices and my supervisor came to the front desk when the customer left. She said that the boss didn't want us to tell people how they can save money at the store. I clarified that I was providing accurate information. She said that if they know about the discount we can charge them less, but if they don't we are expected to break the rules and charge them more. I thought this was wrong, so I spoke to my supervisor in private the next day. I told her that I thought the practice was wrong.

While many employees would not bother to contest this practice, thankfully this outspoken saleswoman did. When addressed appropriately, her dissent will save customers money and will move the company to adhere to greater ethical standards when dealing with customers.

Supervisor Inaction

Some of the accounts to this point reveal that management often fails to address employee concerns the first time those concerns arise. Rather, it may take several attempts to draw corrective action from management. When concerns go unheeded, employees' original motives for expressing dissent come to incorporate management inattentiveness. This can be a powerful force, so powerful that it stands as one of the justifications employees provide for going around their boss (Kassing, 2009b). The example below reveals how this happens.

> I worked at a bar that was also a restaurant. It just so happened that one of the bartenders was stealing money from the safe on a regular basis. I told the manager who brushed it off. So I told the other bartenders what was going on because he was stealing portions of our tips. It got really bad, the guy was getting worse and worse. So I went to the general manager and told her what was going on.

Confronted with the unethical behavior of a coworker, this bartender has to raise her concern multiple times. Fascinatingly, the company was willing to tolerate theft rather than investigate an esteemed member of their staff. The bartender, in turn, came to realize that she could no longer work for a company that was unresponsive to repeated expressions of dissent and gave her notice. What began with unethical behavior grew to incorporate intolerable levels of supervisory inaction.

Supervisor Performance

Not all supervisors are qualified to perform their assigned duties. Nor do they have the interpersonal composure necessary to manage people well. Therefore dissent often stems from problems with the qualifications and style of managers (Kassing, 2009b). Moreover, people in managerial roles can abuse the power of their position, dispensing punishment, admonishment, and harassment unjustifiably – performing as such to create and protect authority and power (Trujillo, 1985). Bosses act as tyrants when they blame subordinates, second-guess staff, and hold unreasonably high standards for employees. Additionally, tyrannical bosses display mercurial mood swings, disparage employees, obsess over loyalty and obedience, and exercise raw power for personal gain (Bies and Trip, 1998). Kassing (2009b) saw evidence of this when employees reported that their supervisors "tried to make a statement to all employees by being very rude and bossy," practiced "micromanaging," and "always wanted you to know that [they were] in charge." So management's poor performance or inappropriate displays of power, or both, can prompt dissent.

This was evident in the account provided by a branch manager of a bank who questioned the performance of her supervisor at multiple levels. She shared: "My newly hired supervisor wasn't qualified to manage sixteen branches. She avoided phone calls, played favoritism, and never was a branch manager herself." In a mere twenty-three words, the branch manager levels several serious allegations against her supervisor. In this case, an unwillingness to communicate regularly with staff, a propensity to play favorites, and a general lack of experience prove incendiary. These perceived deficiencies combine to provoke organizational dissent.

Supervisor Indiscretion

Although we would like to think that those who hold positions of power understand and accept the responsibility that accompanies these roles, this is not always the case. Managers can make bad personal and professional choices. They can engage in untoward behavior, defraud companies, or fail to uphold important organizational standards. Either way, employees find enough fault with supervisors' indiscretion that it serves as a potent trigger of organizational dissent (Kassing, 2009b). In previous work, indiscretions included clocking in for hours not worked, running personal errands on company time, manipulating commission reports, stealing from the organization, dating subordinates, and drinking alcohol on the job. Evidence of such indiscretion can be seen in this employee account:

> I experienced favoritism when my manager was having affairs with two other female agents in the office. This situation caused a lot of drama in my office. As the manager funneled the best leads and prospects to these females. I found it stressful to work in this environment. I also resented the good leads going to my coworkers who were having relationships with my manager. I eventually spoke with my manager's supervisor and explained the situation.

This particular supervisor's cavalier dating practices create drama and tension in the office which he is meant to manage. It also disadvantages those employees who are not involved romantically with him. Unfair and irritating, the supervisor's indiscretion leads directly to organizational dissent.

Dissent and Ethics

Values drive our determination of what is right and wrong, what is proper and improper, what is ethical and unethical (O'Leary, 2006). For some, ethics is as simple as considering how we would like to be treated in any given situation (Maxwell, 2003). But ethics in organizational settings gets complicated quickly. Because we hold membership in and loyalties toward two distinct groups, we acknowledge and respond to ethical obligations to both our organization and society at large (Seeger, 1997).

Just as the meaning and role of dissent can fluctuate with one's perspective, so too can the relationship between dissent and ethics. Dissent can serve a protective function for the public, can signal a need for an organization to take corrective action, or can be a form of catharsis for individuals. Indeed, "these different emphases carry quite different ethical meanings, according to which dissent may be condemned or lauded" (Maclaglan, 1998, p. 123). Gorden (1988) recognized that employee voice can be constructive or destructive, but questioned for whom: the public at large, the organization, or the individual? Similarly, the beneficiary of dissent makes whistleblowing difficult to assess. The nature of whistleblowing proves troubling to evaluate, as it may serve some public good but damage the organization. At once it is constructive and destructive – depending on one's ethical standpoint.

Ethical standpoints in relation to dissent include concern for the organization and its stakeholders, concern for the public, and concern for oneself and one's family/friends (Maclaglan, 1998). Judgments about blowing the whistle, then, must take into account our ethical obligations to multiple constituents, some of which will override others in particular situations. For example, we may choose not to dissent when perceived wrongdoing subsides and little can be done about it retrospectively. Putting our career and livelihood at risk in this situation would make little sense. In contrast, a heinous grievance that endangers the public – say, a faulty product or the unexpected and uncontrolled release of hazardous waste – may prompt us to blow the whistle regardless of perceived risks to ourselves and our families.

Is giving consideration to our ethical standpoints and the related loyalties they invoke enough? Not necessarily. There are clear ethical considerations that we should bear in mind when dissenting, particularly with regard to whistleblowing (Maclaglan, 1998). First, dissenters should exhaust all possible outlets for expressing concern within organizations before going public. Second, whistleblowers must give their motives serious reflection.

Dissent should not occur for selfish or political reasons. Take the politician who regularly attended meetings of the higher education board of regents in an unnamed state. He used this forum to disagree with proposed tuition hikes. His dissent was dramatic and highly disruptive during the meetings, so much so that attendees quickly came to realize that it was fueled by political motives rather than a genuine concern for students' well-being and rising education costs. Finally, whistleblowers need to be certain of the facts. It short, it would be questionable to blow the whistle on organizational wrongdoing that can not be substantiated or corroborated.

Beyond questions of expressing dissent, ethics are relevant to organizational dissent in other meaningful ways (Shahinpoor and Matt, 2007). First, dissent heeded restores dignity to employees. This happens when organizational leaders treat dissenters seriously and with respect. As such, dissent humanizes relationships between employees and management, signaling mutual respect and understanding as well as an equal stake in the venture. Management and employees who carefully and conscientiously handle dissent demonstrate ethical treatment toward one another. Second, acting out of principle, the dissenter seeks to improve the organization through his or her own integrity. The employee with integrity recognizes the need to stand in opposition to the organization and musters the courage to do so. In this way, organizational dissent recaptures individual integrity that may have been sacrificed under the strain of conformity and the threat of reprisal. Third, dissenters choose to stay and voice rather than exit their organizations – to try and make things better from within. This in and of itself is an ethical choice as well. So, ethically speaking, dissent restores dignity, recaptures integrity, and signals commitment.

Ethics, perhaps more than any other triggering event, has been associated with organizational dissent (Graham, 1986). Matters of principle, where ethics are in play, spur organizational dissent (Westin, 1986). Ethical issues drive dissent even in organizations that constrain employee voice (Hegstrom, 1999). And, when left unaddressed, ethical concerns lead to whistleblowing (Near and Miceli, 1985, 1995; Stewart, 1980). The ethical concerns that trigger dissent are clear in the report provided by this member of upper management:

> I was at a publicly traded company and discovered that my direct supervisor was engaging in illegal actions to manipulate the stock price for the benefit of select insiders. I strongly expressed that I was uncomfortable with his actions. Several other executives tried to pressure me to go along. The CFO offered me financial rewards if I participated. I escalated my issue to the board of directors.

This manager observed and confronted some of the very same unethical practices that led to the demise of such companies as Enron and WorldCom. The invitation to become complicit in the ongoing fraud demonstrates how corporate officers appealed to a sense of company loyalty, as well as to a sense of duty to serve and protect fellow management partners. These attempts failed, though, as the manager refused to perpetuate the misconduct. Instead, his individual moral compass led him to blow the whistle internally. He was ostracized and alienated for a year or so before receiving a severance package in return for his resignation.

Thus, it is clear that ethics play a major role in determining when and how to express dissent (Seeger, 1997). But predicting what that role will be is challenging, as any number of ethical obligations can surface and compete in a given dissent episode. The example below illustrates this point well.

> My employer asked me to sign insurance applications with deceptive information on them – which could jeopardize my insurance license. He wouldn't stop the requests and I told him directly that if he wanted the business he would have to sign them. Because I would not.

The supervisor's conduct forces the employee into an undesirable situation. Her moral feathers have been ruffled. For not only is the behavior in question unethical, her noncompliance with it is disregarded. Moreover, the request puts her in a professionally tenuous position. Nonetheless, her ethical obligations to herself, her profession, and general standards of honesty trump loyalty to the organization and deference to supervisory authority.

While there are many dissent-triggering events, ethics hold a fundamental place in the experience and expression of organizational dissent (Kassing, 1997; Kassing and Armstrong, 2002; Seeger, 1997) – so fundamental, in fact, that employees understand the need to stress the principled nature of their dissent even when an issue is primarily personal. Doing so mobilizes ethical concerns alongside personal ones and shifts purely personal-advantage dissent towards principled dissent (Kassing, 2009b).

The employees have spoken. And they have shown us how many aspects of organizational life can become dissent-triggering events. When concerns are serious and likely to draw some response, they have a good chance of triggering organizational dissent, particularly when the risk of retaliation is low. The employees represented in this chapter have depicted the varied landscape of actual dissent-triggering events. In doing so they have revealed how any number of factors can lead to organizational dissent and how those factors often combine to increase the potency and currency of a dissent claim. And, in the end, they reminded us of the relevancy of ethics to dissent – revealing how challenging and difficult ethical choices about expressing dissent can become. The next chapter examines the ways in which employees actually express dissent.

Discussion Questions

1 This chapter touches on the idea that people may be morally obligated to express dissent. Is this true? In what circumstances would people be obligated to express dissent? When would we expect people to express dissent and be disappointed if they failed to do so? Can we expect people in organizational settings to feel obligated to express dissent? Can management, company policy, or organizational culture mandate organizational dissent?
2 There are several barriers that block the expression of organizational dissent. Which of these have you observed in your own work experience? Leadership shortcomings? Binary thinking?

Diffusion of responsibility? Futility? Loyalty? Are there additional barriers that you have observed that are not discussed here? What is the nature of these barriers and how do they function to impede organizational dissent?

3 Considering your individual tolerance for dissent and examples from your own work experience, use figure 4.1 to plot out some specific dissent triggers. Which dissent triggers emerged in high-risk conditions? Which emerged in low-risk conditions? What conclusions can you draw about dissent triggers when you compare those that surfaced in high-risk conditions with the ones that appeared in low-risk conditions?

4 There are numerous examples of organizational dissent in the chapter. Think of your own example of dissent. Now consider what triggering events were involved. Was there a primary triggering event that led you to express dissent? Or was there a combination of triggering events that developed over time and linked with one another? If so, what were the triggering events and how did they work in concert with one another?

5 What is the relationship between ethics and dissent? What factors contribute to the ethical expression of dissent? In organizational settings, which ethical standpoints come into play when we consider expressing dissent?

5

How Do Employees Express Dissent?

Our lives begin to end the day we become silent about things that matter.
– Martin Luther King, Jr (1929–1968)

There is a powerful sentiment captured in Dr King's words: that standing up for what is right is paramount to our very existence. This is true in our social, political, and family lives, and very much relevant to our organizational lives. We commit much of ourselves to the places we work: our time, energy, and identity. What happens in our organizational lives matters. When confronted with the need and desire to speak out about things that matter, we exercise free choice. These possibilities are captured simplistically yet powerfully in the children's picture book *Big Moon Tortilla* (Cowley, 1998). In this story, young Marta Enos stumbles over her worktable when she moves quickly to retrieve one of her grandmother's aromatic and inviting tortillas. She can smell them from across the yard and cannot resist the urge to get hold of one. Her homework spills on the floor and is swept outdoors by the wind, soon to be chomped up by the local dogs. In Marta's haste to retrieve what remains of her homework, a playful puppy knocks off and breaks her glasses. She is distraught. At this point her grandmother takes her aside and sings her a Native American healing song:

When we have a problem we must choose what we will be.
Sometimes it is good to be a tree, to stand up tall in the desert and look all ways at once.

Sometimes it is best to be a rock, to sit very still, seeing nothing and saying nothing.
Sometimes when you have a problem, you have to be a strong mountain lion,
fierce and ready to fight for what is right.
Sometimes the wisest thing is to be an eagle and fly.
When the eagle is high up, it sees how small the earth is.
It sees how small the problem is, and it laughs and laughs.

The healing song provides Marta with a range of choices, just like employees who confront problematic situations at work. We can observe like a tree, remain reserved and removed from an issue like a rock, dismiss it as trivial like an eagle, or engage with it fiercely like a mountain lion – ready to fight for what is right.

While any one of these choices would be appropriate in a particular context, this chapter is about the last choice: the choice to engage and express organizational dissent, to be lion-like and fight for what is right – to avoid being silent about things that matter. This chapter focuses very particularly on the way in which employees express dissent as well as the factors that directly influence the expression of dissent. To begin, it reviews two predominant models of organizational dissent developed over a decade apart (Graham, 1986; Kassing, 1997).

Models of Organizational Dissent

There are many factors that affect how, why, and when employees express organizational dissent. Organizational scholars have developed explanations to pull these factors together in some meaningful way (Berry, 2004; Graham, 1986; Edmondson and Munchus, 2007; Kassing, 1997; Martin and Rifkin, 2004). Two prominent models are reviewed here (Graham, 1986; Kassing, 1997), paying particular attention to points shared between them.

Graham (1986) developed a model to explain the occurrence of what she called *principled organizational dissent*, or dissent that occurs when people recognize and become aware of perceived wrongdoing in their respective organizations. To complement and extend this work, Kassing (1997) introduced a model that considered multiple forms of dissent expressed to various audiences. Graham's model is narrower in focus, being limited exclusively to explaining principled dissent, whereas Kassing's model attempts to explain dissent across a broad range of issues, not just those tied to matters of principle. This difference aside, both focus on the individual as the locus of analysis, and both begin with some theoretical discussion of the factors that contribute to organizational dissent – essentially, some discussion of the factors that position particular issues and situations as dissent-triggering events (see chapter 4).

For Graham (1986), dissent begins when an employee observes wrongdoing. This alone, however, does not move one immediately to express dissent. People work through several considerations initially. First, they must consider how serious the issue is. Is it serious enough to warrant attention? Second, how much personal responsibility does a given employee feel regarding the issue? To be clear, this need not refer to feeling personally responsible for causing or being involved with the issue, but rather feeling more or less responsible about the need to report it. Third, how feasible is a response to the issue? According to Graham, then, principled dissent most likely occurs when issues are serious, personal responsibility is engaged, and responsiveness is relatively assured.

In Kassing's model, dissent starts when "a triggering agent exceeds an individual's tolerance for dissent" (1997, p. 322) in such a way that an individual experiences incongruence between what they expect and what they actually experience. Such incongruence, in turn, causes employees to see past organizational decision premises – those values promoted in order to render employees more likely to act in ways that favor the organization – and reflect instead upon their own decision premises. Triggering agents shake people out of the status quo of organizational life, requiring them to think about the implications of a given action or situation in personal as well as organizational terms. From this perspective, dissent occurs when people forego organizational decision premises in lieu of individual ones.

Together these works clarify the facets that determine which issues wind up leading to organizational dissent and dovetail in an interesting way. Kassing's (1997) model suggests that the dynamic interplay between self- and organizational interests comes into relief when we experience incongruence between what we expect to happen and what actually does happen. So, for example, we might expect our colleagues to operate ethically, but discover that they have colluded to defraud customers. Incongruence of this magnitude should be traceable to certain events or issues in the workplace that warrant the type of assessment Graham's (1986) model prescribes. That is, determining how serious the issue is and how much responsibility we have to report it – and then assessing the likelihood that expressing dissent will provoke some response or corrective action. Making these determinations, however, is complicated. It will require employees to work through and tack back and forth between decisions premises that favor the individual and those that benefit the organization.

Employees in traditional organizations that resist dissent likely base their estimations about the seriousness of issues, the responsibility tied to reporting them, and the probability of garnering responses in organizational decision premises. As a result they will be less likely to express dissent. Rather they will consent according to standard operating procedures. Hegstrom (1990) called this the mimetic condition. Employees are expected and required to adopt and mimic organizational values and management imperatives. Accordingly, they potentially undervalue the seriousness of issues, misjudge their responsibility to address them, and underestimate the probability of garnering responses.

When employees preference individual decision premises, they act on what they believe is most appropriate in the situation versus what the organization prescribes. This occurs in what Hegstrom labeled the dissent condition and leads to expressive and unexpected messages that voice "dissent from prevailing organizational positions" (1990, p. 146). To clarify, this does not necessarily mean that people will act exclusively in their own best interests, but rather that they will decide on how to proceed based on what feels right and appropriate to them. Keep in mind that

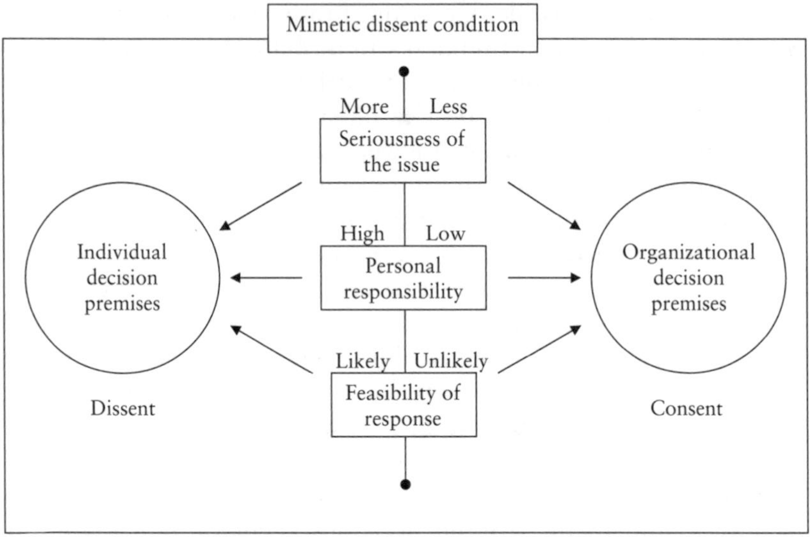

Figure 5.1 Decision premises and assessment of dissent-triggering events

whistleblowers often suffer tremendously for their decisions to report wrongdoing (Stewart, 1980; Rothschild and Miethe, 1999). They do not choose to challenge their organization merely because it will benefit them in some way, but rather because they believe it is the right thing to do. This is not to say that dissenters do not benefit personally. Successful dissent could lead to favorable outcomes in any number of ways (Kassing, 2007). So dissenters do and will benefit. Choosing to adhere to one's own decision premises, though, should not be conflated with behaving in a way that merely benefits the dissenter. Actually dissenters can adhere to their own decision premises in a given situation and protect the company, coworkers, and customers in addition to themselves.

The relationships between decision premises and assessments about seriousness, responsibility, and feasibility of a response are depicted in figure 5.1. Organizational and individual decision premises work as polarizing forces, pulling people's assessments in one direction or the other. Accordingly, dissent is more likely to occur when individual decision premises lead people to assess issues as serious, their responsibility as high, and the likelihood of a response as feasible. Consent is more likely to occur when organizational decision premises are mobilized in making assessments and people deemphasize the seriousness of the issue, their responsibility tied to it, and the likelihood that it will merit a response from management. A caveat is needed here, though. The suggested links between decision premises and assessments made about dissent triggers apply when organizations fail to foster dissent, when they operate in a mimetic condition (Hegstrom, 1990). In organizations that welcome and manage dissent well, there should be much greater alignment between individual and organizational decision premises and therefore less polarization in how assessments about dissent-triggering events are made. Indeed, "permission to dissent balances organizational and individual values and needs" (ibid., p. 146).

Workplace bullying provides a provocative case for examining these connections. Failure to respond appropriately to those victimized by a bully undermines our commonly held beliefs that people will do the right thing, that companies will protect their employees, and that hard work will be rewarded (Lutgen-Sandvik, 2008). Workplace bullying stems from a clear disconnect between what we expect from people and organizations with regard to fair treatment and actual behavior perpetrated in contemporary workplaces. It can trigger resistance and dissent (Lutgen-Sandvik, 2006).

Often employees dismiss the seriousness of early and initial displays of aggressive behavior because they have become so commonplace in many organizations (Lutgen-Sandvik et al., 2007) – only to find out later that a persistent pattern of enduring harassment has emerged (Lutgen-Sandvik, 2008). The significance of workplace bullying is overlooked at first. It is only after repeated offenses that people come to recognize the gravity of the situation and to forego an organizational decision premise that assumes tolerance and normalization of bullying behavior for an individual one that marks such acts as unacceptable.

Moreover, people are often hesitant to report bullying if they are not themselves targeted. Members of a workgroup may tolerate bullying behavior out of concern that they too will become victims (Harvey et al., 2006), allowing fear to blanket any responsibility they may feel to report it. The desire both to keep the status quo and to avoid mistreatment dismisses any felt responsibility for reporting workplace bullying. Yet the effects of bullying can spill over to others in the workgroup, so responsibility cannot be sequestered so easily. In her examination of employees' accounts of workplace bullying, Lutgen-Sandvik recalled how one individual was "glad when [a coworker] was cornered" (2008, p. 109) because it substantiated his claims, forcing others to see the behavior for what it was – to recognize the seriousness of the harassment and the need to take responsibility for reporting it. When employees rely on their own decision premises to assess workplace bullying, they should find it intolerable and take responsibility for reporting it.

Additionally, organizations can be remiss in addressing workplace bullying. Companies can normalize aggressive behavior, fail to sanction bullying, and neglect to develop formal policies against either (Salin, 2003). As a result the costs for perpetrators diminish and stabilize while bullies remain free to continue violating the expectations of victims. Despite the fact that the feasibility of a response may seem unlikely in settings where bullying persists unchecked, the desire to draw a response will be strong. Accordingly, people may forego organizational decision premises that imply nothing can be changed for individual ones that demand that something be done. Examination of workplace bullying shows, then, how individual decision premises position it as something quite serious that demands our responsibility and the attention of management.

Once an event triggers dissent, the dissenter must determine how to respond. For Graham (1986) this involves selecting an appropriate behavioral response: reporting to a supervisor, choosing another formal reporting channel like an oversight office, externally sharing one's dissent as a whistleblower, or resorting to some form of direct action like quitting. Kassing (1997) places an emphasis on verbal expressions of dissent to particular audiences other than governing bodies and the media – that is, expressions of organizational dissent other than whistleblowing. Hence, people share dissent with management via articulated dissent, with coworkers using antagonist dissent, and with nonwork friends and family members by expressing displaced dissent.

Both scholars give consideration as well to the factors that would help employees judge how best to express dissent. Graham (1986) grouped these factors into sets of determinants. She provides determinants for issue awareness (e.g., job tenure, level in the organization, possession of strong normative standards), perceived issue seriousness (e.g., frequency of issue's occurrence, number of observers), personal responsibility attribution (e.g., assigned responsibility for reporting and oversight, personally assumed social responsibility), and perceived feasibility of response (e.g., risk of reprisal, self-confidence as a change agent, estimation of protection for dissidents). These groupings provide a rather comprehensive list of factors that determine how and when one chooses to express principled dissent.

Kassing (1997) suggested that making sound decisions about expressing dissent requires employees to sift through three layered spheres of influence: individual, relational, and organizational. Individual influences concern the predispositions and expectations people bring with them from outside of organizations and how they behave within organizations. These might include individual communication predispositions, personality traits, and orientations to power and conflict. Relational influences comprise "the types and quality of relationships people maintain within organizations" (ibid., p. 324) – the primary relationships we keep with supervisors, coworkers, and colleagues. Organizational influences involve the ways in which people "relate to and perceive organizations" (ibid.). This set of influences takes into account organizational tolerances for dissent and norms about employee feedback, as well as the socialization practices and corporate cultures fostered by organizations.

Thus, both models establish, yet group differently, basic considerations that affect how employees choose to express dissent. Key among these is the notion that dissenters likely will face hostility and retaliation in unsupportive climates that stifle employee input. In fact, Kassing (1997) reasoned that all influences come together to inform employees' responses to two fundamental questions: first, Will dissent be perceived as adversarial or constructive? and second, Will dissent lead to retaliation? Graham stipulated that dissenters "can be rewarded, ignored, or punished for pursing an issue" (1986, p. 36).

Graham's (1986) model concludes by giving consideration to the organizational response to dissent, Kassing's (1997) by outlining three ways in which dissent can be expressed to particular audiences under certain conditions. Dissent gets shared with management as articulated dissent when employees believe that they will be viewed as constructive and that they will see little or no retaliation. In contrast, displaced dissent expressed to friends and family outside of work should occur when dissent will be seen as adversarial and likely lead to retaliation. Employees choose this audience rather than audiences within their organization because it negates concerns about being perceived as adversarial and facing punishment. Antagonistic dissent in some ways bridges these two conditions. By expressing dissent to coworkers individuals can still be seen as adversarial but can do so with considerably less risk – that is, they can express dissent in an adversarial/low-retaliation condition. In follow-up studies the antagonistic dissent label was replaced with latent dissent and later with lateral dissent, while the articulated dissent moniker was changed to upward dissent (Kassing, 1997, Kassing and Armstrong, 2002).

Forms of Organizational Dissent

Together these two models, as well as literature on whistleblowing (Park et al., 2008) and dissent expression (Garner, 2009b; Kassing, 2002), provide a typology of the ways in which organizational dissent can be expressed. Figure 5.2 presents a classification scheme of these possibilities. The graphic is split into two large sections denoting dissent expression as either inside (internal) or outside (external) the organization. Recall that whistleblowing is a subset of organizational dissent (see chapter 2) and therefore makes an appearance here as well. It can be differentiated

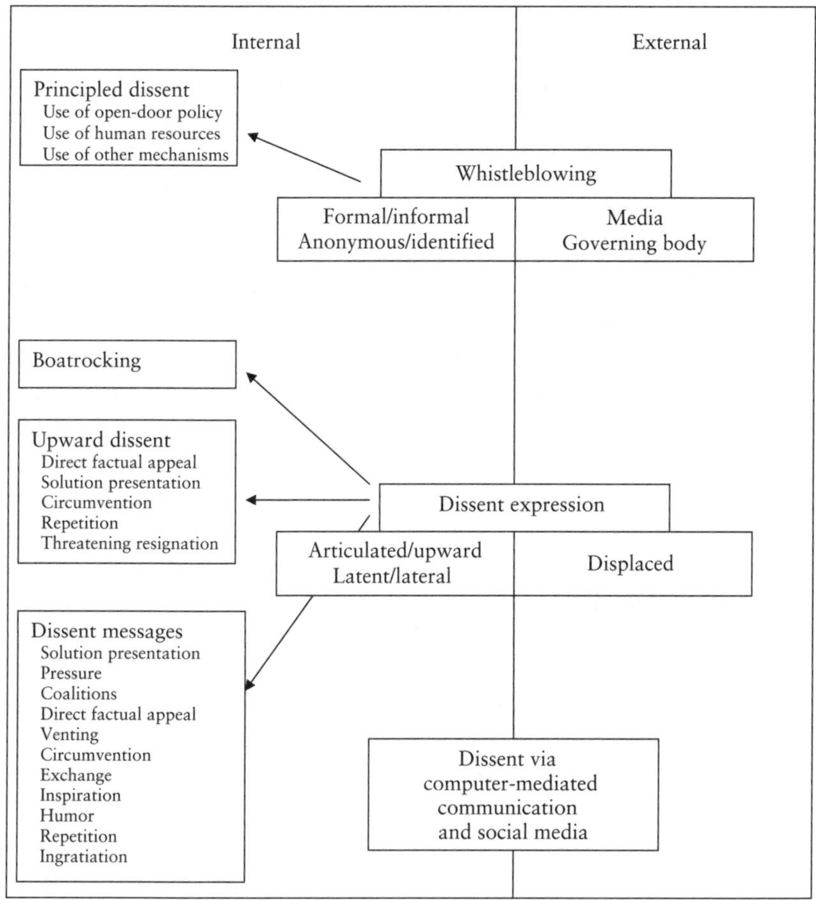

Figure 5.2 Typology of organizational dissent

as happening within or outside of an organization. Within an organization we may see whistleblowing that is either formally or informally reported and done so anonymously or identified. Graham (1986) suggested that employees could use formal reporting procedures within the organization to express principled dissent. Doing so is akin to internal-formal whistleblowing. This may entail taking advantage of an open-door policy, bringing the concern to human resources, visiting with an ombudsperson, or using some other formal or informal mechanism. Whistleblowing outside the organization can be directed to the media or some governing/regulatory body. Like whistleblowing, dissent expression can be expressed internally or externally. Internally it will take the form of articulated/upward dissent or latent/lateral dissent. Externally it will be voiced as displaced dissent (Kassing, 1997).

Dissent expression can be further differentiated in terms of upward dissent strategies (Kassing, 2002), dissent messages (Garner, 2009b), and boatrocking (Redding, 1985; Sprague and Ruud, 1988). Boatrocking refers to the expression of dissent in a "direct, straight-forward manner – within the boundaries of an organization" (Redding, 1985, p. 246). Redding positioned whistleblowing as "the most drastic of all forms of dissent" (ibid., p. 255), while promoting the need for boatrocking to combat the dominant operating premise of American organizations: "If you want to get along, go along" (ibid., p. 245). For Redding, boatrocking was necessary to counterbalance the prevailing "management knows best" ideology. He conceded that boatrocking was confrontational, but cautioned that it could be offered "in the spirit of helpfulness" as well (ibid., p. 255). In an empirical examination of boatrocking, Sprague and Ruud (1988) interviewed employees from high-tech companies in Silicon Valley. They found that most boatrocking occurred in face-to-face interactions with supervisors, that it derived primarily from employees' desires to make "the company a better place to work" (ibid., p. 185) and that employees "were overwhelmingly glad they took the opportunity to express their disagreement even in the cases where communication was less than ideal and/or employees were unsuccessful in changing company policy" (ibid., p. 184).

Two other typologies of dissent expression round out the possibilities. The first of these, Kassing's (2002) typology of upward dissent strategies, presents a set of five strategies employees use for expressing dissent to supervisors and management. These are examined just briefly here, as the following chapter provides a much more comprehensive treatment of each. Accordingly, employees can support their dissent claim with factual evidence garnered through first-hand experience with the workplace issue, which is known as a direct factual appeal, or they can bolster their evidentiary approach by presenting a solution to the perceived issue – employing the solution presentation strategy. Employees also can go around their supervisor to someone higher in the chain of command (circumvention), they can threaten to quit their job if the problem is question is not addressed (threatening resignation), or they can repeatedly raise the issue over the course of time (repetition). Although these strategies clearly seek to draw attention to a dissent claim, they vary considerably with regard to how they achieve that end (Kassing, 2005, 2007, 2009a, 2009b).

Recognizing the parallels in the above strategies with traditional upward influence strategies, Garner (2009b) expanded on earlier work by examining dissent messages. A few important distinctions are worth noting here. First, Kassing (2002) identified exclusively upward dissent strategies, whereas Garner's work took into account both upward and lateral dissent expression. Second, Garner focused specifically on messages, whereas Kassing explored strategies. Messages support strategies. They are building blocks used in the service of strategies. As such, there are more messages than strategies. Indeed, Garner found eleven distinct types of dissent messages, some of which clearly reflected the strategies they would be deployed to support (see figure 5.2). These included direct factual appeal, solution presentation, circumvention, and repetition messages.

Additional dissent messages were pressure, coalitions, venting, exchange, inspiration, humor, and ingratiation. Pressure messages rely on negative actions and intimidation to draw attention to dissent. They would be apparent when employees use the threatening resignation strategy. Those using coalition messages find allies who share their dissent claim so that the contested issue appears to stem from a collective rather than a single individual. Venting messages require sharing one's anger and frustration about the dissatisfying condition. Exchange messages entail offering favors or recalling obligations. Inspiration messages involve appealing to commonly held values and morals. Humor messages incorporate sarcasm, jokes, and offhand comments. And ingratiation messages appeal to recipients' egos by making them feel that solutions offered were their ideas. Regarding the frequency with which people use these dissent messages, Garner (2009b) found that employees reported using solution presentation and direct factual appeal messages most often and pressure and exchange messages least often.

In sum, there is an array of organizational dissent expression – ranging from whistleblowing to coalition-building, from boatrocking to humor, and from solution presentation to venting. Organizational dissent research has progressed from a focus on whistleblowing (Stewart, 1980) to encompass examinations of boatrocking (Redding, 1985; Sprague and Ruud, 1988) and principled dissent (Graham, 1986). This, in turn, has given way to the exploration of dissent audiences (Kassing, 1997, 1998), dissent strategies (Kassing, 2002, 2005, 2007, 2009a, 2009b), and dissent messages (Garner, 2009a, 2009b). But what causes employees to practice such variation when expressing organizational dissent? The upcoming sections of this chapter address that question by offering a closer inspection of the dissent goals and the individual, relational, and organizational influences that affect the expression of organizational dissent.

Dissent Goals

Organizational communication, like communication in other contexts, is goal driven (Waldron, 1999). We seek to meet and achieve particular goals when we communicate at work. This is true as much for organizational dissent as for any other type of communication occurring within organizations. As noted earlier in this chapter, employees express dissent when they face a matter of principle – when they confront the incongruence that arises when their expectations of what should happen in a given situation are out of phase with what actually does happen. At a fundamental level the goal of dissenters is to address the issue at hand. But doing so does not preclude employees from achieving and pursuing other goals as they strive to address the issue of concern. Thus, there may be other goals enabled when employees express dissent.

In a recent study, Garner (2009a) identified primary and secondary goals relevant to organizational dissent. Primary goals concern what one wants to achieve in a given interaction, whereas secondary goals concern how one pursues the primary goal. Secondary goals take into account identity concerns, managing conversations and emotion, and building or protecting personal and relational resources. Secondary goals attend to the long-term implications of an influence attempt, whereas primary goals are more narrowly focused and situation specific. A review of research on goals pertinent to interpersonal communication, romantic relationships, and upward influence led Garner to identify an initial set of seven primary goals relevant to organizational dissent: providing guidance, getting advice, obtaining information, gaining assistance, seeking emotional support, changing the audience's opinion, and changing the audience's behavior. Of these, obtaining information was the most important, followed by getting advice, changing opinion, and emotional support. Apparently employees express dissent with the goal of seeking clarity about the issue of concern and circumstances surrounding it, but hope to affect change and vent their frustrations as well. What proved most important to employees, though, was the secondary goal of identity – demonstrating once again the powerful connection between employee resistance and workers' identities (Ashforth and Mael, 1998; Murphy, 1998). And, interestingly, the least important secondary goal was personal resources, revealing that employees resist dissenting in response to self-serving goals even though they often are suspected of doing so (Sunstein, 2003). While goals drive the choices people make about expressing dissent, they are only one of many factors.

Individual, Relational, and Organizational Influences Affecting Dissent Expression

Not all people feel either comfortable expressing dissent or confident about their ability to do so. In reality, people differ in their propensity to become dissenters. Their senses of powerlessness and preferences for avoiding conflict can influence how likely they will be to express dissent (Sprague and Ruud, 1988). These and other differences manifest as individual factors that influence organizational dissent. Certain personality traits and communication predispositions appear to lead people to favor either upward or lateral dissent. Those who possess an internal locus of control believe that they control their fate directly. Not surprisingly, they report expressing comparatively more upward dissent. In contrast, employees express more lateral dissent when they believe that factors outside of their control influence their lives (Kassing and Avtgis, 2001). Similarly, people who enjoy arguing prefer upward dissent compared with those who tend to be more verbally aggressive. The latter channel their dissent to coworkers more readily (Kassing and Avtgis, 1999).

Our organizational standing plays a role in how we choose to express dissent too. For instance, younger employees with less overall work experience reported expressing more displaced dissent to friends and family outside of work than their older and more seasoned colleagues (Kassing and DiCioccio, 2004). Similarly, latent dissent appeared to be more prevalent among employees who had fewer employers and less work experience but greater job tenure in their present organization – that is, for employees who had learned the ropes in their respective organizations with regard to dissent expression norms, but had less exposure to how dissent functioned within different organizations (Kassing and Armstrong, 2001). A common finding across studies is that managers regularly express more upward dissent than nonmanagers. By comparison, nonmanagers seem to favor expressing lateral dissent to coworkers and displaced dissent to friends and family outside of work (Kassing and Armstrong, 2001; Kassing and Avtgis, 1999; Kassing and DiCioccio, 2004).

At the individual level, employees also take into account how they feel about their respective organizations when determining with whom to share dissent. Do they feel committed to their organization? Satisfied with their work? Loyal to their company? Or none of the above? Dissent expression varies in response to these factors. For instance, employees who report higher levels of satisfaction also report expressing more upward dissent to management, whereas those registering lower levels of organizational commitment tend to express lateral and displaced dissent. Employees who believe they exercise more personal influence in their organizations also express comparatively more upward dissent, whereas those who believe they exercise less personal influence report using more lateral and displaced dissent (Kassing, 1998). A pronounced sense of powerlessness can lead to feelings of burnout, and – as one recent study indicated – dissent can suffer. It showed that employees who experienced symptoms of burnout reduced their expressions of lateral dissent (Avtgis et al., 2007). Organizational identity is important to the expression of organizational dissent as well (Kassing, 2000a). Employees whose self-esteem was linked more closely to their organizational identities expressed more upward dissent than their counterparts who reported lower levels of organization-based self-esteem (Payne, 2007). Additionally, when they believed that their organizations were more tolerant of dissent, employees reported high levels of identification with their companies and shared dissent readily with management (Kassing, 2000a).

Relational influences simply concern the types and quality of relationships people maintain with supervisors, managers, coworkers, and colleagues (Kassing, 1997). Early research revealed that employees chose to express dissent most often in face-to-face interactions with their supervisors (Sprague and Ruud, 1988). Not surprisingly, when employees feel they have a strong relationship with their supervisor they express more upward dissent to management and direct less lateral dissent to coworkers (Kassing, 1998, 2000b). Although supervisory relationship quality is clearly important to the expression of organizational dissent, the significance of coworker relationships should not be overlooked. Indeed, concern for coworkers surfaced in preliminary dissent research (Sprague and Ruud, 1988). Subsequent work revealed that coworker concerns were a more important dissent trigger than ethical issues for both lateral and upward dissent (Kassing and Armstrong, 2002). These findings demonstrate the centrality of workplace relationships to the expression of organizational dissent.

Organizational influences consist of the structural and cultural facets of organizations (see chapter 3). Organizational structure concerns the formal, systematic arrangements that dictate reporting, tasks, and relationships – specifically the number of levels in a hierarchy, the span of control managers possess, and the communication within and across departments (Daft, 2010). The mere size of an organization, for example, can affect whistleblowing, with employees feeling more comfortable and influential when expressing dissent in smaller companies (Miceli and Near, 1992). But size alone does not make for more or less dissent. Other aspects of organizational structure are relevant too. King (1999) stipulated that variation in organizational structure would have a direct impact on organizational dissent, particularly whistleblowing. He postulated that, in centralized-vertical-bureaucratic organizations, where dissent is met with retaliation or ignored, fewer channels exist for expressing dissent and employees believe they can exercise little influence. As a result employees tend to express dissent externally. Conversely, in hybrid structures, where decision-making is decentralized among business units while administrative functions remain centralized, communication and the exchange of information flows without difficulty between divisions and upper management. King stipulated that, in these arrangements, dissent should be expressed internally within organizations.

Structural and cultural elements come together in a given organization's climate, and organizational climate, perhaps more than many relational and individual influences, informs employees' decisions about expressing dissent. Because organizations can respond to the issue, to the dissenter, or to both (Graham, 1986), organizational climate becomes a significant predictor of which will be the case. Organizations that afford freedom of speech in the workplace deal with the issues at hand and create a climate that invites dissent – a place where employees feel comfortable and secure expressing disagreement (Hegstrom, 1990; Pacanowsky, 1988). Moreover, the way in which organizations react to dissenters serves to inform subsequent dissenters about the likelihood of drawing fair or punitive responses from management (Graham, 1986; Kassing, 2002).

Several scholars have recognized the predominant role that organizational climate plays in determining dissent (Graham, 1986; Hegstrom, 1990; Kassing, 1998, 2000a, 2008). For example, Hegstrom (1990) argued that organizations can foster dissent climates that recognize, tolerate, and in some instances even cultivate dissent. Or they can maintain mimetic conditions whereby employees feel the pressure to acquiesce and go along with management directives. In this last condition, dissent remains restricted and subdued – relegated to only the most intolerable and unethical issues (Hegstrom, 1999). Kassing (1998, 2000a) generated empirical support for these propositions, finding that upward dissent increased when employees trusted top management and when they believed that their organizations provided ample workplace freedom of speech. Equally it decreased when employees distrusted management and felt little freedom of speech at work. The effect of organizational climate apparently extends to peer reporting of unethical behavior. Researchers found, for instance, that an organization's participatory culture was the strongest predictor of teachers' intentions to report wrongdoing (Richardson et al., 2008).

So there are many influences that affect the expression of organizational dissent. But which of these are the most significant? In an effort to determine the relative strength of different factors, Kassing (2008) asked employees to judge how important a list of possible considerations was in their determination of the need to express dissent. Employees rated a series of possible considerations which collapsed into three groupings: (a) organizational climate or employees' perceptions of management's willingness and ability to address employee concerns, (b) adversarial position/retaliation or employees' concerns about being perceived as adversarial and experiencing retaliation, and (c) organizational attachment or the combination of employees' levels of organizational identification, loyalty, and commitment. Interestingly, employees rated adversarial position/retaliation considerations as least important for both upward and lateral dissent expression, the implication being that, once they have sorted through considerations related to organizational climate and organizational attachment, employees have a clear sense of whether they will be perceived as adversarial or constructive and whether they will be met with retaliation or acceptance. In addition, employees rated all three factors higher when contemplating upward versus lateral dissent. And managers and nonmanagers did not differ in their ratings of dissent considerations – suggesting that, regardless of rank and status, "a template may exist for how employees arrange and weigh dissent considerations" (ibid., p. 351). Unfortunately, items used to assess the impact of relational factors dropped out of the analysis, preventing comparisons between relational factors and the individual and organizational considerations examined.

The discussion to this point has centered on traditional organizations – workplaces with conventional attributes such as clear reporting lines, clear differentiation between employees and management, and clear directives with regard to roles, responsibilities, and conduct. But not all organizations are created equally. Some in fact look and feel quite different to the ones just described. These are workplaces that have little formal structure and a more egalitarian approach to the assignment of roles and responsibilities, as well as the distribution of rewards. How dissent functions in alternative work arrangements is considered next.

Organizational Dissent in Alternative Organizing Structures

Most research on organizational dissent has been conducted in traditional for-profit organizations (Hegstrom, 1999; Kassing, 1998; Sprague and Ruud, 1988). But dissent will occur whenever organizational structures exist that call for consensus and coordinated activity. And in light of these pressures we can expect to find organizational dissent. Although there are many alternatives to traditional for-profit businesses, we can look to a few examples to develop a sense of how dissent functions in these organizations (Cheney, 1995; Garner and Wargo, 2009; Rothschild-Whitt, 1979).

Collectivist-democratic organizations represent a clear departure from traditional organizing (Cheney, 1995; Rothschild-Whitt, 1979). In such arrangements authority resides in the collective rather than in individuals and groups like CEOs and management. Instead, all members contribute to the enterprise in relatively equal terms. Decisions are reached through negotiation and consensus, while employees have considerable say over processes. In this way members achieve and maintain status equality. For the most part traditional bureaucratic divisions of labor are absent. Employees share roles, tasks, and information in order to demystify specialized knowledge. Thus, the vast majority of employees are on equal footing. They understand the diversity of tasks and roles and they possess knowledge appropriate to realize their own success and that of the organization. Such equality gives rise to emotionally charged interactions, but surprisingly a tendency to avoid conflict persists. This is due to the highly personalized nature of working relationships. People who have self-selected into these work arrangements share common interests and perspectives. They connect personally with one another. As a result workplace relationships become a valuable part of the endeavor and consequentially criticism and dissent take on a very personal tone.

Similar patterns of communication regarding dissent were revealed in the Swedish workforce. Here equality is achieved through the provision of meaningful voice, realized through codetermination programs that foster democratic dialogue (Gorden et al., 1994). Accordingly, management is required legally to negotiate with unions and to facilitate employee representation on boards of directors. These arrangements give employees a seat at the organizational decision-making table. Yet Gorden and his colleagues found that communication patterns tended toward seeking consensus, avoiding conflict, and rarely offering corrective feedback. Although the mandates were in place to foster employee voice, employees neglected the opportunities afforded them. Yet at the same time they reported that they desired more democratic dialogue. This hints at the possibility that employees want assurances that they will be afforded opportunities to share their concerns, even when they routinely neglect to take advantage of those opportunities.

In perhaps the most comprehensive examination of alternative organizing structures, Cheney (1995) observed the communication and organizing practices of the Mondragon cooperatives of Spain. The Mondragon cooperatives stand as one of the world's largest and most enduring organizations characterized by democratic organizing principles. Equality, equity, and solidarity constitute the bedrock upon which the cooperatives were built. These values come to life through a system that combines individual incentives with group cooperation and welfare. In fact, all members are also part owners and all members are represented in organizational decisions through an elaborate democratic voting structure. Profits (up to 70 percent) are shared with workers and reinvested back into the larger cooperative enterprise. Remaining funds get funneled into local communities. Although no single cooperative is incredibly large, the overall operation is impressive. During the period of Cheney's study there were 150 smaller local cooperatives employing some 23,000 people – making it the fifteenth largest firm in Spain. According to Cheney, communication was the key to democratic organizing. In particular, he noted that members realized democratic organizing values through discussion. It was in the access to and structure and content of discussions that members practiced and reinvented their democratic organizing principles. Through debate, discussion, and dissent they came to reevaluate and reassess the meaning of solidarity. After spending considerable time in the cooperatives it became apparent to Cheney that democracy demands "an acute need to maintain a dynamic, self-reflective and comprehensive communication system" (ibid., p. 195), one in which dissent would certainly be instrumental.

Churches represent another particularly interesting organizational structure. They have clear leaders and followers, but responsibility and direction often advance from a divine source (Dixon, 2004). This places dissent in an interesting position. Dissenters not only disagree with organizational policies and practices, but with church doctrine divined by church leaders from some higher power. This calls into question both the doctrine and those who interpret it. According to the Catholic Church, for example, spiritual law dictates that members of the priesthood should be male and remain celibate. Although held by the faithful as a universal truth, these doctrines have been called into question routinely by reformist-minded church members, clergy, and theologians. Calls for such reform have become a customary form of dissent within the Catholic Church, particularly in the US.

In April of 2002, Pope John Paul II called cardinals from across the United States to Rome for a multi-day meeting to address the sexual abuse scandal that had erupted. Through the years the Church had periodically faced allegations of sexual abuse by priests and successfully managed to deal with each. But this was different. This time around allegations of a single priest's misdeeds led to public pressure to disclose other such missteps. Soon the US Catholic Church admitted that eighty priests in the Boston area faced allegations of sexual abuse. From Boston the crisis spread to Miami, St Louis, Chicago, Philadelphia, and Los Angeles. And a single frightening truth emerged: "Cardinals and Bishops were placing repeat offenders where they could continue their pattern of abuse" (Dixon, 2004, p. 64). Two dozen priests from across the country faced dismissal or suspensions as a result of allegations of sexual abuse. Needless to say, the scandal threatened to undermine the credibility and, some would argue, piousness of the Catholic Church.

Struggling with doctrine that proved arcane for contemporary churchgoers, the American Catholic Church began to call for major reform – critical pieces of which were calls to relax the vow of celibacy and to allow women into the priesthood. The Church faced a "growing tide of dissent by its American based laity, theologians, and clergy" (Dixon, 2004, p. 66) alongside the sexual abuse scandal. In her analysis of the Church's response to the crisis, Dixon concluded that "the Catholic Church, in their initial formal responses to the 2002 scandal, were not concerned with image restoration or the care of the victims, but instead with silencing the voices of dissent that had emerged, threatening to undermine its teaching" (ibid., p. 66). This was achieved through remarks made by the pope in his opening address and in the letter produced by the cardinals at the conclusion of the meeting.

The pope's remarks invoked the divine authority of the Catholic

Church and its fundamental mission to watch over and shepherd the "spiritual good of the people it leads" (Dixon, 2004, p. 77). The latter rhetorical move positioned reformers as antithetical to the spiritual good of parishioners. It worked to "place dissent where the church likes it best, outside the theological doors" (ibid., pp. 77–8). Whereas the pope's remarks strategically reasserted the authority of the Church, the closing statement of the American cardinals at the Vatican spoke in no uncertain terms about dissident reformist ideals. It made clear that pastors were responsible not only for promoting the correct moral teachings but equally for reprimanding dissenters – in short, to restore fidelity to Catholic teachings. "Their statement of orthodoxy served to remind dissenters, in both the church and the academy, that their relationship with the church was subject to Cardinals' approval" (ibid., p. 80). Through this strategy another chapter was added to the "long history of the Catholic Church's ability to withstand even the most withering attacks of governments and internal dissent" (ibid., p. 75). Ironically, Cardinal Joseph Ratzinger presided over the Vatican meeting of American cardinals. In 2005 he became Pope Benedict XVI and in 2010 faced a global scandal when another wave of allegations of sexual abuse and institutional cover-up came to light in Ireland, the US, Germany, Australia, and Malta.

In other work examining religious organizations, Garner and Wargo (2009) explored dissent within a cross-section of churches from several denominations. They found that church leaders reported that members favored indirect forms of expressing dissent, vented often about frustrations, and generally failed to provide solutions to issues of concern. Leaders said that members often conflated their personal opinions with religious doctrine when expressing dissent and that they threatened to withhold contributions or to leave the church on occasion. An interesting discrepancy in perceptions of dissent was revealed in this work as well. Leaders felt that more latent and displaced dissent was occurring – causing one to lament that "all that discontent just festers" (ibid., p. 384) – whereas members reported expressing significantly more upward dissent to leaders than lateral dissent to fellow members. Organizational and relational factors also seemed to impact members' expressions of dissent. For example, some leaders attributed silence and the lack of dissent to perceived status difference realized through assigned titles. Others suspected that silence was due to a general lack of personal relationships with members of the congregation. And, as with for-profit businesses, there was a positive relationship between upward dissent and workplace freedom of speech and between upward dissent and the quality of one's relationship with the church leader. Interestingly, one particular individual influence – religiosity – seemed to dampen organizational dissent, having an effect on expressions of both upward and lateral dissent.

While we may not work in an organization that adopts one of the unique forms described above, we will certainly encounter non-traditional organizations like churches, community groups, homeowners' and parents' associations, and the like. The purpose and expression of dissent may resemble or differ from what we see in the places where we actually find employment. Nevertheless, the need to express dissent may surface here with equal potency. Understanding the nuances involved in expressing organizational dissent, then, is not limited to how we communicate in the workplace. It will be relevant when we confront organizational constraints in other spheres of our lives – spheres that continue to overlap and blend as a result of varied influences – of which communication technology is one. Communication technology stands as one clear force that continues to erode conventional organizational boundaries. Its impact on and relationship to organizational dissent is considered in the final section of this chapter.

Communication Technology and the Expression of Organizational Dissent

Computer-mediated communication (CMC) and social media continue to advance. Because of these technologies, communication now moves effortlessly across temporal and spatial boundaries. Consequently, employees have begun to voice organizational dissent via these new and social media – using websites and blogs, for example, to share concerns about their respective organizations (Gossett and Kilker, 2006; Sanderson, 2009). CMC and social media often provide a degree of anonymity unavailable in face-to-face interactions. Knowing that retaliation is always a possibility, it is not surprising that employees have turned to CMC and social media to express organizational dissent. Yet risk that accompanies dissent has not abated entirely with the advancement of these new communication platforms. In fact, many dissidents across the world have started using CMC and social media and have paid dearly as a result. One recent inventory listed fifty-two "cyberdissidents" from various countries – activists, writers, and journalists who had been arrested, charged, and imprisoned for posting material on the Internet (Chronicle of Dissent, 2007). And, in some organizational contexts, dissenting via the Internet is an actionable offense (Gossett and Kilker, 2006). Today most companies have surveillance systems in place that monitor email despite the fact that employees have dissented openly about the implementation of such practices (Duane and Finnegan, 2007).

In an early examination of organizational dissent expression via communication technology, Gossett and Kilker (2006) examined counterinstitutional websites. They were particularly interested in how such mechanisms provided voice to employees of RadioShack. They recognized that contemporary organizational forms characterized by outsourcing, independent contractors, multinational corporations, and virtual firms have forced "employees to find informal spaces other than the traditional water cooler or office hallway" to discuss workplace issues and suggested that, "as organizational structures become increasingly fragmented, so do the acts of member dissent and resistance" (ibid., p. 68).

By their estimation at the time, the number of counterinstitutional websites (also known as "suck" or "gripe" sites) surpassed 7,000. And even though such sites tend to be trivialized as mere outlets for disgruntled employees and customers, the amount of traffic on them is far from insignificant. The RadioShack website alone received nearly a million hits per month in 2004 (Gossett and Kilker, 2006). Not surprisingly, RadioShack tried unsuccessfully to shut down the website several times and made posting or contributing to it – even during nonwork hours – a terminable offense. Participants, in turn, remained entirely anonymous through the use of pseudonyms like Shackchick, RadioShackled, and Endless Schakrifice.

There were several interesting conclusions Gossett and Kilker (2006) were able to draw about RadioShacksucks.com. First, a sense of futility regarding the possibility of resolving problems from within the company was prevalent among employees. Site users perceived internal communication mechanisms to be largely ineffective. The website provided a viable alternative for airing concerns. Second, the prolific use of the website revealed a workforce that understood the lack of safe, easy, and effective ways to be heard more than it pointed to a disengaged workforce. Fascinatingly, employees not only wanted management to read their posts but also assumed that they were doing so. In this way, the website served as a mechanism for upward dissent even though it functioned outside of the organization – allowing for externally expressed dissent to be internalized. That is why in figure 5.2 dissent expression via CMC and social media straddles and spans the internal/external divide – signaling the possibility that it can be at once both external and internal. Finally, one-quarter of users were former employees, indicating that, when presented with a viable outlet for expressing organizational dissent, individuals continued to share it even after their tenure with the organization had ended.

So what should we make of counterinstitutional websites? Their emergence likely signals weaknesses in organizational communication infrastructures that need attention. And their existence can function as a valuable and unique source of stakeholder feedback (Gossett and Kilker, 2006). National Basketball Association (NBA) franchise owner of the Dallas Mavericks, Mark Cuban, recognized this possibility when he began using a blog to dissent about officiating and league policies (Sanderson, 2009). Known for being outspoken, Cuban has amassed more than $1.6 million in fines from the NBA for his commentary, including criticism leveraged via his blog. He has come to rely on his blog as a public space for sharing his dissent about the NBA. It also serves as a site for building support for his positions, since blog visitors can post their comments as well. Across some thirty posts, several common themes were detected. Cuban positioned himself as a change agent, routinely critiquing NBA officiating with the intention of improving its quality. Specifically, he alleged that poor officiating was inconsistent and systematically flawed, and that it was hurting the NBA's marketability. Cuban also used his blog to roundly criticize the league for failing to communicate openly with fans, particularly the NBA's failure to address officiating discrepancies publicly. Fans reading and posting to his blog generally supported these positions and collectively formed a community of dissent aimed at the NBA. In essence, Cuban mobilized dissent among fans, showing how powerful CMC and social media can be as a vehicle for collective organizational dissent.

Mark Cuban possesses a luxury to dissent that few others share. His job is secure, his wallet fat. He can take criticism easily because it is unlikely to undermine his employment. And he can afford and absorb the economic costs of dissenting. The rest of us are not as fortunate. We have to give serious consideration to the economic and social implications of expressing dissent at work. We have to think strategically about how to go about doing so, when to refrain from doing so, and with whom we can safely share our opinions. This is no easy undertaking. It can be taxing. And upward dissent remains the most demanding and challenging form of dissent. The strategies for and implications of expressing upward dissent are profiled in the next chapter.

Discussion Questions

1 This chapter uses workplace bullying to illustrate the assessments employees make with regard to the seriousness of an issue, one's responsibility to report it, and management's perceived responsiveness. Would people make these assessments differently in mimetic and dissent conditions? What other workplace concerns can be substituted for bullying

to illustrate how these assessments shape our willingness to express dissent? Provide and explore a few examples.

2 What forms of organizational dissent have you practiced in your workplace? Were these effective or ineffective? Why did they prove effective or ineffective? When ineffective, what other forms of dissent may have worked better?
3 The chapter reviews numerous factors that employees consider when choosing to express dissent. These include the goals of the dissenter, individual differences, relationships, and organizational factors. How do these factors work together to inform employees' decisions about expressing dissent? Which, if any, are more or less predominant? What makes certain considerations more relevant in particular situations or in different types of organization?
4 Dissent is not limited to the places where we work. It surfaces in all kinds of organizations (homeowners' associations, parent–teacher organizations, churches, etc.). How does it differ in these settings? What aspects of dissent expression cross over to organizational encounters in other spheres of our lives?
5 What are the implications of expressing dissent via computer-mediated communication and/or social media? What barriers to dissent expression do these technologies skirt? What additional considerations do they introduce? What are the likely benefits and risks associated with expressing dissent via computer-mediated communication and/or social media?

6

Upward Dissent Anyone?

> All discussion, all debate, all dissidence tends to question and, in consequence, to upset existing convictions; that is precisely its purpose and its justification.
>
> – Judge Learned Hand (1872–1961)

Don't rock the boat. Don't upset the applecart. Don't be a fly in the ointment. Don't go against the grain. Don't stick your neck out. Don't go out on a limb. Don't swim against the tide. Don't make waves. Don't get too big for your britches. Don't go on the warpath. Don't point the finger. Don't run your mouth off. Don't make a mountain out of a molehill. Don't cry over split milk. Don't shoot yourself in the foot. Don't cut off your nose to spite your face. Get off your high horse. Get off your soapbox. Know your place. Know which side your bread's buttered on. Don't bite the hand that feeds you. Discretion is the better part of valor.

In other words, be careful expressing dissent. This assortment of idiomatic expressions says much about our orientation to consensus in the workplace. Idioms powerfully convey, in short order, some aspect of social reality. They give directive and extol some measure of wisdom. In this case, they underscore the currency afforded consensus – indicating that usually it is favored over dissent. Realistically, life is considerably easier when there is agreement, but not always better. To remain healthy and functional, consensus needs the countervailing force of dissent

(Sunstein, 2003). And this is true in organizational settings as much as anywhere (Hegstrom, 1995; Kassing, 1997).

Generally we hold a fundamental belief that speaking up is important and necessary. Stick to your guns. Dig your heels in. Fight tooth and nail. Lock horns. Cross swords. All are idioms that capture the relevancy of disagreement. Yet these directives get subverted by an equally if not more powerful drive to consent. A consistent tension persists between the two. It forces us to choose between going along and being accepted or dissenting and distancing ourselves from the group. In some cases consenting makes sense but remains distasteful. We have a host of idioms that capture this sentiment: Bite the bullet. Bite your lip. Hold your tongue. Put a sock in it. Leave well enough alone. Let sleeping dogs lie. Don't beat a dead horse. Cut your losses. Grin and bear it. Better safe than sorry. From these idioms we gather that it is often best to be quiet – to avoid dissent.

This is due to the fact that dissenting is risky and that it makes people uncomfortable. As Judge Learned Hand pointed out, dissent questions and upsets existing convictions. Dissent in the modern organization is no exception. To the contrary, in organizational settings where free speech historically has been restricted (Sanders, 1983) the risk of dissent is amplified (Waldron and Kassing, 2011). And, although employees can dissent about workplace issues outside of their respective organizations (see chapter 5), few would argue with the position that expressing dissent up the chain of command to supervisors and management is the riskiest of all forms of dissent occurring within organizations (Waldron and Kassing, 2011). Organizational dissenters put their reputations, standing, economic viability, and employment status at risk. Expressing upward dissent to management is not something employees take lightly (Kassing, 2002). The purpose of this chapter is to take a closer look at how employees actually express upward dissent. To that end five predominant upward dissent strategies are reviewed and explored (ibid.). Then, a series of recommendations for employees expressing organizational dissent is shared.

Direct Factual Appeal

The direct factual appeal strategy involves "supporting one's dissent claim with factual information derived from some combination of physical evidence, knowledge of organizational policies and practices, and personal work experience" (Kassing, 2002, p. 195). Direct factual appeals are a form of active-constructive voice (Gorden, 1988) – active "in the sense that employees actively collect evidence, summon experience, and direct their claims" and constructive "in the sense that employees position themselves as cooperative by grounding their assertions in facts, evidence, and workplace experience" (Kassing, 2002, p. 196). In so doing, employees avoid unfounded opinions, unnecessarily aggressive attacks, and misdirected complaints.

Organizational members using direct factual appeals appear measured and proactive. Garner (2009a) found that the need to manage one's emotions and to be protective of one's personal resources was a negative predictor of direct factual appeal use, whereas identity and conversation management were positive predictors. Together these findings suggest that employees set aside the need to vent and gain personal advantage when using this strategy and instead remain conscientious about the identity implications of expressing dissent and the necessity of managing such interactions carefully. Packaging one's dissent alongside evidence from any number of sources shifts attention away from the individual dissenter and toward the issue at hand. As a matter of fact, when people were asked to rate the competence of upward dissent strategies, direct factual appeals were rated as comparatively competent, second only to solution presentation (Kassing, 2005).

By incorporating evidence, direct factual appeals represent a form of truth telling. But when organizational powers promote consensus, even reasonable appeals can fall on deaf ears. Consider the case of Ronald Cathcart, who worked as Washington Mutual Bank's (WaMu) chief risk officer from 2006 to 2008. In early April of 2010 Cathcart testified before a US Senate panel investigating the financial crisis and mortgage industry collapse. In his testimony he described how he tried to warn WaMu about its risk profile even as he was increasingly being excluded from executive meetings. He was no longer receiving copies of board meeting materials or being put on board meeting agendas. Feeling obliged to share his concerns, he cited "weak operational controls in the bank's credit platform" and "indicated that the company's loss numbers were increasing at unprecedented rates" (Corkery, 2010). Cathcart erroneously assumed that his corporate colleagues would appreciate and respect his warnings, particularly as they were rooted in factual evidence and professional experience. He was, after all, the chief risk officer – hired for his expertise in ascertaining financial risk. Perhaps his direct factual appeals proved too ominous. They certainly revealed a reality that other senior executives were not ready to see. Indeed, he testified that he was neutralized by senior management to the point that he "was no longer able to discharge [his] responsibilities as Chief Enterprise Risk Officer of WaMu." His appointment was terminated shortly thereafter by the chairman of the board. WaMu would have done well to heed his warnings. Federal regulators took over the bank's assets, totaling $307 billion, in late September of 2008 – marking the largest bank failure in American history (Dash and Sorkin, 2008).

With the collapse of WaMu the stakes were higher than in most cases, and the consequences of failing to respond to upward dissent were devastating. But this is in no way a reflection of the effectiveness of the strategy. To the contrary, direct factual appeal can be very effective, producing results that span beyond the parties involved. This was evident in the account provided by a laboratory technician concerned about proper adherence to lab protocol regarding the storage of samples. A general lack of adherence to set protocols warranted attention. The lab tech reported:

> We have a protocol for storing samples used in our particular laboratory. They are stored separately to avoid cross contamination. Several times I found that the samples were stored improperly by another department. I went to my department manager and informed her of this problem. I documented in writing in my analysis logbook that the samples had been stored improperly. That documentation went to the project manager who had to advise the employee that proper protocol

> had not been followed. At that point a lab wide memo was issued addressing the problem.

As a result of direct factual appeal that incorporated specific written documentation, a memo addressing the concern ends up distributed across the organization to remind employees of the importance and necessity of following a critical organizational policy. Upward dissent is clearly effective in this instance. If employees initially had become lax about following the policy because it was flawed in some way, then they might choose to generate evidence of shortcomings and produce a solution to share with management. Doing so is known as solution presentation.

Solution Presentation

Having a solution to an observed problem gives employees a strategic advantage when expressing dissent. It provides a plan of action for addressing the concern at hand. But, perhaps more importantly, it demonstrates a willingness to be proactive in addressing a dissatisfying condition. Taking a proactive stance signals a desire to work with rather than against management, to seek a solution that works for both employees and their management counterparts. Solutions provided by employees address a range of issues, take many forms, and vary in their apparent viability (Kassing, 2002). Management may receive limited, underdeveloped, and unrealistic solutions from employees. They would be remiss, based on the quality of such solutions, to question employees' intentions to be proactive about workplace issues. Put another way, the feasibility of a solution provided is less pertinent than the act of offering one in the first place.

Not surprisingly, employees rated solution presentation as the single most competent upward dissent strategy (Kassing, 2005) – that is, the one that they believed had the greatest applicability across situations, should be used before other strategies, and was most appropriate and effective for dealing with serious issues. Like direct factual appeal, solution presentation is an example of active-constructive voice (Kassing, 2002). Developing solutions is a constructive expression of concern, whereas proposing solutions is an active response to workplace issues. The goals people reported employing when practicing solution presentation strike a balance between trying to exercise some influence and attempting to be better informed. Providing guidance and changing opinions, as well as getting advice and obtaining information, were significant predictors of solution presentation. And, like direct factual appeal, the secondary goals of identity and conversation management were mobilized, while desires to vent frustrations and create personal advantage were repressed (Garner, 2009a). In essence, solution presentation affords employees the opportunity to exercise influence while being collaborative and proactive.

Solutions presented can be used in place of or accompany direct evidence (Kassing, 2002). For example, a financial planner found it troubling that he had no alternative investment opportunities to offer his clients and that he lacked the knowledge to push these products even if they were made available. The financial planner became frustrated with the limitations this placed on his ability to provide well-rounded advice to investors, and he eventually grew fed up with management's failure to address these concerns. He decided to take matters into his own hands and develop a solution. He reported:

> There is a general lack of alternative investment choices available to clients, and the need for additional asset classes of investment vehicles for us. To address this problem, I met with mutual fund companies to gather information about their programs and presented these to management to show our lack of alternative investments.

This financial planner did his homework. After being rebuffed in his earlier attempts to draw attention to the issue, he was prepared with a solution to the perceived problem. To enhance the likelihood that his solution would be taken seriously he understood the need to generate evidence to support his position. He did so by gathering the appropriate information from mutual fund companies. This gave his proposed solution some real footing – a strong chance of being adopted. If it was to fall on deaf ears, however, and the financial planner still felt strongly enough about pursuing the issue, he may consider circumvention. That is, he may decide to take his concern to someone higher in the chain of command.

Circumvention

Circumvention entails expressing dissent to someone higher in the chain of command than one's immediate supervisor (Kassing, 2002). Basically it involves going around one's boss to express dissent. Therefore it carries considerable risk (Waldron and Kassing, 2011), particularly risk related to diminishing the quality of one's superior–subordinate relationship (Kassing, 2007). Circumvention is used considerably less often than direct factual appeal and solution presentation strategies, and understandably employees view it as less competent than these approaches (Kassing, 2002, 2005). However, it does occur with some regularity within organizations (Kassing, 2007). Circumvention takes place when employees find supervisors to be unsympathetic to dissent or assume that that will be the case. Employees reported practicing circumvention when "they presumed that their immediate supervisors were unable to respond, disinclined to respond, or ineffective when responding to employee dissent" (ibid., p. 200). It also occurred when dissent-triggering events involved supervisors' behavior (Kassing, 2002, 2009b).

The goal of gaining assistance primarily drives circumvention (Garner, 2009a). This makes sense, as circumvention requires reaching out beyond one's immediate supervisor to seek support from an alternative audience. When direct supervisors fail to address issues, these alternative audiences potentially provide access to a network of influence that would otherwise remain obstructed. There is a clear and potentially risky trade-off here, though. The promise of receptiveness available at higher levels of the organization outweighs the expectation of working through the issue with one's immediate boss.

In their dissent accounts, employees described speaking directly to their bosses on numerous occasions before going to someone higher in the chain of command (Kassing, 2009b). In these cases, supervisor inaction was the issue that forced circumvention. Seeing that they were making little or no headway with their direct supervisors after repeated attempts, employees eventually realized that they would need to turn to a higher authority to voice their concerns. Supervisors who ignored issues, claimed to have already addressed them, or addressed them in a substandard manner found themselves circumvented by their subordinates. Supervisors' failures to address issues when given the chance provided the justification necessary for most employees to feel comfortable practicing circumvention. Employees came to understand that supervisors would continue to do nothing unless pressure came from elsewhere in the organization.

On some occasions employees made quick judgments about their supervisors' willingness to address concerns, assuming inaction on their part (Kassing, 2009b). These judgmental shortcuts seemed to stem from a degree of relational history, emerging from a backdrop of familiarity with how the supervisor routinely behaved. Although swift judgments of this nature may have been accurately grounded in superior–subordinate relational dynamics, they still voided any opportunities the supervisor may have had to address the issue. Employees practicing circumvention in these circumstances displayed considerable self-confidence and self-assurance in their judgments. Such confidence served to shift the emphasis away from judgments dissenters made about their supervisors and placed it squarely on the latter's presumed inability or unwillingness to deal with organizational dissent.

Finally, supervisor inaction was evident when employees felt that their superiors misjudged how serious issues were, and inevitably neglected to respond. In one example, an employee shared her concerns about a corporate trainer with her immediate supervisor. In her estimation the trainer lacked professionalism, as he made inappropriate comments and jokes during the training session. Yet her supervisor did not find these behaviors offensive. Knowing that she would make little impression on someone who did not see the issue as serious, she took her concern to someone higher in the chain of command (Kassing, 2009b).

A second reason employees provided for expressing dissent via circumvention was supervisors' performance (Kassing, 2009b). Employees found fault with how poorly supervisors performed their assigned duties and with how they performed in their role – often bullying, badgering, and dispensing unwarranted harassment. Performance issues with supervisors' skills and expectations were cited. Supervisors lacked the requisite skills to manage scheduling, to conduct performance reviews, to provide accurate information about organizational policies, and to offer clear and helpful feedback. Regarding expectations, employees found fault with being held to a higher standard than their peers and used these differential expectations as grounds for circumventing their bosses. Managers were circumvented as well when they capriciously wielded power and asserted authority as part of managerial performances (Trujillo, 1985). Supervisors fond of saying no to employee requests simply because they could, as well as those who bullied and harassed employees, fell prey to circumvention.

Employees also practiced circumvention in response to supervisor indiscretion (Kassing, 2009b). This took the form of exposing bosses who breached company policies and behaved unethically. Supervisors were cited for cheating employees out of overtime, stealing from their organizations, logging hours not worked, running personal errands on company time, displaying favoritism, and manipulating commission reports. Along with these serious infractions, supervisors' behavior that put employees and the public in harm's way was called into question. For example, they were cited for downplaying substandard products and environmental concerns caused by corporate waste. Finally, circumvention as a result of supervisor indiscretion shed light on poor personal choices made – dating subordinates and drinking on the job, to name a couple. Circumvention cast these transgressions as questionable in the eyes of other organizational members.

So employees circumvent supervisors due to their inaction and incompetence, as well as for their unethical behavior. While some of these reasons naturally strike a chord of seriousness and resonate as matters of principle, others begin as less serious and more personal in nature. Ironically, they gain credibility and

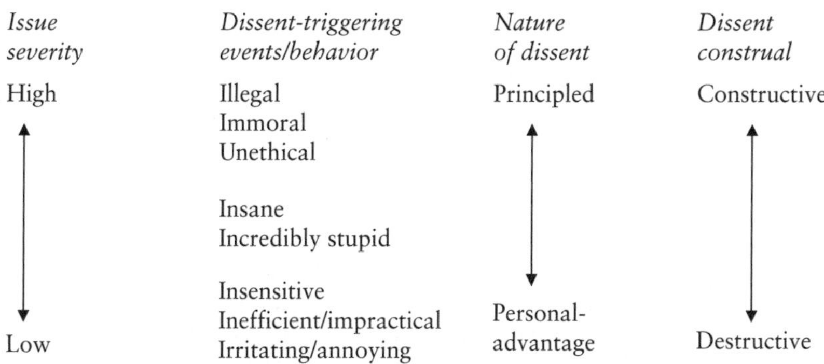

Source: Kassing (2009b). Reprinted by permission of SAGE publications.

Figure 6.1 Constructive versus destructive circumvention

legitimacy each and every time supervisors dismiss them, for such dismissals provide both momentum to an ongoing dissent claim and additional incentive for practicing circumvention. The longer the issue goes unaddressed by supervisors, the more powerfully it gets tethered to perceptions of fairness and respect for employees. Employees seize upon these possibilities and when necessary position less serious, personal-advantage dissent so that it becomes construed as more constructive (see figure 6.1). How dissenters, and others in the workplace, construe circumvention evolves from perceptions about the nature of the issue and how principled and serious it appears to be.

But what are the consequences associated with expressing dissent via circumvention? Circumvention led primarily to relational deterioration between superiors and subordinates, which manifested in relational strain, hard feelings, and hostile work environments (Kassing, 2007). But there were other outcomes present as well (see table 6.1). Compromise occurred when employees and their supervisors interacted in a way that signaled mutual respect and protected each other's status despite the obvious breach in the chain of command. While the relationship may have suffered in these cases, efforts to move forward in a respectful manner allowed for relational repair. Neutrality resulted when employees observed

Table 6.1 Typology of relational outcomes

Deterioration	Subordinates noted a decline in superior–subordinate relationship quality and/or work conditions.
Compromise	Supervisors and subordinates addressed the concern at issue or the circumvention, or both, in a way that protected their status and their mutual identities.
Neutrality	Subordinates reported no notable change in the relationship because circumvention produced ineffectual outcomes or because circumvention exposed inadequacies regarding how supervisors initially handled issues.
Development	Subordinates reported being thanked and feeling appreciated when circumvention produced favorable outcomes for supervisors.
Understanding	Supervisors tacitly approved of and deemed legitimate the issues raised by employees that they did not or could not address effectively.

Source: Kassing (2007). Reprinted by permission of SAGE publications.

no significant changes in their superior–subordinate relationship. This happened in two situations. The first was when circumvention attempts proved ineffectual. In these instances supervisors were vindicated when upper management gave little or no consideration to employee claims. Second, and contrastingly, it took place in situations where circumvention attempts were effective and exposed supervisors in some way. Exposed supervisors deflected attention away from their failures to act. This safeguarded employees from subsequent retaliation that would possibly bring additional scrutiny upon supervisors. In a few cases circumvention actually led to relational development, as employees were thanked and applauded for taking a stand. Finally, understanding arose when employees and their supervisors perceived that circumvention was warranted and supervisors recognized that employees' dissent claims were legitimate, rational, and logical. Overall superior–subordinate relational decline was the most prevalent outcome by far. Yet some other relational outcome emerged in half the cases considered.

The outcomes of circumvention can be considered from an organizational perspective as well (Kassing, 2007), and these

Table 6.2 Typology of organizational outcomes

Successful circumvention	
Favorable for the dissenter	Circumvention allowed employees to achieve goals and to compel supervisory action.
Organizational improvement	Circumvention led to corrective action that addressed either workplace conditions or corporate policies and practices that were beneficial to other employees as well as or in addition to the dissenter.
Triggering agent sanctions	Circumvention resulted in some form of reprimand or sanction for the dissent-triggering agent (i.e., supervisors, coworkers, customers).
Unsuccessful circumvention	
Absence of corrective action	Circumvention failed to produce any or enough corrective action on the part of management.
Disadvantageous for dissenter	Circumvention created confrontational representations of dissenters and produced retaliation.

Source: Kassing (2007).

can vary considerably (see table 6.2). Some outcomes, such as favorable responses to the dissenter, triggering agent sanctions, and organizational improvement, derive from successful cases of circumvention. Others, for example, absence of corrective action and disadvantageous outcomes for the dissenter, result from unsuccessful circumvention.

The predominant outcome was a favorable response for dissenters, such that they achieved their respective goals and compelled supervisory action that had been absent or missing. For example, employees were successful in soliciting raises, having transfers approved, and protecting their jobs. This finding, juxtaposed against the predominant relational outcome of decreased superior–subordinate relationship quality, reveals the inherent paradox that underlies circumvention. To achieve the desired outcome of circumvention an individual must risk damaging his or her relationship with an immediate supervisor. But there is much to be gained by doing so.

On top of the favorable outcomes for dissenters, circumvention also might bring about some degree of organizational improvement. In certain situations it resulted in the adjustment of organizational policies and practices that benefited other employees too. Organizational improvement generally derived from circumvention that required clarifying, correcting, or amending organizational policies. For instance, circumvention about overtime and safety issues produced efforts to shore up related policies.

Another outcome resulting from successful circumvention involved sanctions being leveled against the dissent-triggering agent. Supervisors primarily – but at times coworkers and customers – received reprimands that ranged from mild to severe. On the mild side, people were given warnings and reprimanded; on the severe side they were terminated, suspended, or sanctioned with disciplinary action.

On occasions when circumvention was unsuccessful it led to two outcomes: absence of corrective action and disadvantageous consequences for the dissenter. These occasions were reported less frequently in comparison to the successful ones described above, but were noteworthy nonetheless. Absence of corrective action resulted when employees believed that not enough had been done to address the dissent concern. While many dissenters experienced superior–subordinate relational deterioration, a few suffered in even more explicit ways. They were branded as adversarial and ended up severely reprimanded, demoted, or in some cases fired. These reactions, which proved unequivocally to be disadvantageous for dissenters, bring into relief the attendant risk that generally accompanies dissent, particularly circumvention. Although comparatively less competent and more risky than other upward dissent strategies, circumvention can be rather effective. Likewise, threatening resignation can be effective, but risky.

Threatening Resignation

Employees express this upward dissent strategy when they use "the threat of resignation as a form of leverage for obtaining responsiveness and action from supervisors and management" regarding a dissent claim (Kassing, 2002, p. 201). Kassing provided the account of a groundskeeper at a golf course to illustrate the practice in action. The groundskeeper was being tasked with filling a sand trap in a way that put the tractor he was driving at risk of flipping over. He twice averted disaster before telling the top dresser on the course that they needed to devise a better way to fill the bunker. The supervisor disagreed and the employee threatened to quit because of the "unsafe conditions" (ibid.). The supervisor then acquiesced, and the groundskeeper remained safe and kept his job. The employee recognized the serious risk he faced in this particular situation and used it to justify his threat to resign.

In such circumstances, when a pronounced and acute risk is apparent to employees, threatening resignation becomes a plausible and viable option. It is a response that produces an immediate ultimatum for a supervisor: fix the situation or lose the employee. In this way it creates a sense of urgency that was lacking. But, like the boy who cried wolf too often, it is not a strategy that can be used regularly or repeatedly. Instead, it is an option of last resort (Kassing, 2009a). It would be foolish, for example, for the aforementioned groundskeeper to quit because he did not want to fill the sand trap at all or because he disagreed with how little sand they were using to fill it. These are not grave enough issues to warrant such a decisive and demanding reaction from employees.

Employees understand well the implications of threatening resignation. Beyond putting one's employment at risk, this strategy compromises one's identity and relational standing (Garner, 2009a). So it is not surprising that employees rated threatening resignation as the least competent upward dissent strategy (Kassing, 2005), or that they positioned threatening resignation as part of a larger group of pressure tactics that involved threats, intimidation, and outright demands (Garner, 2009b). In addition, research findings indicate that the goal of securing or protecting personal resources was the strongest predictor of pressure tactics, accompanied by a lack of concern for identity and conversation management goals (Garner, 2009a). Thus, threatening resignation suspends identity and appropriateness concerns for the direct achievement of personal goals. This obviously is not a strategy to be used widely or often. It clearly has limited applicability. Indeed, employees report using threatening resignation and pressure dissent messages less frequently than other possible choices (Kassing, 2002; Garner, 2009b), which begs the question: When does threatening resignation occur?

Threatening resignation seems to occur in at least three situations. First, when employees or customers, or both, are placed at risk, as the example above and the one that follows illustrate. Upon leaving work late one night a restaurant worker was accosted by two teenagers who demanded she let them in her car. One struck her car window multiple times with a rock until she "could see the cracks forming." The restaurant worker escaped safely, but clearly was upset by the incident. The next day she reported the events to her manager. He subsequently told the remaining female staff to refrain from leaving work alone. She recounted that people were concerned for about a week, but soon forgot all about the incident. She remained concerned, though, and felt something needed to be done when the following happened.

> All of our lights in the parking lot were broken. Someone had cut the wires and none of the lights worked. I told the manager about the lights that night because I was concerned about the incident that had happened to me and he did not seem too concerned at all. So my manager and all of the other guys left the restaurant that night and left me and three other girls there to close the restaurant by ourselves. I was furious. [The next day] I went to talk to him about the previous night and I basically told him that if the lights weren't fixed and the policy of girls not closing alone wasn't fixed then I was going to quit. He didn't give me an answer. Now that I look back at it I think he felt I was overstepping my bounds by telling him what to do and he did not like that. In the situation I felt that I was right and he was wrong, so I didn't care if I was overstepping. I honestly did not think these were unreasonable requests, considering what had just happened to me. My manager fixed the lights and then implemented the no girls were allowed to close by themselves policy.

Like the previous account, this one details a situation where expectations collided about employee safety and the responsibility of management to protect workers. After a harrowing experience it does not seem unreasonable for this employee to demand that better safeguards be put in place. To her these are sensible requests, but to see them realized she recognizes that she needs to confront the supervisor and demand action. She feels justified in deploying this forceful tactic because the situation requires action. In the end, she was successful in bringing about the desired change. As we have seen employees do with circumvention, the restaurant staff member construed this as a matter of principle in response to a serious issue that warranted immediate and direct attention (Graham, 1986; Kassing, 2009b).

Second, employees may threaten resignation when confronting a serious affront to their integrity and image. Threatening resignation helps focus attention on the offense. Consider the account provided by a marketing director working for a start-up energy drink manufacturer and distributor. During tradeshow season, the marketing director and the company's graphic designer were expected to produce a display for the National Association of Convenience Stores. The entire process, which spanned several weeks, was governed by tight deadlines that had to be met. The marketing director left Friday evening assured that the graphic designer would turn in the necessary and remaining graphics to complete the design by that day's deadline. However, the marketing director found himself caught in the sights of his supervisor's wrath when the deadline was missed. He recalled:

> I woke the next morning with a phone message from my direct supervisor. The tone of the message was threatening. In the message, he blamed me for missing our deadline and called me a "f. . .ing retard." Our graphics guy did not send the completed files. Instead of reacting, I gave the incident some good thought and I scheduled a meeting with my boss on Monday to address the incident. I began the conversation immediately with threatening my resignation. I did not discuss the events, or defend my position until after saying "I don't appreciate the phone message you left me. If you don't apologize, then I quit." I felt it was necessary to threaten my resignation because of the severity of the incident. I was

> disrespected and more importantly, my boss made assumptions and arrived at conclusions without making any attempt to identify why the deadline was not met. I viewed it as a personal attack and knew that if I did not make it a priority to address the phone message he left with me, it would happen again. Ultimately being treated in that way was not OK with me. My integrity had been challenged and my decreased confidence was a direct result of my supervisor's behavior.

Although disturbed by the accusations and assumptions his boss made regarding his commitment and attention to this project, the marketing director responded carefully. His threat to resign did not result from an emotional outburst as might be expected when a boss cusses out an employee. Rather it was part of a thoughtful and deliberate effort to set the record straight, to correct erroneous assumptions, and to repair a damaged identity. In this instance, threatening resignation was a measured and calculated response. It highlighted the inappropriateness of the supervisor's behavior and the absolute need for it to be corrected. The ultimatum was powerful but simple: apologize and show some respect or lose a valued employee.

Third, threatening resignation seems appropriate when employees believe that situations with their supervisors or employers have reached an impasse – when situations become untenable or intolerable. Threatening resignation underscores the problematic circumstances and exhibits one's desire to leave if the situation cannot be rectified accordingly. A young saleswoman captures this condition well in her dissent account. She joined the sales force of "a well-known gift company" right out of college. She had a large sales territory and reported directly to a sales manager out of state. She received limited training, but was expected to meet with her sales manager on a weekly basis to continue her training. Unfortunately he often cancelled these meetings. Despite her lack of training the saleswoman was successful and attained many new accounts – so many that she eventually received an award for opening the most new accounts. In the interim she requested to have the training meetings that had fallen by the wayside reinstated. After these meetings resumed she reported that she noticed some changes in her supervisor's behavior. She remembered:

> On more than one occasion, after I had opened a new account he would contact me and inform me that he would be taking over that account. He gave me various reasons as to why. The final straw for me came when I was in the process of opening the largest account in the state for the company and my sales manager informed me that he would be closing the deal. This was about 6 months into the position and I was very frustrated. I tried speaking with him first about my frustrations and mentioned that I did not understand why he would need to be the one to close the account. The conversation did not go well and he threatened to fire me if I did not let it go. I left this meeting feeling even more frustrated and wrote a resignation letter. I requested another meeting with him and handed him the letter and explained that I could not work for him any longer unless the circumstances changed.

The saleswoman ended up leaving the organization, as the supervisor did not respond to her threat to quit. He clearly acted of his own volition, though. She was contacted by the corporate office a week later and asked why she had neglected to turn in her weekly paperwork. Apparently, her supervisor failed to inform the corporate office of her resignation. Although it was unsuccessful in bringing about change, threatening resignation was not a complete loss. The saleswoman's professional identity was bolstered by addressing the unsatisfactory situation head on. Once the corporate office learned of her resignation she was invited back. She refused the offer, though – knowing that she could not return to the same troubling environment that forced her resignation in the first place. She learned something valuable about her tolerance for dissent in the process.

Threatening resignation can be quite powerful, but costly when it fails. The saleswoman profiled here found herself out of a job, whereas the other dissenters examined found that conditions improved. But job loss is a real possibility when it comes to threatening resignation, so it is a strategy that demands careful consideration. As such, threatening resignation is a form of dissent that gambles with the power of employee exit (Gorden, 1988). This appears to be why employees use it so infrequently (Kassing, 2002). When threatening resignation, employees reveal their limits regarding safety, integrity, and ethical issues. They show supervisors how far they can be pushed before they will push back. Sometimes employees reach that breaking point rather instantaneously, as is the case with acute safety concerns and offensive personal affronts. Other times they come to that conclusion over time when they realize that their integrity has been eroded through modest but consistent attacks or when they recognize that unethical situations will not change unless they take a stand. In these instances, threatening resignation is a strategy to which employees resort after first attempting other strategies (Kassing, 2009a). Organizing strategies relative to one another is a crucial consideration of the repetition strategy discussed next.

Repetition

As the name suggests, repetition involves "repeated attempts to express dissent about a given topic at multiple points across time with the intention of eventually attaining receptivity to the dissent issue" (Kassing, 2002, pp. 197–8). Repetition sits as moderately competent when compared to other strategies – less competent than direct factual appeal and solution presentation, more competent than circumvention and threatening resignation (Kassing, 2005). This indicates that employees recognize the trade-offs implicit in repeatedly reintroducing their concerns to management – the balance that needs to be struck between keeping the topic alive and overstating it. Dissenters using repetition report wanting primarily to provide guidance, but also to gain assistance and to change behavior (Garner, 2009a).

Whereas other upward dissent strategies prescribe particular tactical approaches (i.e., generating evidence, providing a solution, going to someone higher in the chain of command, and threatening to quit), how to enact repetition remains somewhat amorphous. There is no clear trajectory of how it should be enacted, no schemata outlining what to say when, no timeline detailing what should be done next. Therefore, Kassing (2009a) reasoned that repetition could incorporate all other strategies, and

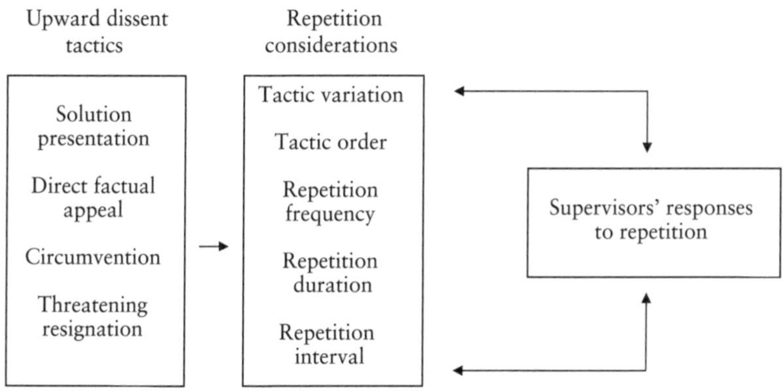

Source: Kassing (2009a). Reprinted by permission of SAGE publications.

Figure 6.2 Factors affecting repetition

suggested that other upward dissent strategies served as tactics deployed during repetition.

Employees have to take several factors into consideration when constructing repetition strategies (see figure 6.2). There is the matter of how and when to use those other strategies. Knowing that upward dissent strategies vary with regard to perceived competence (Kassing, 2005), it makes sense to suggest that some strategies would be deployed more often and before others. So tactic order – which tactics are used earlier versus later in one's repetition strategy – and tactic variation – how tactics are ordered with regard to one another – are two considerations. Timing is important as well. There are several temporal aspects that should be given consideration: first, repetition frequency, or how often an employee raises a concern; second, overall duration, or how long repetition lasts across time; and, third, the time that elapses between dissent episodes. Together these factors affect supervisors' responses to repetition, which in turn inform the subsequent choices employees make about their ongoing efforts to continue dissenting about the same issue.

Employees reported using direct factual appeals most often during repetition, followed by solution presentation and circumvention. Threatening resignation was used least frequently

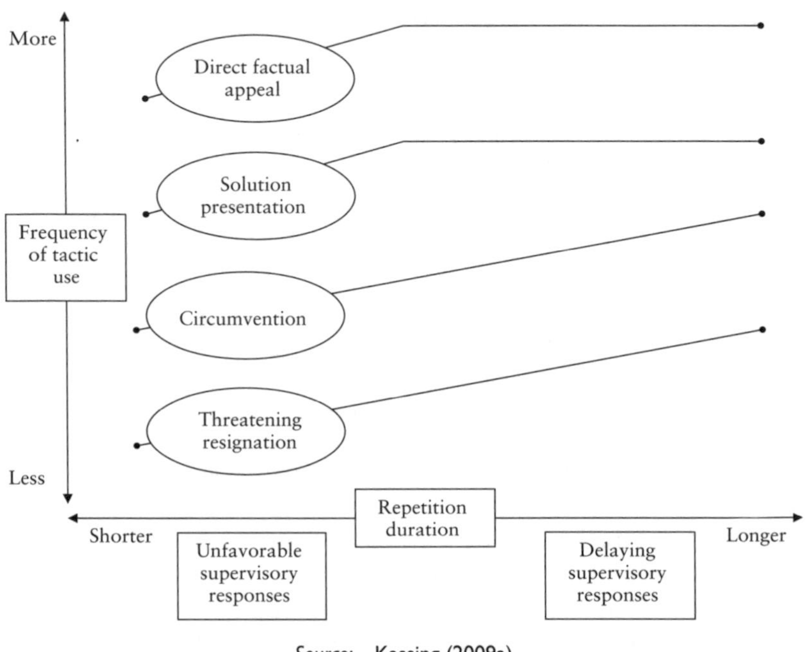

Source: Kassing (2009a).

Figure 6.3 Empirical findings regarding repetition

(Kassing, 2009a). Over the course of repetition, employees reported that their use of direct factual appeals and solution presentation increased from the first time they raised the issue to the next but remained consistent thereafter. By comparison, they reported using more circumvention and threatening resignation tactics as repetition continued. This reveals an overall trend toward adjoining more competent strategies with less competent ones, or trading more balanced approaches for those that could produce more immediate results as repetition progresses (see figure 6.3).

Employees reported that they stretched repetition over time when they perceived that their supervisors used delaying responses (Kassing, 2009a). That is, repetition lasted longer when employees perceived that their supervisors neglected to address or waited to address issues, when they made excuses for failing to address issues, and when they dismissed and ignored issues. Employees shortened repetition when supervisors appeared to be responding unfavorably to ongoing dissent claims. They terminated repetition sooner when they perceived that supervisors became irritated, aggravated, and annoyed with them. However, the total amount of times employees raised an issue and the time they let lapse before raising it again did not relate to supervisors' responses to repetition, leading to the conclusion that determining the duration of repetition in response to supervisory reactions overrides the particulars of how many times and how often dissent should be expressed. Basically, supervisors' responses influenced the overall duration of repetition, but not the specific sequential enactment of it.

We can look to the recent financial crisis for another illustration – this time an illustration of how repetition unfolds. Richard Bowen became the business chief underwriter for CitiMortgage in 2006. In this position he was responsible for making sure that purchased mortgages met the company's credit policy standards. This was no small undertaking, as CitiMortgage was in the business of buying up and selling mortgages to the tune of $90 billion annually. Bowen testified before the Financial Crisis Inquiry Commission in April of 2010 about the unbridled financial risks that were being taken at CitiMortgage during his tenure. He reported that he repeatedly warned his colleagues about risk issues he had identified, about the risk practices he witnessed that "made a mockery of Citi credit policy" (Citigroup executives, 2010).

At issue was oversight of the credit standards used in buying and selling mortgages. Citi purchased $50 billion annually of prime mortgages that were underwritten elsewhere. It then proceeded to sell those mortgages to other investors like Fannie Mae and Freddie Mac. Citi did not underwrite these mortgages, but it did offer "reps and warrants" that attested to the fact that each and every mortgage sold met its underwriting credit standards. Bowen discovered, after a sample of mortgages purchased by Citi was reviewed internally, that an alarming portion of the purchased and sold mortgages were defective:

> In June of 2006, I discovered that over 60% of the mortgages in delegated flow were defective. And by defective I mean the mortgages were

> not underwritten to Citi policy guidelines. Citi had given reps and warrants to the investors that these mortgages were not defective. And the investors could force Citi to repurchase many billions of dollars of these defective mortgages. This represented a large risk of loss to the shareholders of Citi. I attempted to get management to address this critical risk issue. I started issuing warnings in June of 2006. These warnings were in the form of email, weekly reports, committee presentations, and discussions. I even requested a special investigation from the management that was in charge of internal controls. And that investigation confirmed that we had very serious problems. And I continued my warnings through 2007. But Citi continued to purchase and sell even more mortgages in 2007. And defective mortgages during 2007 increased to over 80%.

From his testimony we can see that Bowen relied heavily on direct factual appeals with his colleagues. He issued warnings via several mechanisms and in a variety of settings. These were based on his knowledge and understanding of the corporate policy regarding credit guidelines, the evidence generated from an earlier internal audit, and his own personal experience as an underwriter. As part of a solution to the problem he requested an internal investigation, which generated further and even more damning evidence to support his claims about the company's risk – bolstering his continued direct factual appeals on the matter. Yet, as Bowen continued to express repetitious upward dissent, the problem continued unabated.

Knowing that the company would face serious financial risk if the lapses in credit practices continued unaddressed, Bowen decided to take his case to the top – to the board of directors and members of the Citi executive team. In early November of 2007 he sent an email to the chief financial officer and the chief auditor of CitiGroup. In the email, he testified:

> I outlined the business practices that I had witnessed and had attempted to address. I specifically warned [the corporate officers] about the extreme risks and unrecognized financial losses that existed within my business unit. I also requested an investigation. And I asked that this investigation be conducted by officers of the company outside of my business unit.

After repeatedly airing his concerns, Bowen circumvented the chain of command and brought the issue to two of the corporation's highest ranking officers. In his estimation circumvention was necessary because his repeated warnings had gone unheeded and the situation had worsened. As part of his repetition strategy, he circumvented other managers who failed to react or respond when given the chance, but he did so by adjoining other comparatively more competent upward dissent strategies with circumvention (Kassing, 2009a). Bowen incorporated direct factual appeal by providing evidence of the faulty practices and an informative firsthand account. He engaged in solution presentation when he requested that another investigation – this time an external one – be conducted. Bowen seemed to be acting out of a desire to provide guidance to the corporate leaders who oversaw his organization. He knew that he needed to demonstrate the precarious financial position of his firm and that he would need their assistance to bring about the necessary changes in auditing required to avert financial disaster. So, even though he resorted to circumvention, his motives were clear and his use of other tactics sensible.

Richard Bowen's experience demonstrates how repetition can span several years and involve the use of other upward dissent tactics as part of a larger and ongoing strategy. Ultimately, he was unsuccessful in his efforts to draw attention to an issue through dissent. He clearly faced some of the barriers discussed earlier (see chapter 4) – futility and diffusion of responsibility, for example. While high profile, his case in some ways is not so unusual. It simply chronicles an employee trying to express dissent as effectively as possible despite clear constraints.

Recommendations for Employees Expressing Organizational Dissent

First, dissenting employees should anticipate feeling isolated (Shahinpoor and Matt, 2007). Dissenters set themselves apart from the organization (Kassing, 1997). They do so in such a way that their "identity and personhood are exposed" (Shahinpoor and Matt, 2007, p. 39). This is the price for failing to go along, for refusing to consent. Dissenters essentially need to be prepared to stand out. Being exposed is a concern, but one that can be mitigated by the content of dissent expressed. Thus, dissenters should give serious consideration to the nature of their disaffection in light of the risks associated with expressing disagreement (Waldron and Kassing, 2011). Organizational members who routinely dissent about personal-advantage issues can be branded as troublemakers and bad apples rather quickly. Those that dissent about matters of principle may be exposed, but likely will be respected (Nemeth et al., 2001). Thus, expressing principled dissent will prove safer than making noise about personal issues. However, the two often mix (Hegstrom, 1999). So whenever possible it would be wise to emphasize principled aspects, even when dissent evolves from a very personal perspective (Kassing, 2009b).

Next, employees should consider their goals when dissenting and the most appropriate audiences for hearing dissent. Employees dissent for many reasons and choose to share their concerns with managers, coworkers, family members, and friends outside of work (Garner, 2009a; Kassing, 1998). Dissent about a frustrating situation, for example, should be directed towards coworkers so that some commiserating can occur. Dissent about a flawed facet of operations should be shared with management so that change can occur. Dissent about suspected misconduct should be revealed to an audience that will protect the dissenter (e.g., an ombudsperson or a trusted confidant). Understanding one's motives for dissenting is important as it will inform the audiences to whom that dissent should be channeled. And the audiences that hear dissent will be instrumental in determining its outcome.

Additionally, employees should think about the effect dissenting might have on their relationships with coworkers and supervisors. It could improve relationships with receptive managers but lead to relational deterioration with managers who demand compliance. The implications for superior–subordinate relationship quality become amplified when employees determine that circumventing their supervisors or threatening to quit is necessary. These strategies could prove successful but carry considerable relational

Table 6.3 Recommendations for employees expressing organizational dissent

For dissent in general

1. Expect to stand out.
2. Contemplate the content of dissent in light of the risks associated with expressing it.
3. Acknowledge dissent goals.
4. Bear in mind the relational effects of expressing dissent.
5. Think about how long dissent expression should persist.

For whistleblowing in particular

1. Anticipate denials of wrongdoing.
2. Attain and produce solid evidence as warranted.
3. Brace for retaliation.
4. Prepare evidence of effective performance to refute accusations of poor performance.
5. Document retaliation when it occurs.
6. Assume that subtle harassment will occur.
7. Refrain from responding to subtle harassment emotionally and excessively.
8. Build support among coworkers to confirm harassment.
9. Be wary of official reporting channels.
10. Understand the legal statutes that protect whistleblowers and their limitations.
11. Ensure that legally and morally justifiable motives are apparent.
12. Differentiate what is objectionable from what it truly misconduct.
13. Make certain that allegations are accurate.
14. Consider the most appropriate means for reporting wrongdoing.

costs (Kassing, 2007). Similarly, endless dissent directed toward coworkers could strain these relationships after a while. It takes considerable time and energy to deal with dissent, something dissenters should keep in mind. Finally, employees should attend carefully to how long they ought to persist in expressing dissent about the same issue (Kassing, 2009a). It may be best to discontinue dissent when managers are unresponsive, or it may make sense to endure when supervisors continue to neglect dissent (see table 6.3).

What can employees expect when they express dissent in response to organizational wrongdoing? And how can they respond? They can expect that managers will deny wrongdoing and should prepare themselves accordingly by amassing solid evidence that is convincing, indisputable, and overwhelming (Martin and Rifkin, 2004). Whistleblowers also should ready themselves for managerial attacks leveled against their character and competence – and for the frustration that will accompany strident denials of any such reprisals. This may involve discrediting, disparaging, humiliating, isolating, or blacklisting dissenters. In response, whistleblowers should secure and accumulate evidence of their performance to counterbalance any personal attacks and should gather and provide evidence of retaliation to combat any harassment.

But not all retaliation will be overt. It can be quite subtle as well. Whistleblowers should be circumspect about the cunning forms of harassment managers may use. This might involve denying access to needed resources and withdrawing routine perks. The subtlety of these acts belies their strategic nature. Managers may undertake these seemingly innocuous and difficult-to-prove offenses to bait whistleblowers into crying foul – using emotional and excessive reactions to paint dissenters as problem employees. Such nuances would be lost on outsiders but may be understood well by colleagues. So dissenters should build support among coworkers who can recognize and appreciate these understated mechanisms of harassment.

Additionally, managers may compel dissenters to use official whistleblowing channels. This too is a strategic move on the part of management. It indicates public support for the employee and his or her related concerns, but at the same time confines dissent to the organizational sidelines, slows its progress in a bureaucratic backlog, and narrows its audience to a few people. Moreover, these channels can sanitize the dissent claim, stripping it of any or most emotionality and outrage. Formal channels also promote the notion that matters are "adjudicated independently and fairly," with the parties involved being on equal footing (Martin and Rifkin, 2004, p. 232). Yet this may not be the case, as formal channels often get corrupted in favor of management (De Maria and Jan, 1996). Dissenters, then, should be wary of official channels and should prevent those channels from nullifying their dissent claims. They should understand that the assurance of justice these channels promise may never materialize. And they should continue to build support for their dissent claim among colleagues while or instead of using formal channels.

There are legal statutes in place to protect whistleblowers from retaliation, but these vary widely. To receive said protections, some statutes stipulate that whistleblowing must be directed to particular recipients, that reports of organizational misconduct must be offered without financial incentive, and that protections extend only to those reporting wrongdoing in the public sector or when employees have voiced concerns internally first. Moreover, particular aspects of whistleblowing can result in the denial of legal protection. In some countries whistleblowing to the media and whistleblowing in bad faith lead to the forfeiture of protections (Miceli et al., 2009).

Thus, whistleblowers should consider their motives for dissenting, their assessments of wrongdoing, the accuracy of their claims, and the outlets available for reporting wrongdoing (Miceli et al., 2009). They should contemplate carefully their motives for reporting wrongdoing. Is it part of a larger personal agenda to get back at an alleged wrongdoer or is it an effort to protect the well-being of employees, the company's reputation, and the public? They should attend as well to their assessment of wrongdoing. Whistleblowers may find something objectionable that by most standards would not qualify as wrongdoing. They should ask: Is the behavior in question truly misconduct or is it merely objectionable? For these reasons whistleblowers should ensure that their concerns are morally and legally justified and that their allegations are offered in good faith. Moreover, their observations and accumulated facts need to be accurate. Finally, whistleblowers should consider the appropriateness of the means chosen for reporting wrongdoing. Reporting internally certainly would be more appropriate than going directly to the media, for instance.

So there are several recommendations that employees should bear in mind when expressing dissent. The burden of expressing dissent, though, should not fall exclusively on the shoulders of employees. Organizations have considerable responsibility too, which leads to a central question: What can organizations do to cultivate and benefit from dissent? Idiomatically speaking, how can organizations refrain from shooting messengers? How can they keep from selling dissenters down the river? How can they avoid throwing them under the bus or leaving them twisting in the wind? How can managers keep their collective heads out of the sand? And how can organizational leaders come to see the shortsightedness in putting issues out of sight, out of mind? They can begin by seeing dissent as a valuable commodity – one that should be exchanged openly within organizations. The final chapter, therefore, considers how organizations can profit from and manage dissent well.

Discussion Questions

1 What is at stake when people express upward dissent? What makes upward dissent particularly risky? How is it more risky than dissent expressed to coworkers or friends and family members outside of work?
2 Why are direct factual appeal and solution presentation preferable in most cases? What about these strategies makes them more appropriate across situations? What makes them more likely to be successful and lead to positive outcomes? How and when do people tend to use these upward dissent strategies?
3 What circumstances make circumvention a viable option? What does one risk when practicing circumvention? What kind of outcomes can employees expect when they practice circumvention? Although circumvention can be risky, it also can be quite effective. What can employees do to make circumvention less risky and more effective?
4 What factors lead employees to threaten resignation? What are the risks associated with threatening resignation? When does threatening resignation seem appropriate and warranted? What are the possible benefits one derives from threatening resignation?

5 What are the major considerations that come into play when employees engage in repetition? How do the other forms of upward dissent fold into and become part of the repetition strategy? How do responses from supervisors affect repetition?

7

Can Organizational Dissent Be Managed Well?

May we never confuse honest dissent with disloyal subversion.
– Dwight D. Eisenhower (1890–1969)

I respect only those who resist me; but I cannot tolerate them.
– Charles De Gaulle (1890–1970)

Perhaps no organization has come under greater scrutiny for failing to accommodate organizational dissent than the National Aeronautics and Space Administration (NASA). Although they are slipping into the annals of history, the fateful events surrounding the decision to launch the Challenger space shuttle in 1986 have been revisited many times in academic case studies exploring a host of issues – including, but not limited to, decision-making, groupthink, and employee feedback – because, in short, NASA failed to attend to dissenting voices that would have provided additional information and most likely a decision to postpone the launch and avert the loss of life (Sunstein, 2003; Tompkins, 2005). Seventeen years later, in 2003, disaster struck a second time when space shuttle Columbia disintegrated upon reentry, resulting once again in the loss of an entire crew and leading to renewed accusations that NASA's inadequate decision-making processes and intolerance of dissenting voices were at fault.

In the wake of these tragedies the agency has since embarked on an ambitious effort to democratize decision-making, to hear dissent, and to create a culture of openness. Following the

Challenger disaster, Wayne Hale was appointed as the deputy program manager and tasked with restructuring the mission management team so that it could better accommodate dissent (Hale, 2009). This was no simple undertaking. Hale reported that "changing the culture to be more welcoming to alternate or dissenting opinions was a task that took a lot of my time and attention." When asked about how the organization was moving forward, he would offer "that we were making progress, making changes, improving the situation, but that changing the culture was hard and we had a long way to go." Hale's confidence grew as reports confirmed that alternative opinions were being welcomed and dissent accepted and considered – leading him to confess that he felt the agency was "doing better than ever." But his confidence was shaken after he left the position and subsequently learned that people in other parts of the organization had failed to share critical information with his staff. Apparently, they were told by middle managers "that speaking up would not be good."

And then there was the video that staff members made to illustrate communication barriers at NASA. It was produced as a team project during a larger exercise in improving innovation and open-mindedness (Greenfieldboyce, 2009). As part of this project, team members shared their stories and anecdotes of life at NASA. In the process they developed a drama that was a composite of their collective experiences. The result was a video that depicts a young engineer at Johnson Space Center in Houston sharing with management what she believes to be a great idea for a new spacecraft design. In response, one supervisor counters with a string of objections, while another simply dismisses the idea. The frustrated engineer eventually dissents, claiming that the current approach is flawed. She is told, "You know that might be, but it doesn't matter. I can't afford to care about that. My job is to make sure the project follows this plan." As managers continue to toe the line, she ends up asking: "How can I possibly contribute and be innovative if I have to ask for approval for everything I want to say?" Management's response: "We're not talking about that here. We don't want to repress dissenting views, or innovation like this. That's not how we operate."

Although fictionalized, the film is based on staff members' real experiences. It served up a sobering wakeup call for NASA – exposing the shortcomings in their ongoing cultural shift. Managers were advocating for organizational dissent while effectively neutralizing it. To their credit NASA allowed the video to be publicly viewed on YouTube for a time and showed it at a manager's retreat. That is where Wayne Hale first saw it. Hale (2009) was so taken back by the video that he wrote about it in a blog post he called "Stifling Dissent." He lamented that "People say the right things in public discussion of how they should act, then behave in the bad old ways in small or private settings," and concluded: "looks like we still have a long way to go."

This case illustrates just how difficult it can be to move an organizational culture mired in consent toward one that makes room for dissent. As Wayne Hale astutely points out, doing so will consume time, drain resources, and exhaust energy. It will be hard work that requires organizational leaders to move past the attitudes captured in this chapter's introductory quotes. Both testify to the relevance and value of dissent while underscoring the difficulties present when addressing it. We often construe dissent as subversive and disloyal and remain intolerant of it. But we have seen throughout this text, and in other important works, that dissent can prove incredibly valuable to society, the institutions designed to govern us, and the places where we work (Hegstrom, 1995; Graham, 1986; O'Leary, 2005; Sunstein, 2003). Thus, pursuing workplaces that are more accepting of dissent – and in return more likely to benefit from it – is a worthy goal.

For some time scholars have lauded the benefits of attending to employee voice within organizations (Hirschman, 1970), particularly dissenting opinions (Hegstrom, 1995; Redding, 1985). Hegstrom contended that "the acid test for an organization's communication system is its reaction to those who dissent" or "how it deals with its own internal critics" (1995, p. 84). Graham positioned organizational dissent alongside external "market discipline" as an internal means for "regulating the quality of organizational performance" (1986, p. 3). Others have suggested that dissent plays a key role in helping an organization acquire "the kind of self-awareness that might enable it to head off some crises before they evolve" (Tyler, 2005, p. 570), reducing risk through the development and maintenance of a collective sense of mindfulness (Novak and Sellnow, 2009). Similarly, Smith (2009) demonstrated the capacity of dissent to expose difficulties in organizational change. Dissent also serves to reveal and uncover corporate malfeasance and organizational wrongdoing (Miceli and Near, 1992, 2002; Near and Miceli, 1995). And it indicates employee satisfaction, commitment, and involvement, as well as employee burnout and turnover (Avtgis et al., 2007; Kassing, 1998; Kassing et al., in press). Dissent, then, is powerful stuff, signaling when communication falters, performance suffers, crises loom, cultural change flounders, ethical behavior slips, and employee morale waxes and wanes. It is valuable corrective feedback, unlikely to be garnered from other sources (Hegstrom, 1995).

There are clear rewards, then, for organizations that cultivate dissent. This final chapter steps back from an individual perspective and takes a broader look at how organizations function regarding dissent. It begins with an examination of the factors that place organizations in underrepresented, optimal, or overloaded conditions relative to organizational dissent. A review of mechanisms used to solicit and capture organizational dissent follows. The chapter closes by presenting specific recommendations that organizations can use when addressing dissent.

How Much Dissent Can an Organization Tolerate?

Dissent is good for organizations, but not all dissent is good. Sunstein cautions, "I do not suggest that dissent is always helpful. Certainly we do not need to encourage would-be dissenters who are speaking nonsense" (2003, p. 7). Unhelpful dissent detracts from meaningful and purposeful dissent. So too does excessive and unfounded dissent. Consider the following example. In November of 2002, a lecturer at Greenwich University in the UK named Suresh Deman blew the whistle on the Commission for Racial

Equality (CRE). Ironically, he alleged that the watchdog group charged with investigating racial discrimination and promoting racial equality was racially motivated in its decision to withhold legal assistance from him (Baty, 2002). He proclaimed that the decision was "nothing but an ongoing campaign of discrimination and victimization against me." Yet an investigation revealed that Deman had filed not one, but two cases against the CRE, and that he had made numerous claims against universities throughout the United Kingdom – including several against his current employer. Increasingly alarmed by the volume of litigation initiated by Deman, and others like him, one university official acknowledged that serial litigants had become an issue for public institutions. What does he mean by serial litigants? Well, Deman filed complaints against three higher education institutions in 2002, nine in 2001, and seven in the year 2000. Knowing that clear safeguards are in place to protect whistleblowers, some employees have begun to take advantage of these opportunities – bringing frivolous legal cases and suing their employers on a number of grounds. Organizations frequently end up settling regardless of a claim's merit, because it is the quickest and most efficient way to appease dissenters. The odds of success often favor would-be whistleblowers, leading to abuses like the one described above.

The content of dissent clearly dictates how valuable it will be for an organization. Recall that dissent can be about matters of principle or driven by a personal agenda (Graham, 1986; Hegstrom, 1999). So the nature of dissent is an important qualification applied to the axiom that dissent is good for organizations. Another relevant qualification relates to the sheer volume of dissent expressed. While speculation about the value of dissent abounds, little is known about how much routinely occurs within organizations. Too much dissent could prove debilitating, clogging lines of communication and stalling critical procedures (Tourish, 2005). The democratic practices necessary to engage with and process disagreement within organizations take time and patience (Cheney, 1995; Stohl and Cheney, 2001). Employees recognize these limitations along with the emotional toll that can be incurred by sharing dissent (Gorden et al., 1994; Rothschild-Whitt, 1979). Processing organizational dissent takes effort, and excessive dissent may redirect time and energy away from other critical tasks.

A third consideration would be how long dissent endures. Does it occur rather instantaneously and subside or does it linger and resurface regularly? Repetitious upward dissent can stretch over time, and when it does employees seem to gauge how long they should continue dissenting based on their supervisors' reactions (Kassing, 2009a). Dissent is ever present in organizations (Kassing, 1997), but its accumulation and the effects of residual dissent remain unexplored. Finally, organizations vary in their tolerance for dissent, with some absorbing more than others (Hegstrom, 1995; Perry et al., 1994). A collection of established mechanisms, informal practices, and communication climates that are more or less open to employee feedback will dictate how much dissent an organization can bear.

Is there an optimal level of dissent – an amount that can be taken on board and processed before it proves dysfunctional? Perhaps, but it likely shifts depending on the aforementioned factors (see figure 7.1) – the nature of dissent, the volume of dissent, the duration and accumulation of dissent, and organizational tolerances for dissent – all of which set parameters that dictate when organizational systems have too little, too much, or optimal levels of dissent.

Figure 7.1 suggests that there are three conditions in which an organization can exist with regard to dissent expression: it can be underrepresented, optimal, or overloaded. The flowing lines and staggered text indicate that the parameters which define these conditions are fluid rather than fixed – shifting relative to one another in a consistent state of flux. Horizontal bands demonstrate how the collection of parameters comes together to determine each condition. Within each condition the nature of dissent is differentiated as personal advantage or principled, the volume of dissent distinguished as greater, moderate, or less. The duration and accumulation of dissent is represented as longer duration with more accumulation, varying duration with some accumulation, or shorter duration with less accumulation. And an organization's tolerance for dissent is noted as high, reasonable, or low.

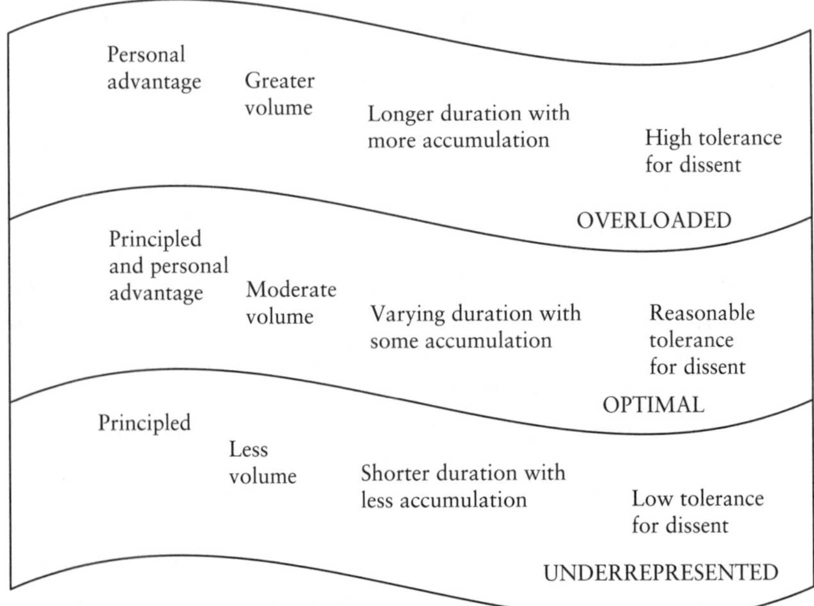

Figure 7.1 Factors determining underrepresented, optimal, and overloaded dissent conditions

Organizations in the underrepresented condition have a low tolerance for dissent to begin, which tends to allow only for principled dissent (Hegstrom, 1999). Dissent accumulates less and does not last long. Employees tend to terminate the continued expression of dissent when supervisors respond unfavorably to it (Kassing, 2009a). Organizations in this condition forfeit the aforementioned benefits derived from attending to dissent. They also become vulnerable to whistleblowing. The probability of dissent seeping outside organizations multiplies when dissenters respond to matters of principle and make little headway in doing so. Unresponsiveness moves undeterred dissenters toward external sources like the media and governing bodies to express dissent (Stewart, 1980). Thus, organizations in the underrepresented condition surrender any benefits derived from dissent and remain exposed to the threat of whistleblowers.

In the overloaded condition, the organization possesses a high tolerance for dissent, hears a greater volume of personal-advantage dissent, and sees the accumulation of dissent. This likely occurs when organizations promise to be receptive to employee feedback but lack mechanisms to effectively process it. As a result, dissent proliferates but rarely gets corralled in a manner that allows organizations to benefit and employees to be heard. Dissent in these circumstances may migrate toward audiences other than management, being shared between coworkers and with friends and family (Kassing, 1997, 1998). Supervisors contribute to the overloaded condition by failing to respond to dissent. Their delaying tactics lead employees to stretch dissent out over time (Kassing, 2009a), keeping it in the system and allowing it to accumulate.

The optimal condition suggests that an organization tolerates dissent at reasonable levels, soliciting enough but not taking on too much. Dissent levels are moderate, with a mix of principled and personal-advantage dissent expressed. Employees voice dissent constructively and do so through a variety of strategies (Kassing, 2002, 2005). Some accumulation of dissent occurs, but generally management deals with it directly and effectively. There is a shared understanding between management and employees that constructive dissent is valuable and that proactive means for expressing it are helpful (Perry et al., 1994). This in turn curtails excessive personal-advantage dissent, which either develops into something more principled as it progresses through the organization or shifts to audiences other than management (Kassing, 1998, 2009a).

Mechanisms Used to Solicit and Capture Organizational Dissent

Organizations have produced and installed several different types of "sanctioned channels for employees to express their content or discontent" (Harlos, 2001, p. 327). These include grievance procedures, appeal boards, ombudspersons, suggestion boxes, ethics

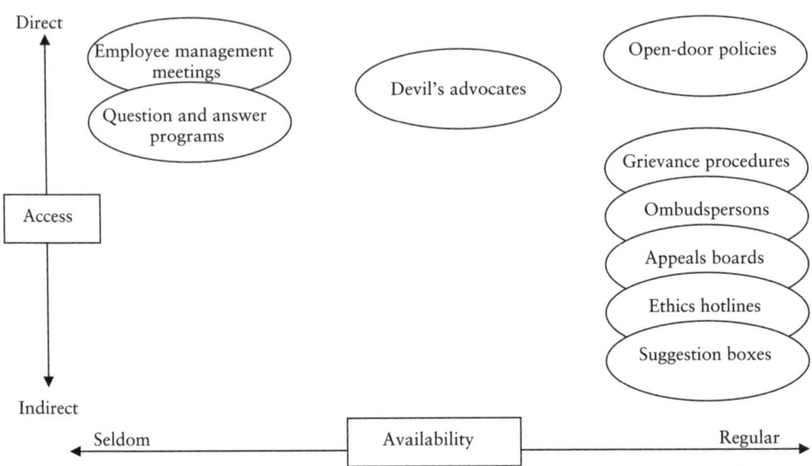

Figure 7.2 Variation in voice mechanisms

hotlines, question-and-answer programs, employee–management meetings, open-door policies and devil's advocates (Graham, 1986; Harlos, 2001; McCabe, 1997; Stanley, 1981). Mechanisms vary widely with regard to access, availability, and accommodation. Some programs provide greater access to management than others. Employees can speak directly with managers in question-and-answer programs or merely leave notes detailing their concerns in a suggestion box. Similarly, there is variation in terms of the regularity with which mechanisms are available. Ethics hotlines have become commonplace in many organizations – available to employees anytime. In contrast, employee–management meetings happen intermittently, usually occurring only every few months. When access and availability are considered together, the variation becomes even more evident (see figure 7.2).

Some mechanisms provide more direct access to management but with comparatively less regularity. Employee–management meetings and question-and-answer programs fit here. Another family of mechanisms, which includes grievance procedures, ombudspersons, appeals boards, ethics hotlines, and suggestion boxes, provides access to management through some indirect point of contact. Dissent expressed in these mechanisms gets

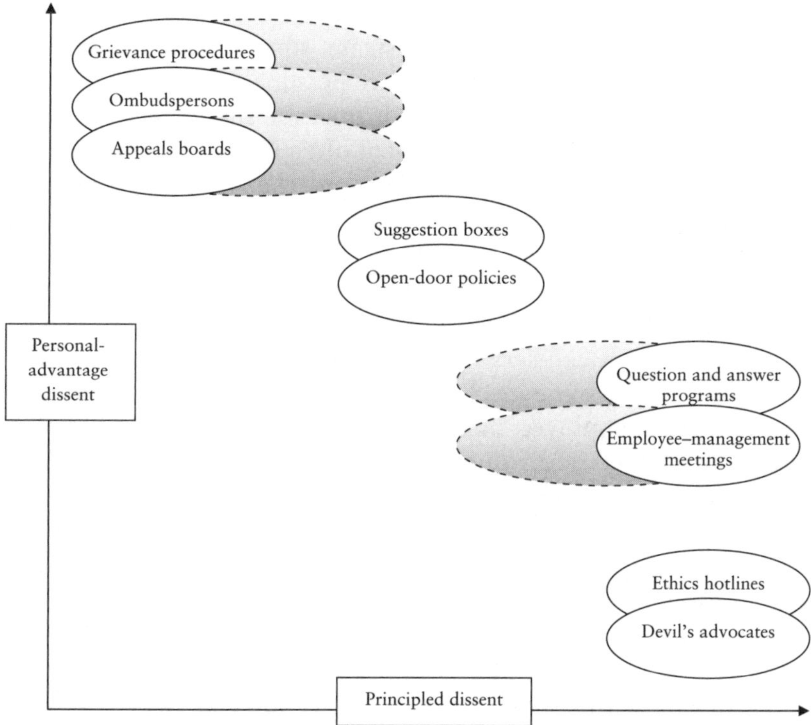

Figure 7.3 Variation in type of dissent accommodated by voice mechanisms

filtered first through another source before reaching management. These can be appointees designated to advance the most pertinent and pressing concerns, employees and peers empowered to make binding decisions about concerns, or staff assigned to administer set protocols governing how concerns get addressed. Open-door policies, on the other hand, provide direct access to management. So too do devil's advocate roles when managers employ them in decision-making processes. However, open-door policies happen with regularity, whereas devil's advocates are restricted principally to decision-making contexts.

Voice mechanisms also vary in their capacity to accommodate different types of dissent (see figure 7.3). Some attract more personal-advantage dissent, whereas others garner more principled dissent. Grievances procedures, for example, usually prescribe that employees demonstrate some form of personal injury, and thus more readily capture personal-advantage dissent. Ombudspersons and appeals boards function similarly. But, as we have seen, personal-advantage dissent often intersects with matters of principle, and employees understand the need to emphasize the principled nature of their otherwise personal dissent claims (Hegstrom, 1999; Kassing, 2009b). Therefore dissent expressed via these mechanisms can stretch to include issues of principle. The shadowed spheres in figure 7.3 illustrate this possibility. Similarly, principled dissent can serve individuals and a greater good at the same time. Thus, some mechanisms, such as question-and-answer programs and employee–management meetings, secure principled dissent that meets individual as well as coworker and organizational needs. In between are mechanisms that acquire all forms of dissent equally (i.e., open-door policies and suggestion boxes). And there are those mechanisms designed to solicit principled dissent exclusively. Ethics hotlines receive feedback about malfeasance, misconduct, wrongdoing, and unethical behavior. Devil's advocates utilize principled dissent with the intention of vetting ideas and decisions thoroughly. A closer look at each will help further differentiate voice mechanisms.

Grievance procedures provide a clearly defined format for filing written complaints that involves "a series of proscribed, documented steps with time limits" (Harlos, 2001, p. 331). They reveal egregious infractions of company policies related to harassment and the fair treatment of employees. While they exist predominantly in unionized workplaces and the civil service sector, they appear in nonunionized for-profit organizations too. Filing a grievance requires one to demonstrate personal injury resulting from organizational action (Graham, 1986). Thus, the procedures tend to capture personal-advantage dissent or dissent claims that combine personal-advantage and principled dissent. And while they should operate free of retribution (McCabe, 1997), this does not always appear to be the case. Filing grievances about their supervisor, for example, resulted in negative performance evaluations for some employees – leading Klaas and DeNisi (1989,

p. 714) to conclude that "the value of voice provided by grievance systems may be limited, given that filing and winning grievances may impose costs upon employees." But grievances that go unresolved can wind up arbitrated by a third party, and this can deter management misconduct that gives rise to questionable behavior in the first place (McCabe, 1997).

Appeal boards are another mechanism for hearing employee grievances. Although there are no universal standards for their composition, they tend to include a balance of managers and peers. Their decisions "are usually treated as final and binding" (McCabe, 1997, p. 351), which serves to instill employee confidence in the appeal system. With regard to organizational dissent, appeal boards represent a formal mechanism for disagreeing with dismissals or disciplinary action. Employees understand that a jury of their peers, not just management, will consider their claim. This emboldens some to bring their complaints forward. When doing so they believe that their concerns have been given just and equitable consideration and recognize that their peers have contributed legitimately to organizational decision-making. For these reasons appeal boards, particularly those that include peers, have been received favorably.

Companies also have instituted ombudsperson offices. This mechanism makes a designated company officer available to hear dissent and grievances (Graham, 1986). Ombudspersons "provide nonbinding and confidential advice to resolve disputes, often handling (but not limited to) complaints of racial and sexual harassment" (Harlos, 2001, p. 331). Typically they can be found in larger organizations where the volume of such complaints justifies the expense of having an office/position. They are therefore comparatively infrequent. Ombudspersons are expected to listen to and investigate employees' claims about organizational misconduct, employee transgressions, and any resulting grievances that accompany these allegations. Thus, they are likely hear both principled and personal-advantage dissent.

Although popularized for a time, traditional suggestion boxes have realized their limited utility, generating little faith and seeing modest use from employees (Harlos, 2001; Tourish, 2005). And managers do not seem to take them seriously either (Tourish, 2005). They are primarily receptacles for the anonymous deposit of concerns, suggestions, or questions. Yet their anonymity can be compromised. Employees in one study claimed that this was the case when they observed managers reviewing handwriting and staff attendance records to identify presumed authors of particular suggestions. They also suspected that certain suggestions had been fabricated because they appeared far too complimentary of management (Harlos, 2001). Hosting suggestion boxes externally, though – as either phone-based or Internet-based outlets – can alleviate anonymity challenges because management no longer has direct access to employee comments. The upside of suggestion boxes is that they can lead to "more timely and candid feedback" than some of the other mechanisms and that they can call attention to micro- as well as macro-issues (Lilienthal, 2002, p. 40). Whereas some mechanisms tend to be outlets for bigger-picture issues, suggestion boxes attract narrow and limited concerns that would fail to draw attention in certain venues.

EmployeeSuggestionBox, a company that provides a web-based application for organizations to outsource their employee feedback processes, appeals to these very possibilities. The company's website claims that the electronic suggestion box they provide offers "an on-demand platform to capture, develop and incorporate good ideas companywide," and that it is available to all manner of employees, including department managers, salespeople, and warehouse staff (employeesuggestionbox.com). Interestingly, there is no mention of the capacity and utility of their resource to capture disagreement or dissent. Rather the company frames the product as a mechanism for making "idea generation a priority for everyone." It also recommends using its electronic suggestion box for conducting opinion polls, brainstorming ideas, collaborating on idea implementation, and rewarding employees. We can expect at times, though, that these processes would incur some measure of dissent. This provider leaves that implied. But clearly the mechanism it supplies could become an important receptacle for eliciting dissent.

Ethics hotlines have been designed to capture organizational wrongdoing and malfeasance – that is, to address principled dissent (Graham, 1986). Historically, they have been set up as telephone numbers that employees can call anonymously to register concerns about misconduct, but they now include Internet-based applications as well (Church et al., 2007). In early assessments about one-quarter of companies reported having ethics hotlines (Barnett and Cochran, 1991). Yet the adoption of ethics hotlines has increased dramatically in the past two decades, by some estimates jumping to over 80 percent (Church et al., 2007). To be effective, ethics hotlines need to be identified to employees and the parameters of their use articulated clearly. This would include stating when they are available for use, what kind of content should be directed to them, whether calls remain anonymous or merely confidential, and whether they are administered by in-house personnel or a third party.

PepsiCo initiated an ethics hotline in 1999 called "Speak-Up!" (Church et al., 2007) and more recently developed a partner website for logging concerns. A third-party vendor administers the 24-hour hotline, which allows all callers to remain anonymous. Employees who call are asked a series of questions about the parties involved, other people they may have informed of the issue, and the types of evidence that they have accumulated to substantiate their report. Each issue receives a case number and a thorough investigation. "Employees are encouraged to use the hotline if they have issues that they cannot resolve with their managers or HR representatives or if they are uncomfortable discussing a matter with any direct members of their team or management" (ibid., p. 161). Additionally, organizational members are encouraged to use the hotline to determine if they have in fact encountered something that constitutes wrongdoing. But the hotline does not stand alone. Rather it reflects PepsiCo's long-standing focus on integrity and ethics, which the company clearly promotes through its code of conduct, that employees have to read and sign annually, its value statement, and its 360-degree feedback process. In essence, the hotline "provides employees with a perceived 'safety-valve' for reporting potentially damaging issues or concerns to the organization through protected channels of communication" (ibid.).

Question-and-answer programs take the form of "occasional or regular meetings between large groups of employees and higher level management for inquiries into organizational policies, practices, and issues" (Harlos, 2001, p. 331). Sometimes these are known as forum or town hall meetings. Question-and-answer programs proved effective for Tandem Computers, which began holding town meetings in the early 1980s (Perry et al., 1994). Upper management hosted and scheduled meetings every six to nine months with the intention of sharing information between management and employees. The meetings served as a vehicle for employees "to gain access to management" and "to give voice to [employee] concerns" – as a forum where they could "publicly question management" (ibid., p. 117). Employees came to expect that any issues raised at the meetings would be addressed. For example, in one meeting an employee dissented about the company's practice of hiring managers from outside the firm instead of making internal promotions. In response, the CEO instantly asked for a show of hands from managers who had worked elsewhere previously and quickly realized that the company had neglected to promote well from within. Upper management vowed to change course straight away. Question-and-answer programs, then, provide direct access to organizational dissent and present management with immediate opportunities to address it.

Employee–management meetings are "occasional or regular meetings between individual or groups of employees and higher level management" (Harlos, 2001, p. 331). Regular meetings of this sort appear to be an effective voice mechanism because of the face-to-face communication they afford employees – allowing for employee recognition, development of support, and the exchange of information. They also provide a venue for airing employee concerns and holding managers accountable. However, employees reported that meetings disintegrated when their bosses used name-calling and yelling to degrade and intimidate them. Rebukes like this ruptured the veneer of civility that was meant to accompany such meetings.

Open-door policies allow organizational members to take their concerns up the hierarchy following chain-of-command steps, and to skip steps when necessary. In essence, employees are given the opportunity to air concerns with people higher in the chain of command than their immediate supervisors. IBM was an early adopter of open-door policies and bolstered its policy with related practices (Graham, 1986). It used skip-level interviews several times a year that required managers to meet individually with all subordinates two levels below them in the chain of command. The practice provided an "upward flow of information and concerns" that remained entirely separate from personnel evaluations and routine feedback processes (ibid., p. 28). IBM also supported a "speak up" program that entitled employees to submit confidential concerns in writing to upper management.

Open-door policies seem to be the most widely used voice mechanism (Harlos, 2001) and are readily available in many organizations. But their popularity should not be conflated with effectiveness. Nearly one-third of employees found that open-door policies were far from reliable. Supervisors with open-door policies aggressively responded to employees bringing concerns, breached confidentiality of complaints waged against coworkers, and failed to respond to important issues, leading employees to say: "Even though you were told that the door is open, God help you if you walked through it" (ibid., p. 324) and, "As much as there is an open door, you have to be careful of what you say when you walk through it" (ibid., p. 332). Yet employees maintained faith in open-door policies, which they believed had the greatest potential to address employee voice. And they determined that these policies failed primarily when breaches of confidentiality occurred. Basically, employees expected managers operating with open-door policies to be communicatively adept, able to recognize employees' desires to be heard and understood, and balance that with employees' needs to have problems proactively addressed. Managers effectively balanced these tensions by monitoring situations, by coaching employees through difficult circumstances, and by justifying why remedial action might be absent. Simply having an open-door policy, then, does not guarantee its success. Commitment from top management and obvious precautions against reprisal are critical for making it clear to employees that they can safely pass through open doors (McCabe, 1997).

Organizations also have implemented the role of devil's advocate in decision-making procedures as a voice mechanism. Accordingly, when debating decisions and discussing possible solutions, someone gets designated as the devil's advocate – charged with finding "everything that is wrong with the plan or position" (Nemeth et al., 2001). The notion of a devil's advocate has its roots in the Catholic Church, where it became an institutionalized part of the tribunals mandated for canonizing saints (Nemeth et al., 2001; Stanley, 1981). Historically the devil's advocate served to refute claims made about candidates' appropriateness for sainthood and ensured that the "best possible arguments" were heard so that church leaders could avoid "making unwise decisions" (Stanley, 1981, pp. 14–15). Widely adopted since, the practice can lead to the reexamination of positions, the consideration of additional alternatives, and the generation of better solutions (Nemeth et al., 2001).

People commonly assume that having a devil's advocate engenders less antagonism within groups and that it generates less dislike for dissenters. This is because it involves role playing rather than actual contestation and genuine disagreement. Knowing that someone may be feigning dissent has led to questions about the veracity of the technique. In fact, Nemeth and her colleagues (2001) stipulated that once people have faced a devil's advocate they may become confident that they have considered all alternatives. As a consequence, they may end up more certain about their initial position and more resistant to reconsidering it. In an empirical examination of devil's advocates versus actual dissenters, these researchers found that authentic dissenters and devil's advocates had similar effects on decision-making groups. Both provoked reports of conflict and dislike. Yet when it came to generating more and better solutions to proposed problems the authentic dissenter was far superior to the devil's advocate. Only the authentic dissenter was effective in influencing group outcomes. The researchers attributed this discrepancy to the fact that authentic dissenters have greater risk than someone instructed to maintain a position. This prompts ambiguity about the level of commitment a devil's advocate holds for a given position, which in turn neutralizes the role player's effectiveness. But for authentic dissenters "the stakes are much higher and far more integral to one's self" (Shahinpoor and Matt, 2007, p. 40). Moreover, people may argue differently with an authentic dissenter than they would with someone role playing. In either case, there are some clear limitations to consider when using devil's advocates as a dissent mechanism within organizations.

Evidently there are many options for how organizations solicit and respond to dissent, and, unlike cooking recipes or stock portfolios, there is no clear formula for determining what will work best. Rather, decisions about accommodating dissent need to be made in light of the specific demands of the work, the resources of the organization, and the features of the workforce – tailored "to fit the endemic operating characteristics of the company" (McCabe, 1997, p. 352). Furthermore, design and consideration of these programs should involve employees. As the NASA video discussed at the beginning of this chapter shows, employees may have considerably different experience with and attitudes about dissent compared with what management preaches. Whenever possible they should be involved in developing mechanisms designed to capture and harness organizational dissent.

While there is no specific formula for choosing and arranging voice mechanisms, there are some common considerations that cut across each: confidentiality, safety, consistency, and authenticity (Graham, 1986; Harlos, 2001; McCabe, 1997). The first two are considerations that sit with employees. Will the information employees share remain confidential? Will dissenting organizational members experience retaliation? Together these determine the viability of the voice mechanism – that is, the degree to which employees actually use the resource. The other two considerations reside with management. Can organizational leaders design authentic programs that employees can trust? Can management administer these programs consistently? These determine the efficacy of a dissent program.

Of course these considerations inform one another – relating

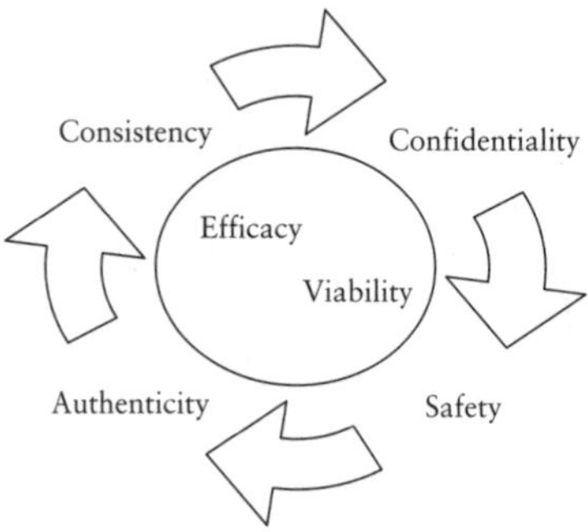

Figure 7.4 Determinants of the viability and efficacy of voice mechanisms

in a cyclical nature whereby the status of one shapes employee responses to another (see figure 7.4). So, for example, when employees believe that programs protect their confidentiality they will feel safe from retribution when using them. They will see these programs as having authenticity because they are administered consistently. In contrast, when programs are inconsistent, employees will question the confidentiality and safety they supposedly offer and end up suspecting their authenticity. The efficacy of programs builds through their authenticity and the consistency with which they are administered. Their viability – how readily employees use those programs – emerges from demonstrated adherence to standards of confidentiality and safety. Programs, then, become effective and viable when all four components work in concert. That is, viability and efficacy are products of consistent administration of authentic programs that protect the confidentiality and safety of employees. Conversely, programs loose credibility and purpose when they are administered inconsistently – authenticity declines as retribution and breaches of confidentiality continue unchecked.

Voice mechanisms are only part of the story. The rest of the plot unfolds with organizational climates and cultures that tolerate and respond well to dissent (Hegstrom, 1990; Graham, 1986; Kassing, 1997, 2000a; Tourish, 2005). Certainly the mechanisms discussed here will contribute to organizational climates that either embrace or reject organizational dissent. But what else can organizations do in this regard? How can they create workplaces that embrace dissent as a viable part of daily operations? As an asset that helps organizations move forward? The final section of this chapter offers some recommendations.

Organizational Recommendations for Cultivating Dissent

Graham (1986) suggests that organizations which value and cultivate dissent emphasize continuous learning and reflection, respect for individual conscience, development of interpersonal trust, and the promotion of independent thought and action among employees. Others call for a flattening of the hierarchy (Hegstrom, 1990; Tourish, 2005). This can be achieved by removing or reducing status symbols of privilege such as reserved parking spaces, executive dining rooms, and large wage discrepancies between upper management and rank-and-file employees (Tourish, 2005). Status differentials can be addressed communicatively as well.

Hegstrom, for example, calls for flattening "the hierarchy, in a communicative sense at least, to reduce the status differential between organizational aristocrats and the middle working classes" (1990, p. 146). He looks to Semco, a Brazilian company that manufactures a range of products, as an example of this philosophy in action. Here decisions are made democratically by people closest to the issues. A host of methods that ensure employee voice and representation are present throughout the enterprise. And company president Ricardo Semler's attitude about organizational dissent is at once historical and contemporary. He applies the historical imperative for conscientious dissent to the contemporary shop floor by associating dissenters with folks such as Henry David Thoreau and Thomas Paine, thereby recognizing the importance of seeing civil disobedience not merely as a sign of revolution, but rather as a necessary step for questioning and realigning commonsense practices that need improvement. Semco as a company and Semler as a president have shown how an organization can develop a climate over time that welcomes and utilizes organizational dissent.

Managers have been creative in their attempts to signal openness to dissent. One, for example, closed each staff meeting with a "satisfaction check." This involved asking staff members to give an overall numerical assessment, ranging from 1 (very dissatisfied) to 7 (very satisfied), to indicate their satisfaction with an operating policy or decision made by the manager. Employee feedback was submitted anonymously, with dissatisfactory reports being shared and discussed in subsequent meetings (Lindo, 1992). A retail manager reported using a "sacred cow roundup" every few months to give her employees an opportunity to dissent about processes traditionally deemed off limits. The practice helped identify issues that interfered with employees' ability to perform their jobs well and created an environment where staff members were "willing to share their frustrations in an open, nonthreatening way" (ibid., p. 16). And a manager in an engineering firm referred to dissenters as "guardian angels" who provided feedback that was tough to hear from a personal-pride standpoint, but extremely helpful when it came to improving processes and avoiding mistakes.

These efforts demonstrate how open dialogue and discussion forums can stimulate dissent (Gottlieb and Sanzgiri, 1996). They provide a valuable link between management and employees that allows for the exchange of ideas – even dissenting opinions – and for the constant evaluation and reevaluation of operating procedures. Reviewing communication systems to ensure that they have the utility to capture dissent should entail examining the vocabulary that sustains such systems. The popular mantra "don't bring me problems, bring me solutions" should be called into question, for instance (Tourish, 2005). Doing so will dislodge consent as standard operating procedure. Tourish adeptly suggests that positive feedback should be subjected to the same standards of scrutiny as dissent usually is. That is, "Managers should adopt a thoroughly questioning attitude to all feedback from those with a lower status, and treat unremittingly positive feedback with considerable skepticism" (ibid., p. 496). Dissecting positive feedback brings to light important questions. What does someone gain by flattering management with positive feedback and lose by expressing dissent? Managers should be trained to recognize and question overly consensual feedback and "to be open, receptive and responsive to dissent" (ibid., p. 498). Furthermore, CEOs and upper management should model openness and receptiveness to dissent.

Aside from cultivating dissent generally, there are particular steps organizations can take to receive and address reports of unethical behavior and organizational misconduct (see table 7.1). Dealing effectively with wrongdoing is important. Mishandling such claims will signal that misconduct can continue and that employees should not bother reporting it. Thus, leaders need to operate with integrity and social conscience, to attend "to what is right, proper, and fair" by making ethics "a key part of dialogue, discussion, and actions" (Gottlieb and Sanzgiri, 1996, p. 1283).

Defense contractor Sundstrand Corporation acknowledged the need to bootstrap its reporting practices after facing a $227 million judgment for ethical violations in the mid-1980s. Company transgressions led to a tarnished image and a sizeable drop in stock values. One outcome of the company's cultural makeover was the development of ethics awareness committees at all of its facilities. The three-person committees comprise a manager, a human resources staff member, and an employee from the shop or clerical pool. The committees meet every other month, and minutes from the meetings are sent to the director of business conduct and ethics. Committees are empowered to solve minor issues immediately, but must consult with the director when major issues arise (Benson and Ross, 1998).

Organizations can be better equipped to accept and address whistleblower reports by doing the following (Miceli et al., 2009):

- focus on the alleged wrongdoing and not on the source of the complaint;
- investigate allegations fully and fairly;
- respond to well-founded complaints with swift corrective action;
- acknowledge successful exposure and termination of wrongdoing when confidentiality measures allow;
- craft and make available multiple communication channels for reporting wrongdoing.

Table 7.1 Organizational recommendations for cultivating dissent

For dissent in general

1. Emphasize continuous learning and reflection.
2. Respect individual conscience.
3. Develop interpersonal trust among and between employees.
4. Promote independent thinking.
5. Encourage employees to take action.
6. Flatten hierarchies through the removal of status differentials.
7. Give employees decision-making authority.
8. Recognize and promote the value of dissent.
9. Check satisfaction and question sacred cows.
10. Develop practices to hear dissent regularly, informally, and in non-threatening settings.
11. Create forums for dialogue and discussion.
12. Empower employees to be decision-makers.
13. Review the capacity of communication systems to accommodate dissent.
14. Scrutinize positive feedback as closely as critical feedback.
15. Train managers to be open, receptive, and responsive to dissent.
16. Model openness and receptiveness to dissent.

For whistleblowing in particular

1. Operate with integrity and social conscience.
2. Emphasize ethics as a key part of dialogue, discussion, and actions.
3. Focus attention on the wrongdoing rather than on the source of the complaint.
4. Investigate allegations fully and fairly.
5. Respond to substantiated allegations with swift corrective action.
6. Acknowledge the successful extinguishing of organizational wrongdoing.
7. Make several channels for reporting misconduct available.
8. Inspire vigilance to shared organizational standards.
9. Foster employee engagement.
10. Create and use viable and credible methods for soliciting reports of wrongdoing.
11. Empower employees to report wrongdoing.
12. Instill accountability for reporting wrongdoing.
13. Extinguish retaliation practices.
14. Protect employees who report wrongdoing.
15. Promote whistleblowing as a courageous act.

The first four help management establish a track record for effectively stamping out organizational misconduct and recognize and celebrate the importance of employee reporting. The last gives employees the opportunity to report wrongdoing to audiences that provide comfort and safety.

In addition to these suggestions, Berry (2004) offers several characteristics of organizational culture necessary for facilitating dissent, particularly whistleblowing. The first is vigilance, realized through shared commitment to organizational standards. Standards must be commonly known so that employees can identify wrongdoing when it occurs. In addition, "a mindful watchfulness for threats to organizational integrity" must be cultivated (ibid., p. 3). Engagement is another important characteristic. Put simply, employees will be more likely to report wrongdoing when they feel they are legitimately involved with their respective organizations. This happens when organizations foster commitment and identification among employees. Credibility should be evident too. Employees must believe in the viability of voice mechanisms offered by their organization. Credibility builds when trustworthy voice mechanisms are in place and employees use them readily. Empowerment – the degree to which employees feel that they are enabled and expected to report wrongdoing – follows. Organizational members who feel empowered will recognize that they have some accountability to their organizations and their coworkers. Thus, accountability is an important characteristic as well. Organizations should foster climates that instill accountability in employees – ensuring that all members understand that reporting wrongdoing is important to the health and well-being of the enterprise.

The aforementioned attributes of organizational culture do much to reduce fears about retaliation. But they do not remove them entirely, because dissent is inherently risk-laden (Waldron and Kassing, 2011). That is why Berry (2004) argues that courage is an additional and critical attribute of organizational cultures that facilitate whistleblowing. Courage can be addressed through protections that provide dissenters with assurances about safety and confidentiality. And it can be realized through clear regard for, articulation of, and adherence to governmental mandates designed to protect whistleblowers. Organizational cultures need to promote whistleblowing as a courageous act – one that emerges from a sense of duty rather than an absence of loyalty.

Time Again

In 2010 much of the world sank deeper into large-scale financial crisis. In May of that year three women once again appeared on the cover of *Time* magazine. They did not share the same defiant look displayed by the whistleblowers celebrated nearly a decade earlier. Instead, they appeared serious and self-assured – imposing, actually. They appeared ready for the unique challenge bestowed upon them. The cover text referred to them in large bold-face type as "The New Sheriffs of Wall Street" – appointed in various capacities to combat the consensus-laden practices that gave way to the financial collapse. They are Securities and Exchange Committee (SEC) Chair Mary Schapiro, Federal Deposit Insurance Corporation (FDIC) Chair Sheila Blair, and Troubled Asset Relief Program (TARP) Oversight Panel Chair Elizabeth Warren. From their respective posts, each aims to clean up the financial sector by welcoming dissent where it has been absent. As women in a traditionally male-dominated industry, they have stood apart for many years as outsiders in their own field. Positioned as such, the "new sheriffs" understand all too well the power of dissenting opinions and the marginalization that accompanies those opinions. And they have what women around Washington call "amplification" – the "extra juice that comes when powerful figures join forces to speak up against entrenched interests" (Scherer, 2010, p. 27). They could be just the right women for the job, able at last to make dissent a valued commodity on Wall Street.

Will NASA continue to make strides in its battle to be more culturally receptive to dissenting voices? Or will it revert to autocratic models of operation? Can it discover the aptitude and find the courage to cultivate a bona fide organizational culture that embraces dissent? Time will tell. Evolution will be necessary, change unavoidable. The organization is facing major layoffs. The space shuttle program is winding down, and new directions for space exploration remain tentative at best. For NASA, the future is uncertain. Still, dissent will be there as the organization steps into its next phase of operation – as it faces the challenges and rewards of redefining itself. Dissent is ever present in organizations. It will surface somewhere, sometime. Will NASA be ready to hear it? Hopefully.

Discussion Questions

1 What does organizational dissent reveal about organizations? How can organizations benefit from accepting, hearing, and addressing organizational dissent?
2 Is there an optimal level of dissent that organizations can tolerate and absorb? What features of dissent are relevant when considering how much of it an organization can tolerate? What factors contribute to or detract from an organization's tolerance for dissent?
3 What mechanisms for capturing dissent have you observed in the places you have worked? Did employees trust these mechanisms? Did they believe they were effective? Did they use them readily?
4 What can organizations do to be better equipped to hear and respond to organizational dissent? What attributes of organizational culture are important for encouraging and handling organizational dissent?
5 What can NASA do as an organization to become more receptive to organizational dissent? NASA is not alone in its inability to process and respond to dissent well. Think of some other examples of companies that have suffered because they failed to respond well to organizational dissent. What can these companies do to improve their capacity for addressing organizational dissent?

References

Addison, C. (writer/director/producer) (2009) *391 San Antonio*. USA: Craig Addison [motion picture].

Alford, C. F. (2007) Whistle-blower narratives: the experience of the choiceless choice, *Social Research*, 74: 223–48.

Ashcraft, K. L. (2005) Resistance through consent: occupation identity, organizational form, and the maintenance of masculinity among commercial airline pilots, *Management Communication Quarterly*, 19: 67–90.

Ashforth, B. E., and Mael, F. A. (1998) The power of resistance: sustaining valued identities, in R. M. Kramer and M. A. Neale (eds), *Power and Influence in Organizations* (pp. 89–119). Thousand Oaks, CA: Sage.

Avtgis, T. A., Thomas-Maddox, C., Taylor, E., and Richardson, B. R. (2007) The influence of employee burnout syndrome on the expression of organizational dissent, *Communication Research Reports*, 24: 97–102.

Barker, J. R. (1993) Tightening the iron cage: concertive control in self-managing teams, *Administrative Science Quarterly*, 38: 408–37.

Barnett, T. R., and Cochran, D. S. (1991) Making room for the whistleblower, *Human Resources Magazine*, 36(4): 58–61.

Baty, P. (2002) Whistleblowers: serial litigant accuses race council of racism, *Times Higher Education Supplement*, November 15. Retrieved from: www.timeshighereducation.co.uk/story.asp?storyCode=172976§ioncode=26.

Bergman, L. (producer) (1996) *60 Minutes: Dr. Jeffrey Wigand, PhD*, February 4. New York: CBS Corporation [television broadcast].

Berlin, L. R. (2001) Robert Noyce and the rise and fall of Fairchild Semiconductor, 1957–1968, *Business History Review*, 75: 63–101.

Benson, J. A., and Ross, D. L. (1998) Sundstrand: a case study in transformation of cultural ethics, *Journal of Business Ethics*, 17: 1517–27.

Berry, B. (2004) Organizational culture: a framework and strategies for facilitating employee whistleblowing, *Employee Responsibilities and Rights Journal*, 16: 1–11.

Bies, R. J., and Trip, T. M. (1998) Two faces of the powerless: coping with tyranny in organizations, in R. M. Kramer and M. A. Neale (eds), *Power and Influence in Organizations* (pp. 203–19). Thousand Oaks, CA: Sage.

Bishop, L., and Levine, D. I. (1999) Computer-mediated communication as employee voice: a case study, *Industrial & Labor Relations Review*, 52: 213–34.

Bodtker, A. M., and Jameson, J. K. (2001) Emotion in conflict formation and its transformation: application to organizational conflict management, *International Journal of Conflict Management*, 12: 259–75.

Bouville, M. (2008) Whistle-blowing and morality, *Journal of Business Ethics*, 81: 579–85.

Brachman, J. (2009) Al Qaeda's dissident, *Foreign Policy*, 176: 40–1.

Broadfoot, K., Carlone, D., Medved, C. E., Aakhus, M., Gabor, E., and Taylor, K. (2008) Meaning/ful work and organizational communication: questioning boundaries, positionalities, and engagements, *Management Communication Quarterly*, 22: 152–61.

Carey, S. C. (2010) The use of repression as a response to domestic dissent, *Political Studies*, 58: 167–86.

Castor, T., and Cooren, F. (2006) Organizations as hybrid forms of life: the implications of the selection of agency in problem formulation, *Management Communication Quarterly*, 19: 570–600.

Cavanaugh, M., and Noe, R. (1999) Antecedents and consequences of relational components of the new psychological contract, *Journal of Organizational Behavior*, 20: 323–40.

Cheney, G. (1995) Democracy in the workplace: theory and practice from the perspective of communication, *Journal of Applied Communication Research*, 23: 167–200.

Cheney, G., and Ashcraft, K. L. (2007) Considering "the professional" in communication studies: implications for theory and research within and beyond the boundaries of organizational communication, *Communication Theory*, 17: 146–75.

Cheney, G., and Cloud, D. L. (2006) Doing democracy, engaging the material: employee participation and labor activity in the age of market globalization, *Management Communication Quarterly*, 19: 501–40.

Chiles, A. M., and Zorn, T. E. (1995) Empowerment in organizations: employees' perceptions of the influences of empowerment, *Journal of Applied Communication Research*, 23: 1–25.

Chronicle of Dissent (2007) Paying the penalty for free expression online, *Index on Censorship*, 36: 122–31.

Church, A. H., Gallus, J. A., Desrosiers, E. I., and Waclawski, J. (2007) Speak-up all you whistle-blowers: an OD perspective on the impact of employee hotlines on organizational culture, *Organization Development Journal*, 25: 159–67.

Citigroup executives (2010) "We warned about mortgage risk," April 7. Retrieved from: www.c-spanvideo.org/program/Day1Pan [video file].

Collins, J. C., and Porras, J. I. (1994) *Built to Last: Successful Habits of Visionary Companies*. New York: HarperCollins.

Collinson, D. (1994) Strategies of resistance: power, knowledge and subjectivity in the workplace, in J. M. Jermier, D. Knights, and W. R. Nord (eds), *Resistance and Power in Organizations* (pp. 25–68). London: Routledge.

Collinson, D. (2005) Dialectics of leadership, *Human Relations*, 58: 1419–42.

Corkery, M. (2010) Now meet two WaMu whistleblowers, *Wall Street Journal Blogs: Deal Journal*, April 13. Retrieved from: http://blogs.wsj.com/deals/2010/04/13/now-meet-two-wamu-whistleblowers/tab/article/.

Cotton, J. L. (1993) *Employee Involvement: Methods for Improving Performance and Work Attitudes*. Newbury Park, CA: Sage.

Cowley, J. (1998) *Big Moon Tortilla*. Honesdale, PA: Boyd Mills Press.

Croucher, S. M., Braziunaite, R., Homsey, D., Pillai, G., Saxena, J., Saldanha, A., Joshi, V., Jafri, I., Choudhary, P., Bose, L., and Agarwal, K. (2009) Organizational dissent and argumentativeness: a comparative analysis between American and Indian Organizations, *Journal of Intercultural Communication Research*, 38: 175–91.

Crowe, C. (writer/director) (1996) *Jerry Maguire* [motion picture]. Culver City, CA: TriStar Pictures.

Daft, R. L. (2010) *Organizational Theory and Design*. 10th edn, Mason, OH: South-Western Cenage Learning.

Dash, E., and Sorkin, A. R. (2008) Government seizes WaMu and sells some assets. *New York Times*, September 25. Retrieved from: http://www.nytimes.com/2008/09/26/business/26wamu.html.

de Forest, J. (2008) The 1958 Harlem school boycott: parental activism and the struggle for educational equity in New York City, *Urban Review*, 40: 21–41.

De Maria, W., and Jan, C. (1996) Behold the shut-eyed sentry! Whistleblower perspectives on government failure to correct wrongdoing, *Crime, Law & Social Change*, 24: 151–66.

Deetz, S. (1982) Critical interpretive research in organizational communication, *Western Journal of Speech Communication*, 46: 131–49.

Deetz, S. (1992) *Democracy in the Age of Corporate Colonization: Developments in Communication and the Politics of Everyday Life*. Albany, NY: State University of New York Press.

Deetz, S., and Mumby, D. K. (1990) Power, discourse, and the workplace: reclaiming the critical tradition, in J. Anderson (ed.), *Communication Yearbook*, 11 (pp. 18–47). Beverley Hills: Sage.

Dixon, M. A. (2004) Silencing the lambs: the Catholic Church's response to the 2002 sexual abuse scandal, *Journal of Communication and Religion*, 27: 63–86.

Dooley, R. S., and Fryxell, G. E. (1999) Attaining decision quality and commitment from dissent: the moderating effects of loyalty and competence in strategic decision-making teams, *Academy of Management Journal*, 42: 389–402.

Duane, A., and Finnegan, P. (2007) Dissent, protest and transformative action: an exploratory study of staff reactions to electronic monitoring and control of e-mail systems in one company based in Ireland, *Information Resource Management Journal*, 20: 1–13.

Dundon, T., Wilkinson, A., Marchington, M., and Ackers, P. (2005) The management of voice in non-union organisations: managers' perspectives, *Employee Relations*, 27: 307–19.

Dworkin, T. M., and Baucus, M. S. (1998) Internal vs. external whistleblowers: a comparison of whistleblowing processes, *Journal of Business Ethics*, 17: 1281–98.

Edmondson, V. C., and Munchus, G. (2007) Managing the unwanted truth: a framework for dissent strategy, *Journal of Organizational Change Management*, 20: 747–60.

Eichenwald, K. (2000) *The Informant*. New York: Random House.

employeesuggestionbox.com (n.d.) Employee suggestion box: on-demand idea collaboration suite. Retrieved from: https://www.employeesuggestionbox.com/Intro/overview.aspx.

Ewing, D. (1977) *Freedom inside the Organization*. New York: Dutton.

Fairhurst, G. T., and Putnam, L. (2004) Organizations as discursive constructions, *Communication Theory*, 14: 5–26.

Fairhurst, G. T., Cooren, F., and Cahill, D. J. (2002) Discursiveness, contradiction, and unintended consequences in successive downsizings, *Management Communication Quarterly*, 15: 501–40.

Farace, R. V., Monge, P. R., and Russell, H. M. (1977). *Communicating and Organizing*. Reading, MA: Addison-Wesley.

Farrell, D. (1983) Exit, voice, loyalty, and neglect as responses to job dissatisfaction: a multidimensional scaling study. *Academy of Management Journal*, 26, 596–607.

Farrell, D., and Rusbult, C. E. (1992) Exploring the exit, voice, loyalty, and neglect typology: The influence of job satisfaction, quality of alternatives, and investment size, *Employee Responsibilities and Rights Journal*, 5: 201–18.

Feistner, E., and Holl, A. (2006) *Mono-Perspective Views of Multi-Perspectivity: Information Systems Modeling and "The Blind Men and the Elephant."* Göteborg, SE: Växjö University Press.

Finet, D. (1994) Sociopolitical consequences of organizational expression, *Journal of Communication*, 44: 114–31.

Gandossy, R., and Sonnenfeld, J. (2005) I see nothing, I hear nothing: culture, corruption and apathy, *International Journal of Disclosure and Governance*, 2: 228–43.

Gandz, J. (2001) Globalization and the legitimacy of dissent, *Ivey Business Journal*, 66: 17–21.

Garner, J. T. (2009a) Strategic dissent: expressions of organizational dissent motivated by influence goals, *International Journal of Strategic Management*, 3: 34–51.

Garner, J. T. (2009b) When things go wrong at work: an exploration of organizational dissent messages, *Communication Studies*, 60: 197–218.

Garner, J. T., and Wargo, M. (2009) Feedback from the pew: a dual-perspective exploration of organizational dissent in churches, *Journal of Communication and Religion*, 32: 375–400.

Garner, J. T., Leahy, A. K., Rubenstein, R. A., and Templeton, K. (2008) Spheres of influence: dissent networks at Enron. Paper presented at the meeting of the International Communication Association, Montreal, Canada, May.

Gayle, B. M., and Preiss, R. W. (1998) Assessing emotionality in organizational conflicts, *Management Communication Quarterly*, 12: 280–302.

Gibbs, J. C. (2003) *Moral Development and Reality: Beyond Theories of Kohlberg and Hoffman*. Thousand Oaks, CA: Sage.

Goodboy, A. K., Chory, R. M., and Dunleavy, K. N. (2009) Organizational dissent as a function of organizational justice, *Communication Research Reports*, 25: 255–65.

Goodheart, A. (2006) 10 days that changed history, *New York Times*, July 2. Retrieved from: www.nytimes.com/2006/07/02/weekinreview/02goodheart.html?ex=1151899200&en=8c51bd1f352d9f24&ei=5087%0.

Gorden, W. I. (1988) Range of employee voice, *Employee Responsibilities and Rights Journal*, 4: 283–99.

Gorden, W. I., and Infante, D. A. (1987) Employee rights: content, argumentativeness, verbal aggressiveness and career satisfaction, in C. A. B. Osigweh (ed.), *Communicating Employee Responsibilities and Rights: A Modern Management Mandate* (pp. 149–63). Westport, CT: Greenwood Press.

Gorden, W. I., and Infante, D. A. (1991) Test of a communication model of organizational commitment, *Communication Quarterly*, 39: 144–55.

Gorden, W. I., Holmberg, K.-A., and Heisey, D. R. (1994) Equality and the Swedish work environment, *Employee Responsibilities and Rights Journal*, 7: 141–60.

Gossett, L. M., and Kilker, J. (2006) My job sucks: examining counterinstitutional web sites as locations for organizational member voice, dissent, and resistance, *Management Communication Quarterly*, 20: 63–90.

Gottlieb, J. Z., and Sanzgiri, J. (1996) Towards an ethical dimension of decision making in organizations, *Journal of Business Ethics*, 15: 1275–85.

Graham, J. W. (1986) Principled organizational dissent: a theoretical essay, in B. M. Staw and L. L. Cummings (eds), *Research in Organizational Behavior*, Vol. 8 (pp. 1–52). Greenwich, CT: JAI Press.

Graham, J. W., and Keeley, M. (1992) Hirschman's loyalty construct, *Employee Responsibilities and Rights Journal*, 5: 191–200.

Greenfieldboyce, N. (2009) Astronaut's video satirizes NASA bureaucracy, *National Public Radio*, February 9. Podcast retrieved from: http://www.npr.org/templates/story/story.php?storyId=100346538.

Gundlach, M. J., Douglas, S. C., and Martinko, M. J. (2003) The decision to blow the whistle: a social information processing framework, *Academy of Management Review*, 28: 107–23.

Hahon, B. (producer), Verboud, M., and Viallet, J. (directors) (2006) *Kill the Messenger*. France: Studio Canal [motion picture].

Hale, W. (2009) Stifling dissent, January 29 [web log comment]. Retrieved from http://blogs.nasa.gov/cm/blog/waynehalesblog/posts/post_1233287218005.html.

Hardy, C., and Clegg, S. R. (1999) Some dare call it power, in S. R. Clegg and C. Hardy (eds), *Studying Organization: Theory and Method* (pp. 368–87). Thousand Oaks, CA: Sage.

Harlos, K. P. (2001) When organizational voice systems fail: more on the deaf-ear syndrome and frustration effects, *Journal of Applied Behavioral Science*, 37: 324–42.

Harris, D. B. (1957) A scale for measuring attitudes of social responsibility in children, *Journal of Abnormal and Social Psychology*, 55: 322–6.

Harvey, M. G., Heames, J. T., Richey, R. G., and Leonard, N. (2006) Bullying: from the playground to the boardroom, *Journal of Leadership and Organizational Studies*, 12: 1–11.

Hegstrom, T. G. (1990) Mimetic and dissent conditions in organizational rhetoric, *Journal of Applied Communication Research*, 18: 141–52.

Hegstrom, T. G. (1995) Focus on organizational dissent: a functionalist response to criticism, in J. Lehtonen (ed.), *Critical Perspectives on Communication Research and Pedagogy* (pp. 83–94). St Ingbert, Germany: Rohrig University Press.

Hegstrom, T. G. (1999) Reasons for rocking the boat: principles and personal problems, in H. K. Geissner, A. F. Herbig, and E. Wessela (eds), *Business Communication in Europe* (pp. 179–94). Tostedt, Germany: Attikon.

Henik, E. (2008) Mad as hell or scared stiff? The effects of value conflict and emotions on potential whistle-blowers, *Journal of Business Ethics*, 80: 111–19.

Hirschman, A. O. (1970) *Exit, Voice, and Loyalty*. Cambridge, MA: Harvard University Press.

Hodson, R. (1995) Worker resistance: an underdeveloped concept in the sociology of work, *Economic and Industrial Democracy*, 16: 79–110.

Hofstede, G. (2001) *Culture's Consequences: Comparing Values, Behaviors, Institutions, and Organizations across Nations*. Thousand Oaks, CA: Sage.

Hubbell, A. P., and Chory-Assad, R. M. (2005) Motivating factors: perceptions of justice and their relationship with managerial and organizational trust, *Communication Studies*, 56: 47–70.

Hwang, S. L., and Geyelin, M. (1996) Getting personal: Brown & Williamson has 500-page dossier attacking chief critic, *Wall Street Journal*, February 1, p. A1.

Jones, C. (2008) Dissent and protest in the House of Lords, 1641–1998: an attempt to reconstruct the procedures involved in entering a protest into the journals of the House of Lords, *Parliamentary History*, 27: 309–29.

Jubb, P. B. (1999) Whistleblowing: a restrictive definition and interpretation, *Journal of Business Ethics*, 21: 77–94.

Kassing, J. W. (1997) Articulating, antagonizing, and displacing: a model of employee dissent, *Communication Studies*, 48: 311–32.

Kassing, J. W. (1998) Development and validation of the Organizational Dissent Scale, *Management Communication Quarterly*, 12: 183–229.

Kassing, J. W. (2000a) Exploring the relationship between workplace freedom of speech, organizational identification, and employee dissent, *Communication Research Reports*, 17 : 387–96.

Kassing, J. W. (2000b) Investigating the relationship between superior–subordinate relationship quality and employee dissent, *Communication Research Reports*, 17 : 58–70.

Kassing, J. W. (2002) Speaking up: identifying employees' upward dissent strategies, *Management Communication Quarterly*, 16: 187–209.

Kassing, J. W. (2005) Speaking up competently: a comparison of perceived competence in upward dissent strategies, *Communication Research Reports*, 22: 227–34.

Kassing, J. W. (2007) Going around the boss: exploring the consequences of circumvention, *Management Communication Quarterly*, 21: 55–74.

Kassing, J. W. (2008) Consider this: a comparison of factors contributing to expressions of employee dissent, *Communication Quarterly*, 56: 342–55.

Kassing, J. W. (2009a) In case you didn't hear me the first time: an examination of repetitious upward dissent, *Management Communication Quarterly*, 22: 416–36.

Kassing, J. W. (2009b) Breaking the chain of command: making sense of employee circumvention, *Journal of Business Communication*, 46: 311–34.

Kassing, J. W., and Armstrong, T. A. (2001) Examining the association of job tenure, employment history, and organizational status with employee dissent, *Communication Research Reports*, 18: 264–73.

Kassing, J. W., and Armstrong, T. A. (2002) Someone's going to hear about this: examining the association between dissent-triggering events and employees' dissent expression, *Management Communication Quarterly*, 16: 39–65.

Kassing, J. W., and Avtgis, T. A. (1999) Examining the relationship between organizational dissent and aggressive communication, *Management Communication Quarterly*, 13(1): 76–91.

Kassing, J. W., and Avtgis, T. A. (2001) Dissension in the organization as a function of control expectancies, *Communication Research Reports*, 18: 118–27.

Kassing, J. W., and DiCioccio, R. L. (2004) Testing a workplace experience explanation of displaced dissent, *Communication Reports*, 17: 111–20.

Kassing, J. W., and McDowell, Z. (2008) Talk about fairness: exploring the relationship between procedural justice and employee dissent, *Communication Research Reports*, 25: 1–10.

Kassing, J. W., Piemonte, N. M., Goman, C. C., and Mitchell, C. A. (in press)

Dissent expression as an indictor of work engagement and intention to leave, *Journal of Business Communication*.
Katz, D., and Kahn, R. L. (1978) *The Social Psychology of Organizations*. 2nd edn, New York: Wiley.
Keenan, J. (2002) Comparing Indian and American managers on whistleblowing, *Employee Responsibilities and Rights Journal*, 14: 79–89.
Keenan, J. (2007) Comparing Chinese and American managers on whistleblowing, *Employee Responsibilities and Rights Journal*, 19: 85–94.
King, G. (1999) The implications of an organization's structure on whistleblowing, *Journal of Business Ethics*, 20: 315–26.
King, W. C., and Miles, E. W. (1990) What we know – and don't know – about measuring conflict: an examination of the ROCI-II and the OCCI Conflict Instruments, *Management Communication Quarterly*, 4: 222–43.
Kipnis, D., and Schmidt, S. M. (1985) The language of persuasion, *Psychology Today*, April: 40–6.
Kipnis, D., and Schmidt, S. M. (1988) Upward-influence styles: relationship with performance evaluations, salary, and stress, *Administrative Science Quarterly*, 33: 528–42.
Kipnis, D., Schmidt, S., and Wilkinson, I. (1980) Intraorganizational influence tactics: explorations in getting one's way, *Journal of Applied Psychology*, 65: 440–52.
Klaas, B. S., and DeNisi, A. S. (1989) Managerial reactions to employee dissent: the impact of grievance activity on performance ratings, *Academy of Management Journal*, 32: 705–17.
Kohlberg, L. (1984) *Essays on Moral Development: The Psychology of Moral Development*. San Francisco: Harper & Row.
Kohn, D. (producer) (2004) *60 Minutes: Lost in Translation*, August 8. New York: CBS Corporation [television broadcast].
Kowalewski, D., and Hoover, D. (1994) Dissent and repression in the world-system: a model of future dynamics, *International Journal of Comparative Sociology*, 35: 161–87.
Krefting, L. A., and Powers, K. J. (1998) Exercised voice as management failure: implications of willing compliance theories of management and individualism for *de facto* employee voice, *Employee Responsibilities and Rights Journal*, 11: 263–77.
Krehbiel, P. J., and Cropanzano, R. (2000) Procedural justice, outcome favorability and emotion, *Social Justice Research*, 13: 339–60.
Krone, K. J. (1992) A comparison of organizational, structural, and relationship effects on subordinates' upward influence choices, *Communication Quarterly*, 40: 1–15.
Kuhn, T., and Ashcraft, K. L. (2003) Corporate scandal and the theory of the firm: formulating the contributions of organizational communication studies, *Management Communication Quarterly*, 17: 20–57.

Kuhn, T., Golden, A. G., Jorgenson, J., Buzzanell, P. M., Berkelaar, B. L., Kisselburth, L. G., and Cruz, D. (2008) Cultural discourses and discursive resources for meaningful work: constructing and disrupting identities in contemporary capitalism, *Management Communication Quarterly*, 22: 162–71.

Lacayo, R., and Ripley, A. (2002) Persons of the year, *Time*, 160, December 30: 32–3.

Larson, G. S., and Tompkins, P. K. (2005) Ambivalence and resistance: a study of management in a concertive control system, *Communication Monographs*, 72: 1–21.

Leary, M. R., and Kowalski, R. M. (1990) Impression management: a literature review and two-component model, *Psychological Bulletin*, 107: 34–47.

Leck, J. D., and Saunders, D. M. (1992) Hirschman's loyalty: attitude or behavior? *Employee Responsibilities and Rights Journal*, 5: 219–30.

Lewicki, R. J., Weiss, S. E., and Lewin, D. (1992) Models of conflict, negotiation and third party intervention: a review and synthesis, *Journal of Organizational Behavior*, 13: 209–52.

Lilienthal, P. (2002) If you give your employees a voice, do you listen? *Journal for Quality and Participation*, 25: 38–40.

Lindo, D. K. (1992) Dissent can be your biggest asset, *SuperVision*, 53: 14–16.

Lutgen-Sandvik, P. (2006) Take this job and . . . : quitting and other forms of resistance to workplace bullying, *Communication Monographs*, 73: 406–33.

Lutgen-Sandvik, P. (2008) Intensive remedial identity work: responses to workplace bullying trauma and stigmatization, *Organization*, 15: 97–119.

Lutgen-Sandvik, P., Tracy, S. J., and Alberts, J. K. (2007) Burned by bullying in the American workplace: prevalence, perception, degree and impact, *Journal of Management Studies*, 44: 837–62.

Maclaglan, P. (1998) *Management and Morality*. Thousand Oaks, CA: Sage.

Maher, T. V., and Peterson, L. (2008) Time and country variation in contentious politics: multilevel modeling of dissent and repression, *International Journal of Sociology*, 38: 52–81.

Markham, A. (1996) Designing discourse: a critical analysis of strategic ambiguity and workplace control, *Management Communication Quarterly*, 9: 389–421.

Martin, B., and Rifkin, W. (2004) The dynamics of employee dissent: whistleblowers and organizational jiu-jitsu, *Public Organization Review*, 4: 221–38.

Maxwell, J. C. (2003) *Ethics 101: What Every Leader Needs to Know*. New York: Center Street.

McCabe, D. M. (1997) Alternative dispute resolution and employee voice in nonunion employment: an ethical analysis of organizational due process procedures and mechanisms – the case of the United States, *Journal of Business Ethics*, 16: 349–56.

McDougall, W. (2009) *Born to Run: A Hidden Tribe, Superathletes, and the Greatest Race the World has Never Seen*. New York: Alfred A. Knopf.

Mesmer-Magnus, J. R., and Viswesvaran, C. (2008) Whistleblowing in organizations: an examination of correlates of whistleblowing intentions, actions, and retaliation, *Journal of Business Ethics*, 62: 277–97.

Miceli, M. P., and Near, J. P. (1992) *Blowing the Whistle: The Organizational and Legal Implications for Companies and Employees*. New York: Lexington Books.

Miceli, M. P., and Near, J. P. (2002) What makes whistleblowers effective? Three field studies, *Human Relations*, 55: 455–79.

Miceli, M. P., Near, J. P., and Dworkin, T. M. (2009) A word to the wise: how managers and policy-makers can encourage employees to report wrongdoing, *Journal of Business Ethics*, 86: 379–96.

Michels, R. (1962) *Political Parties: A Sociological Study of the Oligarchical Tendencies of Modern Democracy*. New York: Free Press.

Miller, K. I. (2008) *Organizational Communication: Approaches and Processes*. 5th edn, Belmont, CA: Thomson Wadsworth.

Miller, K. I., Ellis, B. H., Zook, E. G., and Lyles, J. S. (1990) An integrated model of communication, stress, and burnout in the workplace, *Communication Research*, 17: 300–26.

Milliken, F. J., Morrison, E. W., and Hewlin, P. F. (2003) An exploratory study of employee silence: issues that employees don't communicate upward and why, *Journal of Management Studies*, 40: 1453–76.

Monge, P., and Contractor, N. (2003) *Theories of Communication Networks*. New York: Oxford University Press.

Monge, P., and Poole, M. S. (2008) The evolution of organizational communication, *Journal of Communication*, 58: 679–92.

Moody, J., Bebensee, M., and Carter, H. (2009) Whistle-blowers and technology: a cross-cultural framework for effective corporate malfeasance reporting systems, *Journal of International Business Research*, 7: 89–105.

Moorman, R. H. (1991) Relationship between organizational justice and organizational citizenship behaviors: do fairness perceptions influence employee citizenship? *Journal of Applied Psychology*, 76: 845–55.

Morris, W. (ed.) (1969) *The American Heritage Dictionary of the English Language*. New York: Houghton Mifflin.

Morse, J., and Bower, A. (2002) The party crasher, *Time*, *160*, December 30: 53–6.

Mumby, D. K. (1988) *Communication and Power in Organizations: Discourse, Ideology and Domination*. Norwood, NJ: Ablex.

Mumby, D. K. (2005) Theorizing resistance in organization studies, *Management Communication Quarterly*, 19: 19–44.

Mumby, D. K., and Stohl, C. (1991) Power and discourse in organization studies: absence and the dialectic of control, *Discourse & Society*, 2: 313–32.

Murphy, A. G. (1998) Hidden transcripts of flight attendant resistance, *Management Communication Quarterly*, 11: 499–535.

Near, J. P., and Jensen, T. C. (1983) The whistleblowing process: retaliation and perceived effectiveness, *Work and Occupations*, 10: 3–28.

Near, J. P., and Miceli, M. P. (1985) Organizational dissidence: the case of whistle-blowing, *Journal of Business Ethics*, 4: 1–16.

Near, J. P., and Miceli, M. P. (1995) Effective whistle-blowing, *Academy of Management Review*, 20: 679–708.

Nemeth, C., Brown, K., and Rogers, J. (2001) Devil's advocate versus authentic dissent: stimulating quantity and quality, *European Journal of Social Psychology*, 31: 707–20.

Novak, J. M., and Sellnow, T. L. (2009) Reducing organizational risk through participatory communication, *Journal of Applied Communication Research*, 37: 349–73.

O'Connell, C. (2007) *The Elephant's Secret Sense: The Hidden Life of the Wild Herds of Africa*. Chicago: University of Chicago Press.

O'Connell Davidson, J. (1994) The sources and limits of resistance in a privatized utility, in J. M. Jermier, D. Knights, and W. R. Nord (eds), *Resistance and Power in Organizations* (pp. 69–101). London: Routledge.

O'Leary, R. (2006) *The Ethics of Dissent: Managing Guerrilla Government*. Washington, DC: CQ Press.

Pacanowsky, M. E. (1988) Communication in the empowering organization, in J. Anderson (ed.), *Communication Yearbook*, 11 (pp. 356–79). Beverley Hills, CA: Sage.

Pacanowsky, M. E., and O'Donnell-Trujillo, N. (1982) Communication and organizational cultures, *Western Journal of Speech Communication*, 2: 115–30.

Pacanowsky, M. E., and O'Donnell-Trujillo, N. (1983) Organizational communication as cultural performance, *Communication Monographs*, 50: 126–47.

Park, H., Blenkinsopp, J., Oktem, M. K., and Omurgonulsen, U. (2008) Cultural orientation and attitudes towards different forms of whistleblowing: a comparison of South Korea, Turkey and the UK, *Journal of Business Ethics*, 82: 929–39.

Payne, H. J. (2007) The role of organization-based self-esteem in employee dissent expression, *Communication Research Reports*, 24: 235–40.

PBS (Public Broadcasting Service) (1999) *The Traitorous Eight Traitorously Leave Shockley Semiconductor*. Retrieved from www.pbs.org/transistor/album1/eight/index.html.

Perry, K. L., Hegstrom, T. G., and Stull, J. B. (1994) Tandem Computers' town meetings: enhancing employee voice, in T. B. Joseph (ed.), *Visions of the Corporate Future: Tools and Techniques* (pp. 115–21). *Proceedings of the West Coast Conference on Corporate Communication*. Orange, CA: Chapman University.

Pierskalla, J. H. (2010) Protest, deterrence, and escalation: the strategic calculus of government repression, *Journal of Conflict Resolution*, 54: 117–45.

Porter, L. W., Allen, R. W., and Angle, H. L. (1981) The politics of upward influence in organizations, in B. M. Staw and L. L. Cummings (eds), *Research in Organizational Behavior*, Vol. 3 (pp. 109–49). Greenwich, CT: JAI Press.

Prasad, A., and Prasad, P. (1998) Everyday struggles at the workplace: the nature and implications of routine resistance in contemporary organizations, in P. A. Bamberger and W. J. Sonnenstuhl (eds), *Research in the Sociology of Organizations*, Vol. 16 (pp. 225–57). Greenwich, CT: JAI Press.

Putnam, L. L., and Pacanowsky, M. E. (eds) (1983) *Communication and Organizations: An Interpretive Approach*. Beverly Hills, CA: Sage.

Putnam, L. L., and Poole, M. S. (1987) Conflict and negotiation, in F. M. Jablin, L. L. Putnam, K. H. Roberts, and L. W. Porter (eds), *Handbook of Organizational Communication: An Interdisciplinary Perspective* (pp. 549–99). Newbury Park, CA: Sage.

Putnam, L. L., Grant, D., Michelson, G., and Cutcher, L. (2005) Discourse and resistance: targets, practices, and consequences, *Management Communication Quarterly*, 19: 5–18.

Rahim, M. A. (1986) *Managing Conflict in Organizations*. New York: Praeger.

Rahim, M. A., Garrett, J. E., and Buntzman, G. F. (1992) Ethics of managing interpersonal conflict in organizations, *Journal of Business Ethics*, 11: 423–32.

Rahim, M. A., Magner, N. R., and Shapiro, D. L. (2000) Do justice perceptions influence styles of handling conflict with supervisors? What justice perceptions, precisely? *International Journal of Conflict Management*, 11: 9–31.

Ray, L. K. (2002) The history of the per curiam opinion: consensus and individual expression on the Supreme Court, *Journal of Supreme Court History*, 27: 176–93.

Redding, W. C. (1985) Rocking boats, blowing whistles, and teaching speech communication, *Communication Education*, 34: 245–58.

Richardson, B. K., Wheeles, L. R., and Cunningham, C. (2008) Tattling on the teacher: a study of factors influencing peer reporting of teachers who violate standardized testing protocol, *Communication Studies*, 59: 202–19.

Ripley, A. (2002) The night detective, *Time*, *160*, December 30: 45–50.

Ripley, A., and Sieger, M. (2002) The special agent, *Time*, *160*, December 30: 34–40.

Romero, S., and Atlas, R. D. (2002) WorldCom's collapse: the overview, *New York Times*, July 22. Retrieved from: http://www.nytimes.com/2002/07/22/us/worldcom-s-collapse-the-overview-worldcom-files-for-bankruptcy-largest-us-case.html?pagewanted=1.

Rose, D. (2005) An inconvenient patriot, *Vanity Fair*, 541, September. Retrieved from www.informationclearinghouse.info/article9774.htm.

Rothschild, J., and Miethe, T. D. (1999) Whistleblower disclosures and management retaliation: the battle to control information, *Work and Occupations*, 26: 107–28.

Rothschild-Whitt, J. (1979) The collectivist organization: an alternative to rational bureaucratic models, *American Sociological Review*, 44: 509–27.

Rusbult, C., and Lowery, D. (1985) When bureaucrats get the blues: responses to dissatisfaction among federal employees, *Journal of Applied Social Psychology*, 15: 80–103.

Rusbult, C. E., Farrell, D., Rogers, G., and Mainous III, A. G. (1988) Impact of exchange variables on exit, voice, loyalty, and neglect: an integrative model of responses to declining job satisfaction, *Academy of Management Journal*, 31: 599–627.

Salin, D. (2003) Ways of explaining workplace bullying: a review of enabling, motivating and precipitating structures and processes in the work environment, *Human Relations*, 56: 1213–32.

Sanders, W. (1983) The first amendment and the government workplace: has the constitution fallen down on the job? *Western Journal of Speech Communication*, 47: 253–76.

Sanderson, J. (2009) "Thanks for fighting the good fight": cultivating dissent on blogmaverick.com, *Southern Communication Journal*, 74: 390–405.

Scherer, M. (2010) The new sheriffs of Wall Street, *Time*, 175, May 24: 22–7.

Schlenker, B. R. (1980) *Impression Management: The Self-Concept, Social Identity and Interpersonal Relations*. Monterey, CA: Brooks/Cole.

Schnall, D. J. (1977) Gush Emunim: Messianic dissent and Israeli politics, *Judaism*, 77: 148–60.

Schriesheim, C. A., and Hinkin, T. R. (1990) Influence tactics used by subordinates: a theoretical and empirical analysis and refinement of the Kipnis, Schmidt, and Wilkinson subscales, *Journal of Applied Psychology*, 75: 246–57.

Schwartz, M. (1996) The place of dissent in inquiry, learning, and reflection, *Peace & Change*, 21: 169–81.

Scott, C. R. (1997) Identification with multiple targets in a geographically dispersed organization, *Management Communication Quarterly*, 10: 491–522.

Scott, C. R. (2007) Communication and social identity theory: existing and potential connections in organizational identification research, *Communication Studies*, 58: 123–38.

Scott, C. R., Corman, S. R., and Cheney, G. (1998) Development of a situated-action theory of identification in the organization, *Communication Theory*, 8: 298–336.

Seeger, M. W. (1997) *Ethics and Organizational Communication*. Cresskill, NJ: Hampton Press.

Shahinpoor, N., and Matt, B. F. (2007) The power of one: dissent and organizational life, *Journal of Business Ethics*, 74: 37–48.

Sheppard, B. H. (1992). Conflict research as schizophrenia: The many faces of organizational conflict. *Journal of Organizational Behavior*, 13, 325–334.

Sinclair, A. L. (2003) The effects of justice and cooperation on team effectiveness, *Small Group Research*, 34: 74–100.

Siqueira, K. (2005) Political and militant wings within dissident movements and organizations, *Journal of Conflict Resolution*, 49: 218–36.

Smith, A. (2009) "Worky tickets": exploring dissent at work, *Qualitative Research in Accounting & Management*, 6: 14–25.

Sprague, J. A., and Ruud, G. L. (1988) Boat-rocking in the high technology culture, *American Behavioral Scientist*, 32: 169–93.

Stanley, J. D. (1981) Dissent in organizations, *Academy of Management Review*, 6: 13–19.

Stewart, L. P. (1980) "Whistle blowing": implications for organizational communication, *Journal of Communication*, 30(4): 90–101.

Stohl, C., and Cheney, G. (2001) Participatory processes/paradoxical practices: communication and the dilemmas of organizational democracy, *Management Communication Quarterly*, 14: 349–407.

Stohl, C., and Coombs, W. T. (1988) Cooperation or cooptation: an analysis of quality circle training manuals, *Management Communication Quarterly*, 2: 63–89.

Sunstein, C. R. (2003) *Why Societies Need Dissent*. Cambridge, MA: Harvard University Press.

Tavakoli, A. A., Keenan, J. P., and Crnjak-Karanovic, B. (2003) Culture and whistleblowing: an empirical study of Croatian and United States managers utilizing Hofstede's cultural dimensions, *Journal of Business Ethics*, 43: 49–64.

Tompkins, P. K. (2005) *Apollo, Challenger, Columbia: The Decline of the Space Program: A Study in Organizational Communication*. Los Angeles: Roxbury.

Tompkins, P. K., and Cheney, G. (1985) Communication and unobtrusive control in contemporary organizations, in R. D. McPhee and P. K. Tompkins (eds), *Organizational Communication: Traditional Themes and New Directions* (pp. 179–210). Beverly Hills, CA: Sage.

Tourish, D. (2005) Critical upward communication: ten commandments for improving strategy and decision making, *Long Range Planning*, 38: 485–503.

Tourish, D., and Pinnington, A. (2002) Transformational leadership, corporate cultism and the spirituality paradigm: an unholy trinity in the workplace? *Human Relations*, 55: 147–72.

Tourish, D., and Robson, P. (2006) Sensemaking and the distortion of critical upward communication in organizations, *Journal of Management Studies*, 43: 711–30.

Trujillo, N. (1985) Organizational communication as cultural performance: some managerial considerations, *Southern Speech Communication Journal*, 50: 201–24.

Tyler, L. (2005) Towards a postmodern understanding of crisis communication, *Public Relations Review*, 32: 566–71.

Tyler, T. R. (1998) The psychology of authority relations: a relational perspective on influence and power in groups, in R. M. Kramer and M. A. Neale (eds), *Power and Influence in Organizations* (pp. 251–9). Thousand Oaks, CA, Sage.

Van Buren III, H. J., and Greenwood, M. (2008) Enhancing employee voice:

are voluntary employer–employee partnerships enough? *Journal of Business Ethics*, 81: 209–21.

Van Dyne, L., Ang, S., and Botero, I. C. (2003) Conceptualizing employee silence and employee voice as multidimensional constructs, *Journal of Management Studies*, 40: 1359–92.

Van Maanen, J., and Kunda, G. (1989) Real feelings: emotional expressions and organizational culture, in B. Staw and L. L. Cummings (eds), *Research in Organizational Behavior*, Vol. 11 (pp. 43–102). Greenwich, CT: JAI Press.

Vandekerckhove, W., and Commers, M. S. R. (2004) Whistle blowing and rational loyalty, *Journal of Business Ethics*, 53: 225–33.

Waldron, V. R. (1999) Communication practices of followers, members, and protégés: the case of upward influence tactics, in M. E. Roloff (ed.), *Communication Yearbook*, 22 (pp. 251–99). Thousand Oaks, CA: Sage.

Waldron, V. R., and Kassing. J. W. (2011) *Managing Risk in Communication Encounters: Strategies for the Workplace*. Thousand Oaks, CA: Sage.

Weick, K. (1979) *The Social Psychology of Organizing*. 2nd edn, Reading, MA: Addison-Wesley.

Weick, K. (1995) *Sensemaking in Organizations*. Newbury Park, CA: Sage.

Weick, K. E., Sutcliffe, K. M., and Obstfeld, D. (2005) Organizing and the process of sensemaking, *Organization Science*, 16: 409–21.

Westin, A. F. (1986) Professional and ethical dissent: individual, corporate and social responsibility, *Technology in Society*, 8: 335–9.

White, M. J. (2007) *Against the President*. Chicago: Ivan R. Dee.

Witt, L. A., and Wilson, J. W. (1991) Moderating effect of job satisfaction on the relationship between equity and extra-role behaviors, *Journal of Social Psychology*, 131: 247–52.

Winter, R., and Jackson, B. (2006) State of the psychological contract: manager and employee perspectives within an Australian credit union, *Employee Relations*, 28: 421–34.

Wolfson, S., and Neave, N. (2007) Coping under pressure: cognitive strategies for maintaining confidence among soccer referees, *Journal of Sport Behavior*, 30: 232–47.

Womack, D. F. (1988) A review of conflict instruments in organizational settings, *Management Communication Quarterly*, 3: 437–45.

Zhang, J., Chiu, R., and Wei, L. (2009) Decision-making process of internal whistleblowing behavior in China: empirical evidence and implications, *Journal of Business Ethics*, 88: 25–41.

Index

Note: page numbers in italics denote tables or figures

absenteeism 32, 42, 44, 81, 93
accountability 79, 89, 197
accountancy malpractice 3–4
Addison, C. 14
Adelphia 89
adversarial position 23, 24, 83, 124, 133–4
agri-business 7
airline pilots 40, 42, 43
Alford, C. F. 48
American Catholic Church 137–8
Anderson, Arthur 4
anonymity 48, 49, 125, 140, 141, 186, 194
appeal boards 185
Archer Daniels Midland 7
architectural design firm 66
Armstrong, T. A. 28, 79, 82, 91, 98–100, 101, 102, 104, 114, 124, 130, 131
Ashcraft, K. L. 42, 43, 69, 89
Ashcroft, John 9–10
Ashforth, B. E. 40, 42, 43, 129
assertiveness 37
Atlas, R. D. 4
Australian credit union 44
authenticity 190, 191, 192
autonomy 60–1, 66
Avtgis, T. A. 130, 131, 177

Ball, George 18
banking sector
  branch management 109
  Chinese 91–2
  Washington Mutual 146–7
bargaining tactics 37
Barker, J. R. 23, 77
Barnett, T. R. 187
Baty, P. 178
Baucus, M. S. 49
Beckman, Arnold 15
Benedict XVI, Pope 138
Benson, J. A. 195
Bergman, L. 11
Berlin, L. R. 15
Berry, B. 117, 197
Bies, R. J. 109
Big Moon Tortilla (Cowley) 116–17
binary thinking 93
Bishop, L. 45
Black, Hugo 17–18
Blair, Sheila 198
Blake, William 56, 57
Blank, Julius 14–15

Index

Blind Men and the Elephant parable 56–7, 70, 74, *75*
  decision-making elephant 75–9
  feeling elephant 79–82
  sensemaking elephant 82–5
boatrocking *125*, 126, 128
Bodtker, A. M. 35
Bouville, M. 90–1, 95
Bowen, Richard 165–7
Bower, A. 5
Brachman, J. 20
British American Tobacco 11–12
Broadfoot, K. 69
Brown & Williamson Tobacco Corporation 11, 13, 25, 47–8
bulletin boards, company-wide 45
bullying 121–2
bureaucracy 24, 77
Burke, Edmund 1

car manufacturers 107
Carey, S. C. 20, 21
Castor, T. 67
Cathcart, Ronald 146–7
Catholic Church 136–8, 190
Cavanaugh, M. 45
censorship 90
Challenger space shuttle 174
cheating 94
Cheney, G. 23, 24, 61, 69, 75, 76, 88, 89, 134, 135, 136, 178
Chiles, A. M. 25
The China Syndrome 5, 6
Chinese banking sector 91–2
Chory-Assad, R. M. 82
Chronicle of Dissent 140
Church, A. H. 187
churches 136–9, 190
circumvention *125*, 127, *163*, *164*
  consequences 156
  constructive/destructive *153*
  example 151–2, 167
  justification for 85, 99–100
  organizational outcomes *155*
  relational outcomes *154*, 168–9
  successful/unsuccessful 15–16, *155*
Citigroup executives 165
CitiMortgage 165–7
Clegg, S. R. 58
Cloud, D. L. 88, 89
coalition tactics 37, 127
Cochran, D. S. 187
collectivist practices 16, 24, 91–2, 134–5
Collins, J. C. 93
Collinson, D. 41, 93
Commers, M. S. R. 95
Commission for Racial Equality 177–8
communication
  classical management 58–9
  feedback 63
  goals 128–9
  identity 68–9
  NASA 175
  organizations xii, 65–8
  performance 64
  power 65
  rigidity 94–5
  see also computer-mediated communication
compliance 60
complicity 94
compromise 153, *154*, 157
computer-mediated communication 45, *125*, 139–42
confidentiality 191, 192
conflict 31, 33–4, 35, 51
conflict avoidance 130, 135
conformity 16–17, 23
  see also compliance
consensus 78, 144–5
consent 60, 121
consistency 191, 192
consultative committees 44

Contractor, N. 63
control mechanisms 76–8
Coombs, W. T. 60
Cooper, Cynthia 2, 3–4, 48
cooperatives 136
Cooren, F. 67
Corkery, M. 147
cost-cutting 102–3
Cotton, J. L. 24–5, 76, 102
counterinstitutional websites 140
Cowley, J. 116–17
coworkers 28, 100–1, 107, 168, 170
craft guilds 58
creativity 66, 194
credibility 197
  see also trust
credit union 44
crew resource management 43
critical perspective 65–8, *71*
Croatian management culture 91
Cropanzano, R. 82
Crosby, Stills, Nash and Young 19
Croucher, S. M. 91
Crowe, C. 28
Crowe, Russell 6
Cuba–US relations 18
Cuban, Mark 141–2
cultural differences 64–5, *71*, 90–1, 92
customer service 45, 64, 70, 87–8, 107–8, 119–20
cyberdissidents 140

Daft, R. L. 132
Dash, E. 147
de Forest, J. 19
De Gaulle, Charles 174
De Maria, W. 170
decision-making 99
  elephant parable 74, 75–9
  empowerment of employees 25
  groups 95
  justice 81–2
  NASA 174–5
  organizational/individual 102–3, 119–21
  triggers *120*
  upward influence 39
  voice 44, 60
Deetz, S. 23, 65, 89
Deman, Suresh 177–8
democracy in organizations 24–5
demonstrations 21
DeNisi, A. S. 184–5
deterioration 153, *154*
development 153, *154*
devil's advocate 190–1
dialectical thinking 93
DiCioccio, R. L. 130
direct factual appeal 128, 146–8, 163–4, 166
discursive perspective 66–8, *71*
Disney 64, 93
dissatisfaction 28–9, 43–4, *75*, 80–1, 194
dissent
  avoidance of 144, 145
  content of 178
  defined xii–xiv, 29, 56–7, 194
  disguised 93
  ethics 87, 110–14
  favourable outcomes 14–16, 73, 120, 175
  globalization 21–2
  goals 128–9
  identity 85, 167–8
  latent/lateral 126, 131
  motivation 74, 98
  optimal level 179–81
  repression 20–3
  and society 16–20
  tolerance of 96–7, 177–81
  see also organizational dissent; principled organizational dissent; upward dissent

Index

dissent expression
  as burden 171–2
  computer-mediated communication 139–42
  conditions 179–81
  factors 123, 129–34, *180*
  idioms about 144–5
  lateral/upward 127
  recommendations 167–72
  typology 124, *125*, 126
dissent messages *125*, 126, 127, 128
dissident groups 19–20
Dixon, M. A. 136, 137–8
Dooley, R. S. 95
Douglas, William 17–18
Duane, A. 140
Dundon, T. 44
Dworkin, T. M. 49
Dynegy 89

economic restraints 88–90
Edmonds, Sibel 8–11, 14, 48
Edmondson, V. C. 117
education issues 18–19
Eichenwald, K.: *The Informant* 7
Eisenhower, Dwight D. 18, 174
elephant: *see* Blind Men and the Elephant parable
emotion 35, 48
employee–management meetings 182, 184, 188
employees
  autonomy 60–1
  Chinese banking sector 91–2
  constraints 40–1
  empowerment 25, 85, 197
  fair treatment 87–8, *99*, 100–1, 107, 121, 184
  family metaphor 59–60
  goals 168
  higher order needs 59
  identity 40, 41
  machine metaphor 58, 59
  performance evaluations 38, 39, 94, *99*, 105–6, 184
  rights 23, 76
  safety considerations 106–7, 158–9, 191, 192
  upward influence 35–9
  see also resistance; voice mechanisms
EmployeeSuggestionBox 186
empowerment 25, 85, 197
engagement 197
Enron 5, 48, 63, 89, 113
espionage 9
ethics
  customer service 107–8
  dissent 87, 110–14
  obligations 113–14
  professionalism 69
  in workplace 50
ethics hotlines 182, 184, 186–7
event triggers *95–8*, *99*, *120*, 122–4
evidence 126–7, 146
Ewing, D. 23
exchange tactics 37, 127, 128
exit 44, 80–1, 161

face threatening 94
faculty senate 67–8
Fairchild, Sherman 16
Fairchild Semiconductor 14–16
Fairhurst, G. T. 67, 101
fairness of treatment 87–8, *99*, 100–1, 107, 121, 184
family metaphor 59–60
Fannie Mae 165
Farace, R. V. 62
Farrell, D. 44, 80, 81
favoritism 109, 110
FBI (Federal Bureau of Investigation)
  Edmonds 8–11, 48
  Rowley 2–3, 25, 48
Federal Aviation Administration 40

Federal Deposit Insurance Corporation 198
feedback
  analyzing 194–5
  anonymity 186
  communication 63
  consensual 195
  corrective 177
  dissenters 194
Feistner, E. 56
Financial Crisis Inquiry Commission 165–6
financial planner 149–50
financial sector 198
  see also banking sector
Finet, D. 24
Finnegan, P. 140
firms: *see* organizations
flight attendants 40
foreign policy 18
Franklin, David 5
Freddie Mac 165
freedom of speech 10, 76, 90, 133
Fryxell, G. E. 95
Fullbright, J. William 56, 57

Gandhi, Mahatma 87
Gandossy, R. 94
Gandz, J. 22
Garner, J. T. 63, 70, 84, 85, 124, 126, 127, 128, 129, 134, 138–9, 146, 149, 150, 157–8, 162, 168
Gayle, B. M. 35
gender stereotyping 40, 65
Geyelin, M. 13
Gibbs, J. C. 79
Glamour magazine 5
global capitalism 1, 88–9, 198
globalization 45
Goodboy, A. K. 82
Goodheart, A. 14
Gorden, W. I. 44, 46, 76, 80, 81, 111, 135, 146, 161, 178
Gossett, L. M. 140–1
Gottlieb, J. Z. 194, 195
Graham, J. W. 75, 79, 80, 96, 98, 112, 117–24, 125, 128, 132, 133, 159, 176, 178, 182, 184, 185, 187, 189, 191, 192, 193
Greenfieldboyce, N. 175
Greenwood, M. 45
grievance procedures 184–5
Grinich, Victor 14–15
Grisham, John: *The Rainmaker* 5
groundskeeper 157
Grundlach, M. J. 79
guerilla attacks 21
Gundlach, M. J. 83
Gush Emunim 20

Hahon, B. 9
Hale, W. 175–6
Hamas 20
harassment 121, 184
Hardy, C. 58
Harlos, K. P. 25, 181, 182, 184, 185, 186, 188, 189, 191
harm prevention 99, 106–8
Harris, D. B. 79
Harvey, M. G. 122
healthcare 103
heavy vehicle manufacturing industry 41
Hegstrom, T. G. 25, 97, 98, 104, 105, 112, 119, 121, 132, 133, 134, 145, 168, 176, 177, 178, 179, 180, 184, 192, 193
Henik, E. 48, 49
higher education 112
high-tech company 126
Hinkin, T. R. 37
Hippocratic Oath 69
Hirschman, A. O. 43, 80–1, 176
Hodson, R. 40
Hoerni, Jean 14–15
Hofstede, G. 74, 75

Index

Holl, A. 56
Holmes, Oliver Wendell, Jr 17–18
honesty 107–8, 113–14
Hoover, D. 21–2
House and Senate Intelligence Committees 2–3
House of Lords (UK) 17
Hubbell, A. P. 82
human anatomy 72–3
human relations perspective 59–61, *71*
human resources 61–2, *71*, 125–6
humor messages *93*, *125*, 127, 128
Hwang, S. L. 13

IBM 189
identification 77
identity *71*
  communication 68–9
  compromised 157
  dissent 85, 167–8
  employees 40, 41
  professionalism 69
  resistance 70, 84–5
  whistleblowers 48
impression management 83
independent mindedness 76
Indian management culture 91
indigenous peoples 73
indiscretion 110, 152
industrialization 58
inefficiency *99*, 103
Infante, D. A. 76
influence
  individual/relational 123
  organizational 132
  strategic 38–9
  upward 32, 35–9, 51–2
The Informant 7
ingratiation tactics 37, 38, 127–8
innovation 14–16, 175
The Insider 6
insider trading 113
inspiration messages 127
integrity 49, 107–8, 159, 162
interaction 33–4, 51, 62–3
interdependence 31, 33, 34, 51
Internet 140
intertextuality 67
Irish Republican Army 20
Islamic terrorism 20
Israel 20

Jackson, B. 44
Jameson, J. K. 35
Jan, C. 170
Jensen, T. C. 14, 49, 96
Jerry Maguire 27–8, 53–4, 80
jihad 20
job satisfaction 48–9
job security 45
John Paul II, Pope 137–8
Johnson, Lyndon 18
Johnson Space Center 175
Jones, C. 17
Jubb, P. B. 48, 49, 95
justice 81, 82

Kahn, R. L. 62
Kassing, J. W. 22, 25, 28, 29, 30, 32, 38, 47, 52, 62, 76, 78, 79, 81, 82, 83, 85, 91, 93, 94, 96, 98–100, 101, 102, 103, 104, 108, 109, 114, 117–24, 126, 127, 128, 130, 131, 132, 133, 134, 145, 146, 148, 149, 150, 151, 152, 153, *154*, *155*, 157, 159, 161, 162–4, 167, 168, 169, 179, 180, 181, 184, 192, 197
Katz, D. 62
Keeley, M. 80
Keenan, J. 91
Kennedy, John F. 18
Kent State University 19
Kerr-McGee Corporation 6

Khmer Rouge 90
Kilker, J. 140–1
Kill the Messenger 9
King, G. 132
King, Martin Luther, Jr 116
King, W. C. 34
Kipnis, D. 36, 37, 38
Klaas, B. S. 184–5
Kleiner, Eugene 14–15
Kohlberg, L. 79
Kohn, D. 8
Kowalewski, D. 21–2
Kowalski, R. M. 83
Krefting, L. A. 59
Krehbiel, P. J. 82
Krone, K. J. 35, 38, 39
Kuhn, T. 69, 89
Kunda, G. 64

labor 58, 88–9
  see also employees; workforce
laboratory technician 147–8
Lacayo, R. 2, 5
Larson, G. S. 93
Last, Jay 15
Lay, Kenneth 5
leadership 92, 93
Learned Hand, Judge 144, 145
Leary, M. R. 83
Leck, J. D. 81
Lemmon, Jack 6
Levine, D. I. 45
Lewicki, R. J. 31
Lilienthal, P. 186
Lindo, D. K. 194
Lowery, D. 81
loyalty 3, 44, 49, 80, 95
Lutgen-Sandvik, P. 121

McCabe, D. M. 182, 184, 185, 190, 191
McDougall, W. 71
McDowell, Z. 82

machine metaphor 58, 59
Maclaglan, P. 111
Macleish, Archibald 27, 29
Mael, F. A. 40, 42, 43, 129
Maher, T. V. 20, 21
management
  classical perspective 58–9, *71*
  creativity 194
  cultural differences 91
  and employees 41
  face threatening 94
  interdependence 34
  training 194–5
  upward dissent 145
  vs. whistleblowers 170
manufacturing industries 34, 41, 45, 52, 101
Markham, A. 66
Martin, B. 117, 170
martyrdom 20
Matt, B. F. 112, 167–8, 191
Maxwell, J. C. 110
Mesmer-Magnus, J. R. 48, 49
Miceli, M. P. 33, 48, 49, 112, 132, 171, 177, 195, 197
Michels, R. 24
microprocessors 14
Miethe, T. D. 49, 91, 120
Miles, E. W. 34
Miller, K. I. 58–9, 61, 62, 103
Milliken, F. J. 23
misconduct 95
Mondragon cooperatives 136
Monge, P. 63, 67
Moody, J. 91
Moore, Gordon 15
Moore, Mike 13
Moorman, R. H. 82
moral reasoning 79, 90–1
Morris, W. 29
Morse, J. 5
mortgage industry 146–7
Mueller, Robert 3, 9

Mumby, D. K. 23, 43, 65
Munchus, G. 117
Murphy, A. G. 40, 129

NASA (National Aeronautics and Space Administration) 174–5, 198–9
  video 175, 191
National Association of Convenience Stores 159–60
National Basketball Association 141–2
National Religious Party 20
national security 9–10
National Security Whistleblowers Coalition 10
Nazism 90
Near, J. P. 14, 33, 48, 49, 96, 112, 132, 177
Neave, N. 19
Neff, Michael: *Year of the Rhinoceros* 5
neglect 44, 80, 81
Nemeth, C. 168, 190
networks 63
neutrality 153, *154*
New York City Board of Education 18–19
New York Times 14
Noe, R. 45
non-cooperation 87
Nordstrom 93
normative rules 77–8
Novak, J. M. 177
Noyce, Robert 14–15, 16
nuclear power industry 5, 6, 107

obligations, ethical 90–1, 113–14
O'Connell, C. 74, 75, 79, 82
O'Connell Davidson, J. 32
O'Donnell-Trujillo, N. 64
Ohio National Guard 19
O'Leary, R. 110, 176
ombudspersons 44, 125–6, 168, 181, *182*, *183*, 184–5
open-door policy 125–6, 183, 188–90
optimal dissent conditions 180, 181
organizational dissent 23–5, 30, *196*
  barriers 92–5
  culture for 36, 133–4, 193–8
  differentiated 50–4
  forms of 118, 122, 124–8
  mechanisms 181–93
  models of 117–24
  myths 28–9
  theoretical explanations 71–5
  see also principled organizational dissent
organizational lives 116–17
organizations
  alternative structures 134–9
  biological metaphor 62–3
  bureaucracy 24
  change 99, 101–2
  climate 192–3
  communication xii, 65–8
  control of society 23
  culture 64, 192–3, 197
  economic restraints 88–90
  hierarchies 24, 93–4, 193
  inattentiveness 95–6
  interaction 62–3
  sensemaking 83–5
  size 132
  as social actors 23
  whistleblower reports 195, 197
outliers/networks 63
overloaded dissent condition 180, 181

Pacanowsky, M. E. 25, 64, 65, 132
Paine, Thomas 193
Palestinian Liberation Organization 20
Park, H. 47, 48, 124

participative organizational practices 61–2, 78
Payne, H. J. 131
PBS (Public Broadcasting Service) 15
peer reports 39
PepsiCo 187
performance 64–5, 109, 152, 176
performance evaluations 38–9, 88, 94, *99*, 105–6, 184
Perry, K. L. 179, 181, 188
personality traits 130
Peterson, L. 20, 21
pharmaceuticals 5
pharmacy practice 87–8
Pierskalla, J. H. 20, 21
Pinnington, A. 92, 93
Polier, Justine 19
politics/dissent 90
Poole, M. S. 31, 32, 67
Porras, J. I. 93
Porter, L. W. 36
power
  abuse of 109
  communication 65
  firm structure 89–90
Powers, K. J. 59
Prasad, A. 41
Prasad, P. 41
Preiss, R. W. 35
pressure messages 127, 128
price fixing 7
principled organizational dissent 117–18, 123, *125*, 128, 187
professionalism 69
promotion policy 188
public interest 48
Putnam, L. L. 31, 32, 42, 64, 67

al-Qaeda 20
quality circles 60
question-and-answer programs 182, 184, 188

RadioShack 140–1
RadioShacksucks.com 141
Rahim, M. A. 33, 35, 82
rationality tactics 37, 38
Ratzinger, Joseph 138
Ray, L. K. 17
Redding, W. C. xii, 23, 24, 28, 47, 96, 97, 100, 102, 126, 128, 176
referees in sport 19
relational criterion 81, 153, *154*, 168–9
repetition 127, 162–7, 179
reporting procedures 125–6
repression 20–3
resignation threats 127, 156–62, 163–4
resistance 32, 40–3
  creativity 66
  identity 70, 84–5
  organizational dissent 52–3
  overt/covert 41–2
resources *99*, 104–5
responsibility/roles 79, 94, *99*, 103–4
restaurant chef 102–3
restaurant worker 158–9
retail manager 194
retaliation risk 96–7, 123–4, 133–4, 140, 170, 197–8
revolutions 21
Richardson, B. K. 133
Rifkin, W. 117, 170
riots 21
Ripley, A. 2, 3, 4, 5
risk avoidance 157
risk tolerance 91
Roberts, Sheldon 15
Robson, P. 94
Romero, S. 4
Rose, D. 8–11
Ross, D. L. 195
Rothschild, J. 49, 91, 120
Rothschild-Whitt, J. 134, 135, 178
Rowley, Coleen 2–3, 25, 48

Running Man theory 71–3
Rusbult, C. 32, 81
Ruud, G. L. 97, 98, 100, 101, 103, 106, 126, 128, 130, 131, 134

safety considerations 106–7, 158–9, 191, 192
safety protocols 107, 147–8, 157
salesman 104
saleswoman 160–1
Salin, D. 122
Sanders, W. 23–4, 145
Sanderson, J. 140–1
Sanzgiri, J. 194, 195
Sarbanes–Oxley Act 5
satisfaction check 194
Saunders, D. M. 81
scandals
  corporate 89
  sexual abuse 137
Schapiro, Mary 198
Scherer, M. 198
Schlenker, B. R. 83
Schmidt, S. 36, 37, 38
Schnall, D. J. 20
school supplies 105
Schriesheim, C. A. 36
Schwartz, M. 19
scientific enquiry 73
Scott, C. R. 68–9
secretary role 65
Securities and Exchange Committee 198
Seeger, M. W. 78, 111, 113, 114
Sellnow, T. L. 177
Semco 193
Semler, Ricardo 193
sensemaking elephant 82–5
Serbian military 90
service industries 45
sexual abuse scandals 137
Shahinpoor, N. 112, 167–8, 191
al-Sharif, Sayyid Imam 20
Sheppard, B. H. 33, 34
Shockley, William 15
Shockley Labs 14–15, 16, 25
Sieger, M. 3
Silicon Valley 14, 126
Silkwood 5–6
Silkwood, Karen 5
Sinclair, A. L. 82
Sinn Fein 20
Siqueira, K. 20
60 Minutes 8, 11, 13
Smith, A. 177
SMOKE-FREE KIDS 13–14
social media 45, 139–40
social responsibility 79
society and dissent 16–20
solution presentation strategy 127, 128, 148–50, 163–4
Sonnenfeld, J. 94
Sorkin, A. R. 147
specialization 58
Sprague, J. A. 97, 98, 100, 103, 106, 126, 128, 130, 131, 134
Stanley, J. D. 182, 190
status differentials 48, 49, 193
stereotyping, gender 40, 65
Stevenson, Adlai 18
Stewart, L. P. 10–11, 47, 48, 49, 106, 112, 120, 128, 180
Stohl, C. 60, 61, 65, 178
strategies 37–9, 127
Streep, Meryl 6
stress 103–4
strikes 21, 32
student protests 19
suggestion boxes 185–6
Sundstrand Corporation 195
Sunstein, C. R. 16, 90, 129, 145, 174, 176
superior–subordinate relations 150, 153
supervisors
  boatrocking 126

faults 100
inaction *99*, 108–9, 151, 164–5
indiscretion 110, 152
neglect 169
performance 109, 152
unsympathetic 150
upward dissent 131
Supreme Court (US) 17–18
Swedish workforce 135
systems perspective *71*

tactics, explored 37–8
Tandem Computers 188
Tavakoli, A. A. 91
tenure factors 91
theft 42, 108–9
Thoreau, Henry David 193
Threatening resignation 156–62
Tiananmen Square 19
Time magazine 1–2, 3, 198
tobacco industry 11–14, 12, 13, 14
Tompkins, P. K. 23, 75, 76, 93, 174
Tourish, D. 92, 93, 94, 178, 185, 186, 192, 193, 194
Toyota Motor Corporation 107
tradeshow 159–60
'traitorous eight' 14–16, 25
transformational leadership 92–3
translating work 8–11
Trip, T. M. 109
Troubled Asset Relief Program 198
Trujillo, N. 109, 152
trust 133, 197
Tyco 89
Tyler, L. 177
Tyler, T. R. 81

underrepresented dissent condition 180
unions 44, 45, 135, 184
universal values 92
unobtrusive control theory 76–9
upward dissent *125*, 126, 127
circumvention 150–6
critical organizational policy 148
direct factual appeal 146–8
management 145
repetition 162–7, 179
solution presentation 148–50
supervisors 131
threatening resignation 156–62
trust 133
upward influence 32, 35–9, 51–2

Van Buren III, H. J. 45
Van Dyne, L. 44, 46
Van Maanen, J. 64
Vandekerckhove, W. 95
venting messages 127, 128
Vietnam War 18, 19
Viswesvaran, C. 48, 49
voice mechanisms *32*, 43–6, *182*, *183*
active-constructive 146, 149
compliance 60
decision-making 44, 60
and dissent 32, 53, 167–72
grievance systems 184–5
Hirschman 43, 80–1, 176
RadioShack 140–1
variations 183–4
viability *192*
see also exit

Waldron, V. R. 22, 32, 35, 36, 37, 38, 128, 145, 150, 168, 197
Wall Street Journal 13
Walters, Barbara 5
Wargo, M. 134, 138–9
Warren, Elizabeth 198
Washington Mutual Bank 146–7
Watkins, Sherron 2, 5, 48
Weick, K. E. 84
Westin, A. F. 70, 79, 112
whistleblower reports 195, 197

whistleblowers 1, 7–8
  consequences 49, 90–1, 120
  discredited 13–14
  effectiveness 49–50
  emotion 48
  as employees/ex-employees 47–8, 49
  legal protection 171, 178
  loyalty 3
  managerial attacks 170
  motives 25, 111–12, 171
  recognized 2, 4
  self-sacrifice 91
whistleblowing 33, 47–50, 53–4, *169*
  cultivation of *196*
  facts 112
  in films and books 5–formal/ informal 47, 49, *125*
  freedom of speech 10
  media/regulatory body 126
  and reform 5
  trajectories 10–11
Whitacre, Mark 7
White, M. J.: *Against the President* 18
Wigand, Jeffrey 11–14, 25, 47–8
Wilson, Charles E. 18
Wilson, J. W. 79
Winter, R. 44
Witt, L. A. 79
Wolfson, S. 19
Womack, D. F. 34
workforce 45, 135
  see also employees
working hours 30
workplace conditions 43–6, 50, 121–2
work-to-rules 32
World Trade Organization 22
WorldCom 3–4, 48, 89, 113

YouTube 176

al-Zawahiri, Ayman 20
Zhang, J. 92
Zorn, T. E. 25